A FEAST OF MEANINGS

SUPPLEMENTS TO
NOVUM TESTAMENTUM

VOLUME LXXII

A FEAST OF MEANINGS

*Eucharistic Theologies from Jesus
through Johannine Circles*

BY

BRUCE CHILTON

E.J. BRILL
LEIDEN · NEW YORK · KÖLN
1994

The paper in this book meets the guidelines for permanence and durability of the Committee on Production Guidelines for Book Longevity of the Council on Library Resources.

BV
823
.C45
1994

Library of Congress Cataloging-in-Publication Data

Chilton, Bruce.
    A feast of meanings : eucharistic theologies from Jesus through Johannine circles / by Bruce Chilton.
        p.   cm — (Supplements to Novum Testamentum, ISSN 0167-9732 ; v. 72)
    Includes bibliographies and index.
    ISBN 9004099492 (alk. paper)
    1. Lord's Supper—History—Early church, ca. 30-600. 2. Bible. N.T.—Criticism, interpretation, etc.   I. Title. II. Series.
BV823.C45   1994
234'.163'09015—dc20   93-36639
                                                            CIP

Die Deutsche bibliothek – CIP-Einheitsaufnahme

Chilton, Bruce:
A feast of meanings : eucharistic theologies from Jesus through Johannine circles / by Bruce Chilton. – Leiden ; New York ; Köln : Brill, 1994
    (Supplements to Novum testamentum : Vol. 72)
    ISBN 90-04-09949-2
NE: Novum testamentum / Supplements

ISSN   0167-9732
ISBN   90 04 09949 2

PRINTED IN THE NETHERLANDS

For Prof. Sydney Barr

CONTENTS

PREFACE

The New Testament's eucharistic texts implicitly, and often explicitly, commend the actions they refer to for repetition. What was done, what should be done, with what words and with what objects: the texts reflect the conscious practice of distinct and often separate circles of usage. Each circle of usage influenced the texts we can read today and helped to shape Christianity.

Christianity emerged by the end of the first century out of early Judaism; that development was neither instantaneous nor inevitable. Rather, the forces of the circles of usage which fed the New Testament, taken in aggregate, made for a religious system evidently, even officially, different from Judaism. The stages of development by which eucharistic practices were transformed from declarations of purity within Judaism to declarations of independence from Judaism permit us to trace the emergence of Christianity from Judaism with unusual clarity. At the same time, those stages of development alone enable us to speak of the meanings of eucharist.

Essential gestures to which the texts refer—in association with specified objects—were repeated through the distinctive circles of usage within early Judaism and Christianity as the movement centered on Jesus evolved. When a circle of usage formulated its practice in a way which influenced our texts, it manifested a stage of development. At each stage, the meaning attached to eucharistic practice corresponded to the social context of the circle concerned. The present study identifies the meanings and the contexts which were involved in eucharistic repetition through its various stages.

The exegesis which is practised here is of a generative nature. The task is not to move from the received form of texts backwards, since such a procedure involves the archaeological fallacy, that texts conceal meanings in the way that tells cover artifacts. The meanings which social groups assign to common actions are better taken as productive forces than as inert matter. Eucharistic texts are products of the interaction of the circles of usage in their stages and our task is to identify the meanings of eucharist at each stage. We are to see how, from stage to stage, meaning was generated and then itself

generated fresh meaning. The process is only recoverable if the
meanings involved are generated anew, in the most plausible order
of their generation. Our aim is to understand how the texts were
framed out of the meanings which each circle contributed.

The monograph analyzes, then, discrete stages of meaning within
the development of eucharistic practices and texts, whether their setting is Judaic or Christian. The germ of the argument was provided
by an earlier study,[1] but the analysis is pursued afresh here. An introduction explains why the analytic approach of generative exegesis
should be preferred to conventional readings of eucharist. Then six
chapters deal in sequence with the major stages of meaning inherent
within the eucharistic practices which have most influenced the texts
of the New Testament. The first two stages reflect practices of Jesus:
he initially (chapter 1) encouraged meals as celebrations of Israel's
purity in anticipation of God's kingdom, and then (chapter 2)
claimed that such meals were a more acceptable sacrifice than worship in a Temple which he came to regard as impure. The circles of
Jesus' movement which followed transformed his practice and its
meaning. The circle of Peter (chapter 3) portrayed Jesus in Mosaic
terms, and his eucharist as a sacrifice which confirmed his covenantal stature. In contrast, the circle of James (chapter 4) insisted that
Passover was the only model of eucharist; the attempt was to limit
practice and meaning to the calendar and the people of circumcised
Israel. In differing ways, the Pauline and Synoptic positions (chapter 5) militate against the Jacobean limitation, by stressing the solidarity between the heroic martyr and all believers which eucharist
effects. Johannine theologies (chapter 6) both alleviate evident tensions and change the key of eucharistic practice by linking what is
consumed to the miraculous provision of food to Israel in Exodus
and to the lamb which was at the center of Israel's sacrificial worship. After six stages of development, then, those who join in eucharist are more a new Israel than they are defined within Israel, and
the implications of that dramatic transformation for the literary[2]
and social history of Christianity are suggested in a conclusion.

Analytic study is an acquired taste, encouraged in my case some

---

[1] *The Temple of Jesus: His Sacrificial Program Within a Cultural History of Sacrifice*
(University Park: Penn State Press, 1992) 137-154.

[2] Cf. *Profiles of a Rabbi. Synoptic Opportunities in Reading about Jesus*: Brown Judaic
Studies 177 (Atlanta: Scholars Press, 1989).

twenty years ago by my professor at the General Theological Seminary, the Revd Dr O. Sydney Barr. I gratefully dedicate the volume
to him, with especial thanks for his permission to so do. His com-
ments, and those of two anonymous readers for the pubisher, were
most helpful. Particular notice, finally, should be given to Bernhard
Lang, who sowed the seed of this analysis during my visit to Pader-
born in 1991, and then nurtured some early shoots. I cannot recall
being more stimulated by *wissenschaftliche Freundschaft*, and I hope my
work might be of some use within his history of the sacraments.

B.D.C.

INTRODUCTION

"The Church is the successor of Israel as the people of God, and its Eucharist is the successor of the Passover." That statement is made at the beginning of an influential work, not of systematic theology, but of exegesis![1] The close identification of eucharist and Passover, evidently warranted by the New Testament, has been taken as a point of departure, not only by exegetes, but in pastoral practice. Many congregations of Christians hold what is called a "Seder," a commemoration of Passover, on Maundy Thursday, the day on which the institution of the eucharist is observed. Neither exegetes nor pastors who adhere to a wholly paschal interpretation of eucharist can take comfort from recent scholarly discussion, which has inclined against an identification with Passover.[2]

The image of eucharist as a transcendent Passover suited the interests of Christian theology just after World War II. The emphasis was placed on the ecumenical, "final reunion" of which the meal was a "foretaste,"[3] and apparent deference could be accorded to Judaism, even as a claim of supercession was perpetuated. Of course, the critical understandings of both Judaism and the New Testament have changed since the first publication of Higgins's book in 1952. Judaism of the period of the second Temple, often called early Judaism, is today seen as a much more pluralistic phenomenon than it once was, as a result of publications of the materials found at Qumran and the Targumim, and analytic inquiry into the nature of Rabbinic literature. The once common notion that we can assess the New Testament as a deliberate transcendence of Rabbinic Judaism is today seen to be anachronistic, since Rabbinic Judaism

---

[1] A.J.B. Higgins, *The Lord's Supper in the New Testament*: Studies in Biblical Theology 6 (London: SCM, 1960) 9.

[2] Two good surveys are readily available, Hans-Josef Klauck (tr. E. Ewert), "Lord's Super," *The Anchor Bible Dictionary* 4 (ed. D.N. Freedman and others; New York: Doubleday, 1992) 362-372; Robert F. O'Toole, "Last Supper," *The Anchor Bible Dictionary* 4 (ed. D.N. Freedman and others; New York: Doubleday, 1992) 234-241.

[3] So Higgins, in the last line of his book, p. 89.

is a product of the second century and later. The New Testament
itself is also regarded in a new light. The presupposition that basical-
ly historical reports were subjected to relatively minor degrees of interpretation over time has given way to a recognition that what appears to be history might well reflect the use to which the memory
of Jesus was put in a given community of Christians.

Given that both Judaism and the New Testament are no longer
seen as they once were, our perspective on eucharist must also be
revised. The simple equation between the ''Last Supper'' and Passover, such as Higgins accepted, was the achievement of an often
reprinted book by Joachim Jeremias, *The Eucharistic Words of Jesus.*[4]
It is a classic exercise in the supposition that the Judaism of Jesus'
time was Rabbinic Judaism, and that the New Testament is a kind
of archaeological tell, strata of interpretation covering a precious artifact of history. Discussion of Jeremias's contribution generally has
been needlessly strident:[5] although he too readily projected rabbis
into the first century and too easily assumed that Jesus' *ipsissima verba* were to be found in the Gospels, the data he adduced and the insights he offered remain considerable.

Nonetheless, Jeremias's approach is especially limited in respect
of eucharistic practice. Critical appraisals of Judaism and the formation of the New Testament have undermined the foundations of his
theory of Jesus' eucharistic words. The meaning and observance of
Passover within Judaism must have changed after the destruction of
the Temple: to begin with, having one's lamb slaughtered there was
no longer practicable. Basic changes of that sort are bound to influence other aspects of ritual and the common understanding of the
observance generally.[6] Direct comparison of the New Testament
with Rabbinic Judaism in paschal terms might therefore be misleading from the outset, quite aside from the question of whether Jesus'
''last supper'' in fact was a Seder. And for all that Christians have
incorporated the ''eucharistic words of Jesus'' into their liturgies,
historical accuracy cannot be assumed more in the case of eucharist

---

[4] Jeremias (tr. A. Ehrhardt), *The Eucharistic Words of Jesus* (New York: Macmillan, 1955). John Lowe observes in an introduction that a change in ''*Zeitgeist*'' encouraged the translation of the book, which was first published in 1935 (p. vii).

[5] See Ben F. Meyer, ''A Caricature of Joachim Jeremias and his Scholarly
Work,'' *Journal of Biblical Literature* 110 (1991) 451-462.

[6] See Catherine Bell, *Ritual Theory, Ritual Practice* (New York: Oxford University Press, 1992).

than elsewhere, especially when the texts do not fully agree in their presentation of what was said. The focus from the time of the Reformation upon the statements, "This is my body" and "This is my blood," has perhaps contributed to a distorted picture. Because Christians since that time have disputed the meaning of the statements, it is all too easy to suppose the wording itself is constant from text to text. That is not the case, any more than the theologies implicit in the practices attested are in complete accord. In an environment in which Christians longed for principals of unity which respected Judaism, Jeremias's position provided a way forward: absent agreement in eucharistic theology, we can at least agree that Jesus said certain words in order to link his death with the paschal sacrifice.

The utility of Jeremias's position, then, has outlasted its adequacy as a critical representation of the sources of Judaism and Christianity. The time has come to develop a new perspective. The direction of the development which is proposed here may, in general terms, be associated with the approach of Hans Lietzmann.[7] Lietzmann, in a work first published in 1926, pointed the way towards the present analysis by attending to differing practices within Christianity. He argued that a practice of breaking bread, reflected in the *Didache* and in the liturgy of Serapion (from fourth-century Egypt), derived from Jesus' fellowship at meals, without connection to his death. Ultimately, he attributed that type of eucharist to Jerusalem, in contrast to the type of eucharist as a memorial of Jesus' death. Lietzmann associated that second type with a Hellenistic practice derived from Paul and reflected in the liturgy of Hippolytus (from third-century Rome).

Criticism of Lietzmann's position has been straightforward.[8] The variety of the Synoptic Gospels, in their emphatic association of Jesus' last meal with his death, tells against the argument that they all derive from a single, Pauline innovation. Moreover, Lietzmann defended the peculiar notion that reference in Acts to the

---

[7] Lietzmann (tr. D.H.G. Reeve), *Mass and Lord's Supper. A Study in the History of Liturgy* (Leiden: Brill, 1979), from *Messe und Herrenmahl. Eine Studie zur Geschichte und Liturgie*: Arbeiten zur Kirchengeschichte 8 (Bonn: Marcus und Weber, 1926). See also Reginald H. Fuller, "The Double Origin of the Eucharist," *Biblical Research* 8 (1963) 60-72.

[8] A representative version is offered by Higgins, pp. 56-63; see also Klauck, 366-367.

breaking of bread among the apostles excluded drinking wine, as well as having nothing to do with Jesus' death. It is far more natural to understand the phrases "to break bread" (κλάω τὸν ἄρτον, Luke 22:19; 24:30; Acts 2:46; 20:7, 11; 27:35) and "breaking of bread" (κλάσις τοῦ ἄρτου, Luke 24:35; Acts 2:42) as references to the practices and customs at particular meals which were current in a given community, rather than as exclusions of specific actions and meanings.[9] What the disciples are said to experience during their journey and their stop along the road to Emmaus (Luke 24:13-35) certainly includes reference to Jesus' death and resurrection, and presumably includes whatever drink the two disciples offered the unknown stranger by way of hospitality.[10] The experience as a whole is referred to them as occurring "during the breaking of bread" (ἐν τῇ κλάσει τοῦ ἄρτου, v. 35).

What is wanting in Lietzmann's position is nuance. To be accepted as it stands, we would need to imagine a simple, binary antithesis[11] of two types of eucharist, which survived independently for

---

[9] For a thorough discussion, see Xavier Léon-Dufour, *Le partage du pain eucharistique selon le Nouveau Testament* (Paris: Editions du Seuil, 1982) 30-41. Léon-Dufour himself begins with the presupposition that the phrase refers to a domestic rite within Judaism, in which one acknowledged that one received food from God, and by that acknowledgement "it was inserted into the current of divine power" (p. 30). The postulation of a service of breaking bread derives from the observation of John Lightfoot; see *A Commentary on the New Testament from the Talmud and Hebraica* 4 (ed. J.R. Pitman; Grand Rapids: Baker, 1979 [from the edition of the Oxford University Press, 1859]) 35, 36. The formal development of the rite (and the significance which Léon-Dufour attaches to it) may not have been achieved by the first century, although it was probably assumed that the master of a house would break bread on festive occasions (see b. Berakhoth 46a). His breaking bread was a particular emphasis within the general, ancient, and widespread practice of blessing what was consumed at meals (see m. Berakhoth 6:5-8 and b. Berakhoth 42a-45a). But Lightfoot and Léon-Dufour in any case conclude that, among Jesus' followers after the resurrection, the reference of the phrase was transferred to eucharist. Their conclusion is all the easier to draw, the less phrase is taken to have referred previously to an established rite within Judaism.

[10] The eucharistic motif within the story is widely recognized, see Joseph A. Fitzmyer, *The Gospel According to Luke (X-XXIV)*: The Anchor Bible 28 A (Garden City: Doubleday, 1985) 1559-1560, 1569. Although his approach is inspired by Leitzmann's, Oscar Cullmann found that, even after the period of the New Testament, "The formula 'to break bread' usually meant 'to take a meal.'" See "The Lord's Supper and the Death of Christ," *Essays on the Lord's Supper*: Ecumenical Studies in Worship 1 (with F.J. Leenhardt, tr. J.G. Davies; Richmond: John Knox, 1958) 10.

[11] Cullmann attempts an interesting revision of Lietzmann's argument, by maintaining that "the joy manifested by the early Christians during the 'breaking

hundreds of years. Criticism could have resulted in an investigation of a larger number of variant practices as reflected within the texts of the New Testament, corresponding to distinct circles within early Christianity. An analysis of how originally separate and diverse traditions of eucharistic discipline came to be synthesized would have made Lietzmann's position more plausible. Such an analysis would avoid attributing to Paul alone more influence than he was likely ever to have exerted; it is implausible, for example, that his teaching molded the Synoptic Gospels directly. A further development of Lietzmann's approach, to trace the convergence of traditions and the tendency within the texts for originally distinct practices to be amalgamated, would also account for the diminishing prevalence of diversity within the Church after the period of the New Testament.[12] Within Lietzmann's own period and country, scholars such as Emanuel Hirsch pursued attempts to relate sources within the Gospels to distinct cycles of tradition,[13] so that a further refinement of his theory might have been anticipated.

The tendency of the field—with Jeremias in the forefront—was in the opposite direction, to accuse Lietzmann of positing too much diversity, rather than too little. The result is that one of two positions

---

of bread' has its source, not in the fact that the assembled disciples eat the body and drink the blood of their crucified Master, but in the consciousness they have of eating *with* the *Risen* Christ, really present in their midst, as He was on Easter Day" (p. 16). He then suggests that Paul wished to "*complete*" the eucharistic interpretation by means of a reference to Jesus' death (p. 17). Cullmann's original suggestion, that the Jesus invoked in eucharist is not only as remembered but as risen, is vital to an understanding of how the ritual meals of early Christianity developed. The (literally) enthused claim that the resurrected Lord disclosed himself in the communal meal (as at Emmaus) proved to exert a mighty force towards diversity, as well shall see in what follows. For precisely that reason, however, Cullmann's acceptance of Lietzmann's binary opposition prevented him from making the progress he might have. He was nonetheless an important exponent of Lietzmann's approach, and the publication of his work in *Revue d'Histoire et de Philosophie religieuses* in 1936, as well as its translation into English in 1958, might have been expected to provoke more discussion than it did.

[12] Nonetheless, diversity of practice needed to be countenanced, cf. Caroline Bammel, "Die Einheit des Glaubens und die Mannigfaltigkeit der Bräuche in der christlichen Ueberlieferung nach Irenäus," *La Tradizione: Forme e Modi*: Studi Ephemeridis "Augustiniaun" 31 (Rome: Institutum Patristicum "Augustinianum," 1990) 283-292.

[13] For an appreciative assessment, see Ernst Bammel, "Hirsch und Wellhausen," *Christentumsgeschichte und Wahrheitsbewusstsein: Studien zur Theologie Emanuel Hirschs* (ed. J. Ringleben; Berlin: de Gruyter, 1991) 37-62. Hirsch's analysis is most readily available in *Frühgeschichte des Evangeliums* (Tübingen: Mohr, 1941).

is common. Some scholars, and almost all pastors, maintain the position of Jeremias, complete with some form of the claim of *ipsissimma verba Jesu* and of Jesus' transcendent incorporation of paschal themes within his final meal with his disciples. Others accept that Jeremias was correct in his stress upon the formative importance of Passover within the meal, but see it as invented within the Hellenistic Church, usually by Mark.[14]

What was already a problem of more diversity than his hypothesis would naturally account for is evident in Lietzmann's contribution; in the case of Jeremias and his successors, the problem becomes glaring. Whether one inclines to the view that texts of the last supper are essentially historical as they stand, or to the view that they are at base a literary invention, the stubborn fact remains that there are significant differences of wording, emphasis, timing, and context, as one compares the three Synoptic Gospels, Paul, John, and the *Didache*. If Jesus actually at one particular meal did and said something his followers transmitted to posterity without substantial deviation, why could they not agree whether or not the meal was paschal, what Jesus said exactly, and within what order of events? Then again, if the meal is Mark's literary invention (or someone else's, known or unknown), how did he manage, not only to turn "an etiological myth into historical narrative,"[15] but to engineer its influence far beyond his own document without leaving clear evidence of verbatim copying or other unequivocal signs of borrowing?

The variety of the texts is among the principal phenomena to be explained, and whether one proceeds with Jeremias's hypothesis in its initial form, or with the revisionist appeal to the hypothesis of a literary invention, the current alternatives both manifest a single fallacy. Each of them presupposes that eucharistic texts are best understood as referring simply to the past: Jesus is held to have said and done such and so, and the only issue of importance is whether that is fact or artifice. Each alternative posits a single hero behind the texts, either a willing martyr or a literary genius, who forges meaning in an instant of creativity. The hero acts, and the texts lie inert. But along with their diversity, among the most striking features of eucharistic texts—especially in the Synoptics, Paul, and the *Didache*

---

[14] So Burton Mack, *A Myth of Innocence. Mark and Christian Origins* (Philadelphia: Fortress, 1988) 303.

[15] The characterization is Mack's, p. 299.

—is their insistence that they relate things to be done, words to be said, and not merely events of the past. They are instruments of practice, not simply matters of record, and their practical dimension is a function of the varieties of practice they both reflect and would promote. Eucharist is a case in which the notion of the New Testament as inert matter (imprinted with something that once happened or was once imagined) is obviously misleading.

In the case of eucharist, the texts of the New Testament unmistakably relate practices at least as much as they refer to data. Of course, such may be the position in other instances, as well, but the present concern is not with the documents in general. Rather, critical reading must be guided by the quest to discern those practices within their originating communities which produced texts of eucharist in the New Testament. The importance of practice was clearly signaled by Lietzmann's analysis, only then to be overlooked by the excessively historicist preoccupations (whether by way of assertion or denial) of the post-war period. The binary opposition between the claim of historical accuracy and the claim of literary fabrication, if it is useful anywhere, is counterproductive when the texts at issue reflect diverse practices evolved over time and in different places by distinct communities.

Lietzmann's initiative, then, shows us the way forward. The correction we must introduce is to increase the variety of practices we would countenance (and at an earlier stage, within the New Testament) in order to account for the diversity of our texts. The present inquiry isolates six types of eucharist within early Christian tradition. In each type, meaning can be assigned to specifiable actions and objects for identifiable social groups. A type of eucharist, then, corresponds to a social constituency which contributed to the New Testament. The fact that a type may be characterized does not imply that a source existed in writing which formalized that type. In that eucharist is a matter of practice, we might suppose that various sorts of communication, written and oral, were used to encourage the sort of action which was valued. Paul in 1 Corinthians 11:23-26 gives an example of how a teacher might put in writing what earlier had been a matter of oral instruction, and then, in vv. 27-33, of how he might append his own imperatives for the maintenance of good practice. The type of eucharist Paul represents, then, is as practised within those communities he accorded with, and was promulgated by means of a catechesis which we have no direct access to.

The example of Paul is instructive. He demonstrates clearly that
the type of eucharist he represented was acknowledged by c. A.D.
55. But the fact that 1 Corinthians happens to be the oldest datable
document which mentions eucharist within early Christianity must
not be taken to prove that Paul's type is also the foundational type
of eucharist. In Galatians 2:11-21, written around A.D. 53, he mentions Peter (or Cephas) and James as chief figures in groups to which
he was in opposition during a controversy in Antioch. In that the
issue which divided the groups, and even separated Barnabas from
Paul, was that of fellowship and purity, meals—including eucharistic meals—were evidently matters of contention. Just as we cannot
understand Paul's vehemence unless we infer his eucharistic practice from what he teaches, so his own teaching is only appreciated
as distinctive when we also infer the eucharistic practices of Peter,
James, and Barnabas.

The practices of eucharist which caused contention in Antioch
were all rooted in the common recognition that meals marked the
boundaries of what could be considered pure, appropriate for fellowship in a manner pleasing to God. Galatians 2 will absorb our attention especially in chapter 5, when Paul's view of eucharist is contrasted to James'. For the moment, however, it is unexceptionable
to observe that Paul drew the boundaries of what was pure in a manner which in his own understanding put him at odds with James and
Peter. The entire dispute, however, is predicated on the awareness
that Jesus practised fellowship at meals in a way that established
boundaries of purity in anticipation of God's kingdom. The contention in Antioch was heated precisely because the fundamental concern was continuity with dominical practice.

As we consider a well-known dispute, then, the natural inference
is that a diversity of practices was not only its result, but its cause.
There is certainly no indication that eucharistic practice remained
untroubled by controversy until James and Paul came to be at odds.
Rather, social groups within early Christianity appear to have practised eucharist with actions and meanings cognate with their own
respective ideologies. Paul's type will have differed from James',
and both will have claimed to perpetuate Jesus'.

Our first eucharist type, then, must be Jesus' practice of fellowship at meals. As we shall see, his activity in that regard, and his connection of his meals with God's kingdom, are well attested. What is
also well attested, although it has often escaped attention, is that the

issue of the boundaries and the nature of purity was also a programmatic concern within Jesus' meals. For that reason, chapter 1 develops the importance of the category of purity in an extended consideration of recent contributions.

Although the first type of eucharist remained fundamental, in relating the kingdom to present purity in anticipation of the kingdom's future, the second type actually provided a definitive structure of eucharist. The assertions, "This is my blood" and "This is my flesh," derive from a major shift in the nature of Jesus' meals with his disciples. Where earlier he had celebrated purity as a characteristic of his fellowship, there was a crucial change after he occupied the Temple. During the occupation, he had insisted that his views of purity should be accepted. When they were rejected by the authorities of the Temple, Jesus made the bold claim that the wine and the bread of his fellowship were the "blood" and the "flesh" of a sacrifice more acceptable than what was offered in the Temple. Chapter 2 develops the meaning of the second type in its sacrificial—but not autobiographical—dimension.

In that the first two types of eucharist were developed within the movement under Jesus' own direction, some care is taken to suggest what the Aramaic form of his eucharistic formulation was. The purpose of that exercise is not to suggest that retroversion into Aramaic is a guarantee of *ipsissima verba*. But the meanings of the sayings which are crucial to the understanding of the first two types are more straightforward when they are taken within their Aramaic milieux. Retroversion might therefore be taken to confirm that the first two types of eucharist were indeed at home within the earliest stages of the movement.

The third type of eucharist was at home within the circle of Peter, which was responsible for a cycle of tradition discernible within the Synoptic Gospels. The emphasis upon the covenant was the particular interest of the Petrine cycle: Jesus was portrayed in Mosaic terms as a teacher who founded a manner of approaching God. Worship in the Temple could go on, but only—within the group—on Jesus' understanding of covenantal purity. At its earliest stage, the Petrine cycle was in fact Cephan, a representation of Jesus for his followers in Jerusalem and Galilee after the crucifixion. The incorporation within the cycle of dominical sayings which appear to have originated in Aramaic suggests that the Cephan source also was transmitted in that language. Chapter 3, however, provides our last occasion for retroversion into Aramaic, and notice that the Petrine cycle achieved its most influential form in Greek.

From chapter 4, we confront the texts of the Synoptic Gospels in nearly their present form. The paradigmatic connection between Passover and Jesus' "last supper," now indeed a single and ultimate meal, is shown to be as artificial as it is dominant. The paradigm of Passover is shown to operate in the interests of the circle of James, and the Jacobean perspective on the meal is contrasted with the Petrine perspective. A genuinely paschal understanding implied a highly exclusive definition of eucharistic fellowship, since only circumcised Jews were to take part in Passover. Such exclusivity appears difficult to reconcile with the Petrine inclusion of Gentiles within the Church and the teaching that the meal itself, not extrinsic considerations, established purity. For the group which centered upon James, however, a fully paschal eucharist was a valuable instrument in the establishment of their own authority, a ritual warrant of the privilege of the Jewish family of Jesus and their circle.

The greatest resistance to the Jacobean view came from Paul, who attempted a return to the Petrine paradigm, and stressed the connection with Jesus' death (rather than Passover). The latter emphasis coincided with the emerging assumption in Hellenistic Christianity that "This is my blood" and "This is my body" were to be taken autobiographically. Solidarity with a heroic martyr in a kind of philosophical symposium was a natural understanding of eucharist, and it has clearly influenced the Synoptic Gospels. Chapter 5 goes on to show how the Synoptics accept the Jacobean limitation to Passover, but then take the paschal connection to be symbolic of the way in which Jesus opens inclusion within God's chosen people to all who are in solidarity with him.

Chapter 6 pursues the symbolic development of the paschal theme within John. The feeding of the 5,000—explicitly linked with Passover in 6:4—provides the occasion to explain that Jesus gives flesh and is consumed as the true bread of heaven (6:51). The autobiographical linkage to "body" and "blood" is now in a position of unquestionable dominance. That connection is as natural in the fourth Gospel as is the connection developed in the Revelation between Jesus and a sacrificed and yet triumphant lamb.

The definition of the types of eucharist, within considerations of identifiable circles of practice, remains the chief object of our study throughout. By the close, however, possibilities concerning the nature of the cycles of traditon which some of those circles contributed will have emerged. In the conclusion, we will review our findings, and suggest how the study of the New Testament on the basis of its constituent cycles might proceed. The character of eucharistic practice within early Christianity, considered in the light of its diverse types, will be our final concern.

CHAPTER ONE

THE PURITY OF THE KINGDOM

The Systemic Importance of Purity within early Judaism

Meals, as recognized thirty years ago by Morton Smith, were principal expressions within Judaism of what constituted purity.[1] One ate what was acceptable with those people deemed acceptable. To eat in that manner could more truly be said to create a sphere a purity than merely to express such purity: the meal became an instance of fellowship within a realm that was understood to be divinely mandated.[2]

Israel was understood as a people elected to serve God by producing pure offerings for the Temple, which those designated as priests prepared and sacrificed. The people, the offerings, and the priests were all to be pure. The purity of Israel as a whole was not be be confused with that of priests in particular, and not every animal needed to be as perfect as an offering, but there was a continuum linking the purity of beasts globally and sacrifices specifically, and the purity of Israel globally and priests specifically. For that reason, a priest defined the purity he embodied by what he ate with whom, as did any Israelite.

The power of sacred association, which establishes the purity of foods and people, is a programmatic theme within Leviticus. That

---

[1] See ''The Dead Sea Sect in Relation to Ancient Judaism,'' *New Testament Studies* 7 (1960-1961) 347-360. Smith's characterization of the issue is remarkable for its clarity, and its prescience in respect of subsequent discussion (p. 352):

> Differences as to the interpretation of the purity laws and especially as to the consequent question of table fellowship were among the principal causes of the separation of Christianity from the rest of Judaism and the early fragmentation of Christianity itself. The same thing holds for the Qumran community and, within Pharisaic traditions, the *ḥaburah*. They are essentially groups whose members observe the same interpretation of the purity rules and therefore can have table fellowship with each other. It is no accident that the essential act of communion in all these groups is participation in common meals.

[2] For a more recent discussion, fully informed by anthropological considerations, see Baruch M. Bokser, *The Origins of the Seder. The Passover Rite and Early Rabbinic Judaism* (Berkeley: University of California Press, 1984) 10-13, 53-62.

book demonstrates the systemic importance of purity for any religious appropriation of the Torah. The characteristic imperative of the book amounts to a signature: God is holy, so that Israel is to be holy (11:45; 19:2; 20:7). That holiness which Israel can enact is purity, the dedication to eat only what is clean (cf. 11:46, 47). Failure to maintain purity will result in death (15:31) and expulsion from the land (20:22). The internal logic of the laws of purity is not difficult to discern: essentially it is a matter of eating only what belongs to distinct categories of creation, not to hybrids (chapter 11),[3] of maintaining separation from the fluid emissions of birth and reproduction (chapters 12, 15), and of keeping one's own skin whole (chapters 13, 14), far from the blood, which belongs only to God (17:10-16). The last, vital principle is connected to what is perhaps the most startling and impracticable requirement in the entire book, that *every* ox, lamb or goat must be slaughtered as a sacrifice (17:3-7).[4]

There is, then, a curious twist in the logic of cleanness. Certain things, such as blood and the parts of beasts which are to be offered, are unclean because they belong to the divine alone. But other things, impure beasts and carcasses, are not fit for consumption, whether human (Israelite) or divine. But along either twist, the thread of the argument is the same: the laws of cleanness are Israel's means of maintaining a solidarity of sacrifice with God, apart from which the land may not be retained. Indeed, the astounding claim is here made that the former inhabitants of the land failed to keep the rules of purity and *for that reason* were expelled, so that Israel might suffer the same fate (18:24-30). The land, in Leviticus, is not for Israel; Israel is for the service of God in his land. The conditionality of Israel's presence is cognate with the fierce emphasis on cutting off what is unclean (cf., for example, 7:19-21, 22-27), and separating from the Gentiles (cf., again as mere instances, 18:3; 20:23).

Holiness is an ambivalent force. It is what gives Israel the land, but also what destroys anything that is not compatible with it. The priests are to be the instruments of Israel's compatibility with the

---

[3] Cf. Mary Douglas, *Purity and Danger. An Analysis of Concepts of Pollution and Taboo* (New York: Praeger, 1966).

[4] Deuteronomy 12:15-28 permits the slaughter and consumption of animals outside of Jerusalem, explicitly as nonsacrificial, provided the blood is poured out and the beast concerned is not owed as a sacrifice.

holy, and for that reason they are oddly privileged and punished. They partake of holy sacrifices, and are held to a higher order of sanctity than the generality of Israel (21:6, 8, 14, 15, 22, 23). But when Nadab and Abihu, sons of Aaron, offer incense in a foreign manner, they are consumed in fire, and God announces, "I will be sanctified among those who are near me, and I will be glorified before all the people" (10:1-3). Death then becomes the sanction for breaking the specific requirements of priesthood (cf. 10:6, 7, 8-11; 16:1, 2). God's desire is to consume a part of what is pure, but he will extirpate the impure, and his destruction of what he does not want is more comprehensive than his consumption of what he sets aside for himself. The priests are to keep those laws of purity which they teach, and more, because they are the guardians of Israel's cleanness, their tenuous compatibility with the holy (10:10, 11).

Once it is appreciated that purity not only defines Israel, but establishes Israel's communion with and survival alongside the divine, the divisions regarding purity within early Judaism become explicable. "Early Judaism" may conveniently be dated from 167 B.C., with the entry of an officer[5] of Antiochus IV into Jerusalem and the desecration of the Temple, but it is evident that the radical pluralization of Judaism prior to Jesus, of which Jesus was both a symptom and a result, is rooted in the flawed unity of restored Israel during the period of the Second Temple generally. But Antiochus' campaign triggered both a fissure of interests and a reconfiguration of those interests, in a way which made pluralism in the practice of purity the order of the day. Erection of the temple of Onias in Egypt (in opposition to the Tobiad administration in Jerusalem)[6] demonstrates that how sacrifice was offered, and *by whom*, was held by one, familial group of priests to be a better measure of the acceptability of worship than *where* sacrifice was offered. The manner, the personnel, and the place of sacrifice are all issues which relate to purity; Antiochus' invasion, and Tobiad complicity with him, exacerbated the divisions which each issue might promote.

Another group, defined by a desire to remain faithful to sacrifice in Jerusalem conducted by an appropriate priesthood and a resistance to the demands of Antiochus, became known as "the faithful" (the famous *hasidim*). Attempts have been made in the history

---

[5] Named Apollonius; see 2 Maccabees 5:24-25.
[6] See Josephus, *Jewish War* I, 33; VII, 420-32.

of scholarship to identify the *hasidim* with a particular sect of Judaism during the period of the second Temple, such as the Essenes or the Pharisees, but the adjective "faithful" cannot usefully or legitimately be limited to any one group. In the context of reaction to Antiochus, however, the sense of the term clearly related to one's adherence to covenantal norms of sacrifice, as part of a vehement resistance. Among the resisters was Mattathias, a country priest from Modin, whose son, Judas Maccabeus ("the hammer") introduced the most powerful priestly rule Judaism has ever known, which was known under the name of Hasmoneus, Mattathias' ancestor.[7] Judas, as is well known, turned piety into disciplined revolt, including an alliance with Rome (1 Maccabees 8) and a willingness to break the sabbath for military reasons (1 Maccabees 2:41; *Jewish War* I, 146), which saw the restoration of worship within the covenant in the Temple in 164 B.C. (1 Maccabees 4:36-61). After his death, his brother, Jonathan, was named high priest (10:20), and from that time until the period of Roman rule, the high priesthood was a Hasmonean prerogative (*Jewish War* I, 70).

Those events were too rapid for some, and simply unacceptable in the view of others. In strictly familial terms, the Hasmoneans could not claim the high priesthood as a right, and therefore competition with other families of priests was a factor. Moreover, the suspension of the sabbath for military purposes and the arrogation of the high priesthood *and* the monarchy by the non-Davidic Hasmoneans would have seemed to many to compound the apostasy sanctioned by Antiochus with disciplined but non- (perhaps anti-) covenantal norms of resistance and priesthood. The book of Daniel certainly does not express overt opposition to the Hasmoneans, but it does represent the less activist, apocalyptic stance which many pious Jews adopted as an alternative to the nationalistic and militaristic policy of the Hasmoneans. The eschatology of the prophets during the period of restored Israel is here transformed into a scenario of the end time, in which the Temple would be restored by miraculous means, with the archangel Michael's triumph capped by the resurrection of the just and the unjust (cf. Daniel 12). Folk Judaism of the period also anticipated providential interventions (cf. Tobit), but Daniel elevates and specifies that anticipation until it be-

---

[7] See 1 Maccabees 2:1-9:18; and Josephus, *Antiquities* XII, 265; XVI, 187; XX, 189, 238, 247.

comes a program of patient attention and fidelity, warranted by both heavenly vision and the pseudepigraphical ascription to Daniel (the sage of the Babylonian period; see Ezekiel 14:14).

In the case of the Essenes, opposition to the Hasmoneans became overt. They pursued their own system of purity, ethics, and initiation, followed their own calendar, and withdrew into their own communities, either within cities or in isolated sites such as Qumran. There they awaited a coming, apocalyptic war, when they, as "the sons of light," would triumph over "the sons of darkness:" not only the Gentiles, but anyone not of their vision. The culmination of those efforts was to be complete control of Jerusalem and the Temple, where worship would be offered according to their revelation, the correct understanding of the law of Moses (see *Zadokite Document* 5:17-6:11).[8] Their insistence upon a doctrine of two messiahs, one of Israel and one of Aaron, would suggest that it was particularly the Hasmoneans' arrogation of priestly and royal powers which alienated the Essenes.

Most of those who resisted the Seleucids, or who sympathized with the resistance, were neither of priestly families nor of Essene temperament. Nonetheless, the unchecked rule of the Hasmonean priests in the Temple was not entirely acceptable to them. For that large group, the Pharisaic movement held a great attraction. The Pharisees attempted less to replace the Hasmoneans than to influence their conduct of the praxis of Israel as centered in Jerusalem. For that reason, the Pharisees appear more conservative than the Essenes or competing, priestly families, although their focus upon the issue of purity makes their concerns (if not their policies) emblematic of the period. They sought to define purity principally by means of their oral tradition, and their interpretation of scripture; since adjudications of purity were bound to be complicated in the Hasmonean combination of secular government and sacrificial worship, disputes were inevitable. Josephus, for example, reports that the Pharisees made known their displeasure at Alexander Jannaeus by inciting a crowd to pelt him with lemons (at hand for a festal procession) at the time he should have been offering sacrifice (*Antiquities* XIII, 372, 373). Josephus also relates, from a later period,

---

[8] For what remains a valuable introduction and translation, see Theodor H. Gaster, *The Dead Sea Scriptures In English With Introduction and Notes* (Garden City: Anchor/Doubleday, 1976).

the teaching of the rabbis (probably Pharisees) who were implicated
in dismantling the eagle Herod had erected over a gate of the
Temple (*Jewish War* I, 648-655; *Antiquities* XVII, 149-167), a
gesture both less subversive of the established authority in the cult
than what earlier Pharisess had done and more pointedly a challenge
to Herod. Paradoxically, the willingness of the Pharisees to consider
the Hasmoneans in their priestly function, in distinction from the
Essenes, involved them, not only in symbolic disputes, but in vocal
and bloody confrontations. Alexander Jannaeus is reported to have
executed by crucifixion eight hundred opponents, either Pharisees
or those with whom the Pharisees sympathized, and to have slaughtered their families; but his wife came to an accommodation with the
Pharisees which guaranteed them considerable influence (*War* I,
96-114). It appears clear that, within the Hasmonean period, purity
was a political issue and a symbol, as well as an important dimension
within early Judaism as a religious system: the acquiescence of one
of the dynasty to any Pharisaic stricture implicitly acknowledged
that the Hasmonean priesthood was provisional, and the Pharisaic
movement probably found its original, political expression in opposition to that priesthood (cf. *Antiquities* XIII, 288-298).

The Pharisees accepted and developed the notion that, with the
end of the canon, the age of prophecy in the classical sense had
ceased (cf. 1 Maccabees 4:46). For that reason, they plausibly saw
Ezra and ''the men of the great assembly'' as their source, and their
own, interpretative movement as an extension of his program of
restoration (see ʾAboth 1:1-18; 2 Esdras 14). But in two, vital respects, the Pharisees need to be distinguished from the reforms of
Ezra. First, they identified themselves with no specific priestly or political figure: their program was its own guide, and was not to be
subservient to any particular family or dynasty. Second, Pharisaic
interpretation was not limited to the scriptures, nor was its characteristic focus scriptural: the principal point of departure was the
recollection of earlier teaching of those called ''sages.'' Ultimately,
after the period of the New Testament, the ideology of the Rabbis
(as the Pharisees came to be called) had it that Moses conveyed two
Torahs on Sinai, one written and one oral. Even before that understanding, however, the sages treated the teachings of their predecessors in ''chains'' of tradition as normative. It was not so much that
oral tradition was set alongside scripture, as that oral tradition *was*
scripture until the canon itself could no longer be ignored as the
functional standard of Judaism.

Factionalism among the Hasmoneans, which resulted in rival claims to the high priesthood between Aristobulus and Hyrcanus (the sons of Alexandra, wife of Alexander Jannaeus), culminated in an appeal by both sides to Pompey, who obliged by taking Jerusalem for Rome and entering the sanctuary in 63 B.C. (*Jewish War* I, 152-154). *The Psalms of Solomon* represents a common, pious expression of horror at the events of 63 B.C., which was probably shared by most Pharisees (whether or not the *Psalms* should be taken as specifically Pharisaic). From that period, and all through the reign of Herod and his relatives, the Pharisees' attitude to the government was ambivalent. Some appear to have engaged in a principled opposition to Roman rule and its representatives as such. Today, that group is often known as the "Zealots," but the term is a misnomer. The Zealots were a priestly group of revolutionaries, not rebellious Pharisees, who were associated with Eleazar, son of Simon, during the revolt of A.D. 66-73 (*Jewish War* II, 564, 565; IV, 224, 225). The rebellious Pharisees are also to be distinguished from the movements of prophetic pretenders, who claimed divine inspiration for their efforts to free the land of the Romans (*Jewish War* II, 258-265; VII, 437-446). Other Pharisees normally accommodated to the new regime, but resisted—sometimes violently—Herodian excesses, such as the erection of a golden eagle on a gate of the Temple (*War* I, 648-655). Nonetheless, an apparently Pharisaic group is called "the Herodians" (Matthew 22:16; Mark 3:6; 12:13), which presumably signals its partisanship of the interests of the royal family as the best support of their teaching of purity. They may be associated with rabbis who enjoyed the protection of Herod and his house; the authorities referred to in Rabbinic literature as the "sons of Bathyra" (cf. b. Baba Meṣia 85a) may have been such a group. Others still largely cooperated with the Romans, and with the priestly administration of the Temple, although they might fall out regarding such questions as whether the priestly vestments should be kept under Roman or local control (*Antiquities* XVIII, 90-95; XX, 6-14), or the price of doves for sacrifice (m. Kerithoth 1:7). Neither the Pharisees nor those who supported them may be understood at base as a sect defined by specifiable teachings.[9] They

---

[9] Josephus' presentation of the Pharisees in that way (together with the Essenes and Sadducees) is a function of his apologetic purpose, as well as of his personal ambition. See "Joseph bar Matthias's Vision of the Temple," *The Temple of Jesus*,

shared skepticism regarding the current administration of the Temple and wariness of Roman hegemony, but varied widely in the degree and kind of resistance they would countenance. And through their history, one group typically defined itself in distinction from others in terms of highly specific (but socially constitutional) issues of purity.

The priesthood itself, meanwhile, was fractured further in its response to the fact of Roman governance. Some priests, especially among the privileged families in Jerusalem, were notoriously pro-Roman. The story of sons of the high priest having the surgery called epispasm, in order to restore the appearance of a foreskin (for gymnastic purposes) is well known (see 1 Maccabees 1:14, 15; *Antiquities* XII, 240, 241). There is little doubt but that such families, the most prominent of which were the Sadducees and Boethusians, were not highly regarded by most Jews (see b. Pesaḥim 57a). They are portrayed by outsiders in a negative light, as not teaching the resurrection of the dead (see *Jewish War* II, 165; Matthew 22:23; Mark 12:18; Luke 20:27; Acts 23:8), but the issue may have been one of emphasis: the Torah had stressed that correct worship in the Temple would bring with it material prosperity, and the elite priests attempted to realize that promise. The arrangement in Jerusalem gave them such constant control that they became known as "high priests," although there was in fact only one high priest. But Josephus indulges in the usage, as well as the Gospels, so that it should not be taken as an inaccuracy: the plural is a cultic mistake, but a sociological fact. Caiaphas held an historically long tenure as high priest during the period (*Antiquities* XVIII, 35, 95), and the frequent change of personnel reflects the collective nature of the priestly leadership, as well as Roman caution in respect of a post which might have produced a national leader. Herod himself understood the possibilities of the high priesthood in that regard, which is why he had Jonathan and Hyrcanus, potential rivals (albeit relatives by marriage), murdered, and why he married Mariamme (*Jewish War* I, 431-444; *Antiquities* XX, 247-251). His ambition was for a new Hasmonean dynasty, and it appears that only the notorious greed of his sons, combined with his willingness to have them

---

69-87 and Jacob Neusner, "Josephus' Pharisees: A Complete Repertoire," *Josephus, Judaism, and Christianity* (ed. L.H. Feldman and G. Hata; Detroit: Wayne State University Press, 1987) 274-292.

executed, thwarted its realization. As it was, Herod's grandson and namesake, king of Chalcis, did maintain the residual power of selecting the high priest, although as king of Chalcis he had no ordinary authority over Jerusalem (see *Antiquities* XX, 15, 16). Several priests were also prominent in the revolt against Rome, however, and it should not be thought that such priestly nationalists, among whom were Joseph bar Matthias, better known as Flavius Josephus, emerged only at the end of the sixties (*Jewish War* II, 562-568). The precedent of the Hasmoneans was there for any priestly family to see itself as a possible alternative to Roman rule. Indeed, some priests were not only nationalists, but revolutionaries, who joined with the Essenes, or with rebellious Pharisees, although any alliance of priests with a prophetic pretender is, perhaps, not a likely supposition.

The Pharisees' mastery of the oral medium made them a successful tendency within pluralized Judaism. In the period before written communication was standard among the generality of Jews, the use of memorization and recitation was far more prominent. The Pharisees were in a position to communicate guidance in respect of purity, an emerging understanding of scripture (in the *Targumim*, whose development they influenced), and their own sense of the authority of the sages, without requiring general literacy. There is no reason to suppose, for example, that rabbis of the first century such as Hillel and Hanina ben Dosa were able to read fluently, although each was a formative member of the Pharisaic, and therefore later of the Rabbinic, movements. The Pharisees' willingness to live by craft, rather than by status (see ʾAvoth 2:2)—the most prominent example being Hillel's menial labor (b. Yoma 35b)—also meant that they could move from town to town, promulgating their views. In some respects, their occasional itinerancy in Israel was comparable to that of the Graeco-Roman philosophers of the Mediterranean world (Stoic, Pythagorean, and/or Cynic). The term "Pharisee" is probably an outsiders' name for the movement, and may mean "separatist" or "purist;" participants in the movement appear to have referred to their ancient predecessors (after Ezra) as "the sages" or "the wise," and to their more recent predecessors and contemporaries as "teachers" (cf. *rab* in m. ʾAvoth 1:6, 16; *sophistês* in Josephus). The normal, respectful address of a teacher was "my great one," or "my master," *rabbi*.

During the time of Hillel and Shammai, and until A.D. 70, Pharisaic teaching was targeted at the conduct of the cult in the

Temple, but its influence was limited. Nonetheless, Pharisees appeared to have succeeded reasonably well in town and villages, even
in Galilee, where they urged local populations to maintain the sort
of purity which would permit them to participate rightly in the cult.
Josephus' fellow in the armed resistance against Rome and arch-
rival, John of Gischala, may well have been representing Pharisaic
interests when he arranged for Jews in Syria to purchase oil exclusively from Galilean sources (*Jewish War*, II, 591-594). In any case,
it does appear plain that some Pharisees supported the revolt of A.D.
66-70, while others did not. But while many priests and Essenes
perished in the internecine strife of the revolt and in the war with
the Romans, and while the aristocracy of scribes and elders in
Jerusalem was discredited and decimated, the Pharisees survived
the war better than any other single group. They were well accepted
locally, had long ago accommodated to some marginality, and survived with their personnel and their traditions comparatively intact.
Rabbinic literature itself personifies the survival of the movement in
a story concerning Rabbi Yoḥanan ben Zakkai. According to the
story, Yoḥanan had himself borne out of Jerusalem on the pretense
he was dead, only to hail Vespasian as king; on his ascent to power,
Vespasian granted Yoḥanan his wish of settlement in the town of
Yavneh, the group of Rabbi Gamaliel, and medical attention for
Rabbi Zadok (cf. b. Giṭṭin 56a, b). In that Josephus claims similarly
to have flattered Vespasian (*Jewish War*, III, 399-408), and to have
seen in his coming the fulfillment of messianic prophecy (*War*, VI,
310-315), the tale is to be used with caution, but it remains expressive of the Rabbinic ethos.

The success of the Pharisees in small towns during Jesus' period
became all the more pronounced as their power was largely ceded
to priestly interests in Jerusalem. Many local scribes, but not all,
were likely Pharisees, and the majority would have to account for
Pharisaic views. Scribes are, strictly speaking, simply men who can
read and write, a skill which in antiquity represented some social
and educational attainment. In Israel, given the Roman encouragement of local government, scribes emerged in towns and villages as
a focus of judicial and religious power. From the time of the writing
of the Torah itself, it was accepted that all aspects of God's rule—
ethical, legal and cultic—were articulated by Moses. The ability of
the scribes to read and write made them ideal judges, adjuncts to
priests, teachers, and leaders of worship. Indeed, all those functions

were probably discharged by an interactive group of scribes, people of priestly lineage, Pharisees and other elders, in any given village. It was likely in the same place in a town that cases were settled, purity or impurity declared, lessons given, and the Torah recited from the written form and from memory in Aramaic. There too, disputes would take place among scribes, judges, priests, Pharisees and elders, concerning how the Torah was to be understood and applied. Later Rabbinic literature tends to reduce the disputes of the period to the ''houses'' of Hillel and Shammai, but that is quite evidently a *topos*; because they lacked any central leadership in the period before A.D. 70, Pharisees differed from movement to movement, town to town, rabbi to rabbi, and (during periods of intense discussion and interaction) even day to day.

The structure of a local council also prevailed under Roman rule in Jerusalem. The Greek term *sunedrion* was applied to it, and it has become known as ''the Sanhedrin,'' largely as a result of the Mishnah. Mishnah, a document of the second century, cannot be taken at face value as a guide to events and institutions of the first century, but it does seem clear, from the Gospels and Josephus, taken together with the Mishnah, that the council in Jerusalem was largely controlled by the high priests, but that elders or aristocrats of the city also participated, among whom were Pharisees (and, of course, some scribes, who may or may not also have been priests, elders, and/or Pharisees). Whether there were actually seventy-one members of the Sanhedrin (as in Rabbinic literature) cannot be known with certainty, and the extent of its capital jurisdiction is not known. But the Romans appear to have given the council the authority to execute perpetrators of blatant sacrilege (*Jewish War* II, 228-231; V, 194; *Antiquities* XV, 417). The authority of the council of Jerusalem outside of the city followed the prestige of the city itself, and the acknowledged centrality of the Temple. But a ruling of the council there was not automatically binding upon those in the countryside and in other major cities; acceptance of a given teaching, precept by precept, was the path of influence. Pharisees also taught in and around the Temple, the focus of their discussion of purity, and the Pharisees in Jerusalem were the most prestigious in the movement.

The observance of purity locally, outside of Jerusalem, might be almost entirely conventional, a manner of keeping company with people of one's own social group and purchasing goods from merchants to whom resort is customary. Provided friends and associates keep customs of purity, little thought is needed to remain pure oneself. People and customs from without might also be avoided, but in much village life, that is also a conventional response. The more complex the social constitution of a village, town, or region,[10] the more self-conscious one's selection of contacts, and therefore one's self-consciousness of purity. The Pharisees represent precisely such a self-consciousness within early Judaism, and therefore may be distinguished from the more unreflective practice of non-urban populations generally.

Jesus' Practice of Purity

Jesus' practice of fellowship at meals is well established within the Gospels. The practice of those Christians who developed the texts as they may be read has evidently influenced the presentation of Jesus; a symposial atmosphere is generated around the picture of Jesus and his followers at table which is redolent of eucharistic worship at a later stage.[11] But Jesus' conscious practice of fellowship at meals is attested in pericopae which are not susceptible of analysis as retroversions from a later period.[12] They clearly suggest that

---

[10] Cosmopolitan cities occasion great complications for the maintenance of purity. But during the first century, Galilee was not subject to the degree of urban development which the second century saw; cf. Lee I. Levine, *The Rabbinic Class of Roman Palestine in Late Antiquity* (New York: The Jewish Theological Seminary, 1989) 25-33 and Sean Freyne, *Galilee, Jesus and the Gospels: Literary Approaches and Historical Investigations* (Philadelphia: Fortress, 1988) 143-155. Moreover, as Freyne repeatedly points out, the Judaic sub-culture of Galilee and Jesus' own activity were not principally urban.

[11] Cf. Burton L. Mack, *A Myth of Innocence. Mark and Christian Origins* (Philadelphia: Fortress, 1988) 114-120. Mack's apparent supposition is that "meal practice" must derive from "a symposium atmosphere" (*sic!*), p. 115. Although that global supposition is unwarranted (and undefended, in Mack's work), there are passages which are susceptible of such an analysis. In John 13, for example, a meal has clearly become more a vehicle of teaching than an event within its own terms of reference. Similarly, the incursion of the dispute regarding hierarchy into Synoptic versions of "the last supper" (Luke 22:24-30, cf. Matthew 20:24-28//Mark 10:41-45) better reflects the programmatic concerns of mealtime fellowship within the Church than a particular concern of Jesus' at that stage of his life. Luke 11:37-54 is another good example of controversial material which has been introduced artificially into the setting of a meal.

[12] See, for example, Richard A. Horsley, *Jesus and the Spiral of Violence. Popular Jewish Resistance in Roman Palestine* (San Francisco: Harper & Row, 1987) 178-180, where a fairly representative list of references is provided. He cites Matthew

Jesus' activity in that regard was not incidental. The challenge posed by the texts is not to establish that Jesus ate with people self-consciously: that much is evident. The challenge is rather to determine the contextual sense of that activity, when our texts reflect a social environment distinct from the one which produced them.[13]

Purity emerges as a natural context in which fellowship at meals would exert symbolic power. In two respects, clearly flagged in the Gospels, purity is made the central issue of Jesus' meals. The first respect concerns the eating of foods, the second concerns immediate social contact with people whose status in regard to purity was problematic.

The issue of what Israelites might eat and with whom is of systemic importance within any straightforward reading of the Torah as embodying the covenant with the patriarchs and Moses. Suitable foods and company for consumption and for sacrifice are designated, and many are forbidden. The probability is that many such laws were rooted in the paradigmatic role which pastoral and ruminant nomadism played within the formation of Israel,[14] but by the time of the Priestly source the system had long constituted a self-contained taxonomy.[15] Even after the attempts at systematization which are evident within the biblical text, glaring inconsistencies are apparent. Leviticus 17:1-9 (cf. 7:19-21), for example, prescribes that every animal which is to be slaughtered should be offered at the cultic center as a kind of sacrifice, while Deuteronomy 12:20-28 represents the practice that genuinely non-sacrificial meals could be enjoyed outside Jerusalem, provided that the blood of the beast has been poured into the ground.[16] The adjudication among competing

---

8:11,12//Luke 13:28, 29; Matthew 11:18, 19//Luke 7:33, 34; Acts 2:46; Mark 2:19a (and cf. Matthew 9:15a; Luke 5:34); 6:30-44 (and cf. Matthew 14:12c-21; Luke 9:10-17); 8:1-10 (and cf. Matthew 15:32-39); Luke 14:16-24; Matthew 22:1-10.

[13] Freyne's study addresses that challenge within the construct of "social world;" the present task is to concentrate attention more particularly on the nexus of issues identified by the systems of purity in early Judaism.

[14] Cf. Marvin Harris, *Good to Eat: Riddles of Food and Culture* (New York: Simon and Schuster, 1985) 72-75.

[15] See Mary Douglas, *Purity and Danger. An Analysis of Concepts of Pollution and Taboo* (New York: Praeger, 1966); David P. Wright, "Unclean and Clean (OT)," *Anchor Bible Dictionary* 6 (ed. D.N. Freedman; New York: Doubleday, 1992) 729-741; also Harris, p. 79 and Martin Noth (tr. J.D. Martin), *Numbers: A Commentary* (Philadelphia: Westminster, 1968).

[16] The conception of the non-sacrificial meal is what permits Deuteronomy to

conceptions of purity within scripture, and the application of such
conceptions to unforeseen social contexts are immediate and pressing necessities for any group which seeks to live as the "Israel"
which those scriptures make classic. As groups address such concerns, the purity of persons and of foods is defined. Pharisees simply
represent one tendency of early Judaism in its quest to develop the
purity which was consistent with acceptable sacrifice, a purity whose
symbol and realization might be a common meal.[17]

Jesus' citation of the complaint against him that he is a glutton and
a drinker, a friend of revenue-contractors[18] and sinners (Matthew
11:18, 19//Luke 7:33-35), is widely acknowledged to distinguish
Jesus' practice from John the baptist's in respect of both consumption and fellowship.[19] What might be more attentively considered is
that the saying coordinates the two issues: Jesus eats and drinks, and
with the wrong people. E.P. Sanders has argued that "sinners" in
the passage refers specifically (and even technically) to those he calls
"the wicked:"[20] "He may have offered them inclusion in the kingdom not only *while they were still sinners* but also *without* requiring
repentance as normally understood, and therefore he could have
been accused of being a friend of people who indefinitely remained
sinners."[21] Taken with all the implications Sanders goes on to de-

---

develop the conception, foreign to the scheme in Leviticus, that the flesh of non-
domesticated animals might be clean (cf. 14:15).

[17] For a discussion in regard to a recent controversy, see Appendix 1.

[18] See Fritz Herrenbrück's suggestion of such a rendering ("Abgabenpächter")
for τελώνης in *Jesus und die Zöllner. Historische und neutestamentlich-exegetische Untersuchungen*: WUNT 41 (Tübingen: Mohr, 1990). Herrenbrück's analysis is developed on the evidence of the Ptolemaic papyri and less comprehensive sources from
later periods. His purpose is to challenge the understanding that τελῶναι in the
Gospels are to be equated with *portitores*, collectors in the service of *publicani* within
Roman society. Herrenbrück's preferred models are the τελῶναι of the Hellenistic
world (not Rome itself), local contractors (*Kleinpächter*) charged with the collection
of various revenues for Rome. They are *Abgabenpächter*, revenue-contractors, rather
than tax or toll collectors (p. 37, cf. p. 225, where the suggested English rendering
confuses the issue somewhat). Identification with the *publicani* of the Roman hierarchy should be avoided, since the system involved private contractors who won their
arrangements on the basis of competitive bids, rather than bureaucrats. The papyri
indicate that a τελώνης might collect duties, and taxes generally (direct and indirect), including charges in kind (p. 291). In other words, the contact of a τελώνης
with people and goods of suspect purity would come as a matter of course.

[19] For a fairly representative discussion of the authenticity of saying, cf. Douglas R.A. Hare, *The Son of Man Tradition* (Minneapolis: Fortress, 1990) 259-264.

[20] Cf. E.P. Sanders, *Jesus and Judaism* (Philadelphia: Fortress, 1985) 178, 179.

[21] P. 206. For a fuller development of the criticism which follows, cf. Chilton,

velop, his argument requires that "sinners" (ἁμαρτωλοί) in the passage (and elsewhere) be understood as the "wicked" (רְשָׁעִים) with a precise meaning. Neither such a retroversion nor the meaning postulated by Sanders is anything more than a possibility.

Yet Sanders's contention that the revenue-contractors and sinners are a worse lot than those who in Rabbinic literature are normally styled "peoples of the land" (עַמְמֵי הָאָרֶץ) is unexceptionable: Jesus is accused of eating with those of the ilk of revenue-contractors, who not only *might* be impure (as in the case of a person of the land [עַם הָאָרֶץ]), but who are *ordinarily* impure as a result of routine trade and fellowship with all manner of produce and people. He makes himself a companion[22] of the unapproachable with food and drink which is unacceptable. That the activity of eating and drinking (rather than repentance) is in dispute, and that fellowship with revenue-contractors and other rabble is related to the dispute, are straightforward inferences which are readily explicable within the environment of early Judaism.

From the point of view of understanding the gravamen of the charge against Jesus from its point of origin, the revenue-contractors represent a more suitable focus than "the sinners." There is clear evidence that the tendency of the Synoptics is to generalize the case of "sinners" from that of revenue-contractors, rather than the reverse. In Mark 2:16, for example, "the scribes of the Pharisees" are said to notice that Jesus eats with "sinners and revenue-contractors," although the order is reversed when they speak themselves in the same verse. The instance at hand, of course, is a meal hosted by Levi, a τελώνης himself (vv. 14f.).[23] Evidently, the generative issue is eating with a revenue-contractor and his ilk; as developed and applied within the community of Mark, the passage concerns "sinners" more generally.

"Jesus and the Repentance of E.P. Sanders," *Tyndale Bulletin* 39 (1988) 1-18, a position earlier intimated in the *Journal of Biblical Literature* 106 (1987) 537-539.

[22] The term "fellow" (חַבְרָא) is of course a possible antecedent in Aramaic of "friend" (φίλος) in the saying, although the present argument does not depend upon that possibility. Similarly, "debtors" (חַיָּיבַיָּא)—the usual term for people who sin—is more plausible as an antecedent of "sinners" (ἁμαρτωλοί) than "the wicked" (רְשִׁיעַיָּא). Even after the last term is conceived of—*pace* Sanders—in its Aramaic form, its meaning is too restricted for it to be taken naturally as a reference to people who sin; generally, the term in Aramaic refers to those who are constitutionally wicked, to the point that they persecute Israel.

[23] See Herrenbrück, p. 229, and the parallels.

Luke especially refers to the revenue-contractor (τελώνης) as a point of departure to speak of instances of the more comprehensive designation, sinner (ἁμαρτωλός). For that reason, the story of the "sinful" woman (7:36-50) follows the saying concerning Jesus' eating with revenue contractors and sinners (τελωνῶν καὶ ἁμαρτωλῶν; v. 34). Attempts to specify her sin (which by now amount to a minor literature of their own) run counter to the tendency of the text, which is deliberately aiming at generality.[24] The Lukan point is simply that sinners are ready for forgiveness: that is their justification. Luke may be regarded as promulgating the same point in the presentation of the parables of the lost sheep (15:3-6) and the lost coin (15:8, 9) as stories told on the occasion of both τελῶναι and ἁμαρτωλοί eating with Jesus, to the annoyance of Pharisees and scribes over such fellowship with "sinners" (15:1-3). Uniquely Lukan sayings relate those two images to the repentant sinner (15:7, 10). Similarly, the nameless revenue-contractor of 18:9-14 calls himself a sinner (v. 13), and is justified (v. 14), and Zachaeus (19:1-10) is styled a sinner (v. 7), but is assigned to the realm of salvation by Jesus (v. 9). It is evident that such usages of ἁμαρτωλός are tendentious, and portray sinfulness as an endemic condition from which Jesus offers release.[25]

Even within Luke, however, "sinner" is an ambivalent category, not simply a positive one. Simon Peter's declaration that he is sinful assumes that Jesus should depart from him for that reason (5:8), although Jesus' reaction is of course quite different (5:10). More tellingly, ἁμαρτωλοί are emphatically referred to in a disparaging sense at 6:32, 33, 34. The Matthean analog of the complex of sayings (5:46, 47) refers instead to revenue-contractors (οἱ τελῶναι) and Gentiles (οἱ ἐθνικοί). The preferred categories of both Gospels come to the fore here. Matthew likely betrays a Syrian bias against revenue-contractors in its assumption, comparable to some attitudes represented in Rabbinica, that revenue-contractors, like prostitutes,

---

[24] An excellent analysis of the Lukan sense of the story is developed in David A. Neale, *None but the Sinners. Religious Categories in the Gospel of Luke*: Journal for the Study of the New Testament Supplement 58 (Sheffield: Sheffield Academic Press, 1991), 135-147. In his analysis, "sinners" for Luke is a religious category (p. 97), developed to target those who are willing to repent (p. 147, cf. pp. 193, 194). The contrast with Sanders's understanding of the term is striking.

[25] It is equally clear that the background of such a usage is not likely to have been a definitive category of exclusion from salvation such as Sanders presupposes.

must give up their professions in order to be baptized (see 18:17; 21:31, 32).[26] That is yet another version of the tendency to generalize upon the memory of Jesus' fellowship with revenue-contractors.

Together with Jesus' citation of his enemies' objection to such fellowship in Matthew 11:18, 19//Luke 7:33-35, the story of the calling of Levi (or Matthew), with its notice of a controversial meal at Levi's house (Matthew 9:9-13//Mark 2:13-17//Luke 5:27-32), establishes the importance of Jesus' connections with revenue-contractors. Indeed, that complex typifies the Synoptic perspective in regard to the contractors, in that it closes with the saying, "I came not to call righteous people, but sinners."[27] But the complex also reflects both a practice of unusual fellowship and a willingness to accept τελῶναι into the heart of the movement which are attributable to Jesus. Even allowing for the Synoptic tendency to extrapolate from the example of revenue-contractors to "sinners" as whole, and for the Lukan tendency to portray them in heroic terms, Jesus' programmatic fellowship with them ought to be regarded as a significant factor in his ministry.[28]

Herrenbrück's study permits of a more accurate appraisal of the meaning of such fellowship than had been possible before. Instead of seeing τελῶναι as notorious "traitors" (Sanders's reading),[29] or as among the generality of the trades which resulted in their being "*de jure* and officially deprived of rights and ostracized" (Jeremias's reading),[30] Herrenbrück is able to show in a comprehensive description that revenue-contractors in fact enjoyed positions of relatively high status and wealth within the Roman settlement in Palestine, and that despite tensions with important strands of Pharisaism, they were well integrated socially and religiously within Judaism.[31]

---

[26] So Herrenbrück, pp. 229, 244-259; he distinguishes the assumptions behind Luke 3:12, pp. 250-254.

[27] The Lukan addition, "to repentance," comes as no surprise, in view of the pattern observed above. On the other hand, "sinners" also appears in a saying included in all the Synoptics which assumes that they do not and will not attend to Jesus: he is delivered into their hands to die (Matthew 26:45//Mark 14:41//Luke 24:7). That is the sort of usage which would suit Sanders's position better; but the ambivalence of ἁμαρτωλός, as well as its general applicability (cf. Luke 13:2) suggests that a term in Aramaic such as debtor (חַיָּבָא) lies in its background.

[28] Herrenbrück's analysis therefore makes too sweeping a claim for the historical reliability of the Gospels (cf. p. 228), although it is accurate in its central contention.

[29] Cf. *Jesus and Judaism*, p. 178, cf. 386 n. 16.

[30] *Jerusalem in the Time of Jesus*, p. 311.

[31] Cf. Herrenbrück, pp. 162-227.

Herrenbrück acknowledges the paucity of relevant Rabbinic texts
for the accurate characterization of the τελῶναι, especially because
the circumstances subsequent to the great revolts against Rome have
influenced the portrayal of social and economic conditions during
the first century.[32] It is nonetheless striking that a construction
related to the term for a collector on behalf of a contractor (a *gabbai*,
normally understood as responsible to a *mokhes*) can be used within
Mishnah in respect of the collection of alms,[33] and that contractors
themselves—although viewed with contempt—are assumed to function within the conventions of Judaism in the earliest datable reference.[34] A baraita has it that at an early stage, *gabba'in* and *mokhsin*
were understood to give reliable testimony; later they came to be
seen as untrustworthy.[35] But whatever the views of Pharisees and
rabbis, it does seem clear that at least some *mokhsin* enjoyed considerable repute during the first century. Herrenbrück's parade example is Josephus' reference to John the τελώνης in Caesarea, a
member—and apparently a leader—of a delegation of Jewish nota-
bles in negotiation with Gessius Florus concerning arrangements in
regard to a synagogue.[36]

What made the revenue-contractors (*mokhsin*) unacceptable in the
attitudes of many Pharisees? In Herrenbrück's opinion, suspicion
attached especially to the source of their wealth, the likelihood that
it was fraudulently acquired, and the difficulty of restoring what was
wrongly taken.[37] His interpretation appears plausible, especially
when it is borne in mind that alms were held not to be acceptable
from the treasuries of the *mokhsin* and *gabba'in*, although contributions could be taken from them at home or in the market.[38] The

---

[32] Herrenbrück, pp. 193-195. It is remarkable that his conclusion is commen-
surate with Büchler's, which is cited on p. 195.

[33] Cf. Peah 8:7, where the verbal form נִגְבֵּית appears, and Herrenbrück p. 197.

[34] Cf. Nedarim 3:4, which discusses using the form of an oath with a *mokhes* (as
with a murderer or a robber) to make a false vow; Herrenbrück, pp. 198, 199.

[35] Cf. b. Sanhedrin 25b; Herrenbrück, p. 202.

[36] *Jewish War* II. 277-292; Herrenbrück, pp. 211-213. But Herrenbrück apparently does not consider the possibility that, since Josephus is here concerned to
stress the venality of Gessius Florus, the example of John is given to show the only
sort of Jew who could deal with him (and even he, of course, is betrayed).

[37] See especially b. Babba Qamma 94b, 95a and Herrenbrück, p. 207. It must
be emphasized, however, that the discussion envisages that shepherds, *gabba'in* and
mokhsin might offer restitution without its being accepted.

[38] M. Babba Qamma 10:1, cited in Herrenbrück, p. 203. A similar restriction
obtains for changing money.

principal issue, then, would appear to have been the nature of the activity and especially its involvement with untithed and/or unclean produce, rather than an evaluation of character or motives. The assumption in regard to the acceptability of fellowship with the *mokhes* named Maʿyan in the Yerushalmi is quite instructive: he is there praised for giving a meal for the poor of Askalon.[39] His table might not have been recommended for companions of the Pharisees, but it is an emblem of charitable fellowship within Israel, and may be compared with Jesus' practice of fellowship at meals.

The last passage suggests that revenue-contractors were viewed with suspicion by Pharisees, and yet not considered to be beyond incorporation within Israel, even on the strict construal of purity which the Pharisees—with much variation among them—generally espoused. Whether produce was tithed and whether foodstuffs had been kept clean were matters of systemic importance to Pharisees (see Appendix 1); when those concerns are taken together with the possibility of fraud raised by Herrenbrück, Pharisaic skepticism of revenue-contractors, over and above the perennial doubts raised by taxpayers, appears to have been both inevitable and rational. It seems that as a group their status would have been below that of peoples of the land (עַמְמֵי הָאָרֶץ), judged within conventionally Pharisaic standards of purity.

Jesus' programmatic fellowship with revenue-contractors, particularly at meals (and scandalously at meals provided by revenue-contractors), put him in at least potential conflict with those who saw the purity of such professionals as suspect or untenable. But the heightening of the role of the revenue-contractors within the Gospels,[40] to serve as symbols of what Jesus might offer to non-Jews, must not be permitted to narrow our appreciation of the nexus of issues which systems of purity involve. For apologetic reasons, the Gospels at a Hellenistic stage in their development portray Jesus as consciously transcending questions of purity.

Within the West, an ideology of the transcendence of purity is all but universally approved, within and without theological discourse.

---

[39] M. Ḥagigah 2:2, cited in Herrenbrück with a discussion of variants on the story, pp. 213-216, with Matthew 22:1-10//Luke 14:15-24; Thomas *l.* 64.

[40] *Mutatis mutandis*, the heightening of the role of the עַמְמֵי הָאָרֶץ within the Mishnah should not lead us to imagine a single Pharisaic/Rabbinic position in contrast to a similarly unvaried laxity among people generally.

The ideology has become emblematic of Western values, to the point that communities which invoke issues of purity are commonly treated as sects if they are found within contemporary societies. Examples might include Ḥasidic forms of Judaism and apocalyptic forms of Christianity, both of which typically involve the avoidance of foods, drinks and practices which are current in the wider cultures in which they exist. If communities are seen as primitive[41] (within historical or ethnographic terms of reference), their systems of purity are usually tolerated better by Westerners, since they assume they will never be asked to practise them on a regular basis. Implicitly (but effectively) the practical notion of purity itself is anathematized in the West as being impure; we instead invoke strictures of hygiene and health—most of which have never been demonstrated to us personally—as ontologically warranted. The apparent irony that the ideology results in the treatment of certain groups as impure is predictable, once it is appreciated that, whatever might be claimed within a social system, "purity" is the means by which certain objects and gestures are privileged and paradigmatic. Their "purity" is nothing other than a social sanction and encouragement of their repetition, while "unclean" actions and objects are those which are proscribed or marginalized.[42] Of course, one method of reinforcing

---

[41] The term has understandably fallen into disrepute among many anthropologists, in view of its association with colonialism. In a recent study, however, Marianna Torgovnick (*Gone Primitive: Savage Intellects, Modern Lives* [Chicago: University of Chicago, 1990] 20) has reminded us that "for Euro-Americans the primitive as an inexact expressive whole—often with little correspondence to any specific or documented societies—has been an influential and powerful concept, capable of referring both to societies 'out there' and to subordinate groups within the West." During the course of her study, she further conflates "the primitive" with aesthetic "primitivism," which may or may not be a useful concession to modern usage. In any case, Torgovnick has demonstrated that primitivity may be considered, without accepting the colonial and sexist abuses of which it has been an instrument. Whether or not "primitive" survives as a category, certain alternatives appear too negative by comparison, either because they are expressly privative (e.g., "non-literate," "non-Western," "underdeveloped") or they implicitly anticipate further development (e.g., "simple," "small scale," "fourth world"). If "primitive" must be used cautiously in the present study, to speak of what others have described, that is no more than a provisional usage, in order to refer to societies regulated by custom and usually characterized by attention to kinship, a complex assignment of differing roles to single individuals, and the practice of ritual. For further discussion and references, see *The Temple of Jesus*, 5 and the indexed material regarding purity.

[42] See "Appendix 1: A Response to *Things Hidden from the Foundation of the World*: In the Beginning was the Meal," *The Temple of Jesus*, 163-172.

such a social system of purity is to claim that it is part of the order of the natural world, and that competing systems oppose that order. That is just what is happening when Westerners open their newspapers and magazines, and discover the purity which makes them healthy and learn about the sects and primitives whose opposing views and practices make them quaint, backward, and/or dangerous. Such a reinforcement of Westerners' purity is most likely to occur on a Saturday and a Sunday, when they are off work, and will be especially strong among those who do not attend religious services, since they have more leisure to read and watch television. Small wonder, then, that people who style themselves as secular are the most dedicated to Western purity (which they will call by another name) and the most intolerant of any other form of purity.

The notion that Jesus was positively engaged in a program of purity will, therefore, predictably offend Western apologists of transcendence (religious and secular). In historical and literary terms, however, Jesus belongs within a system of religion which regards purity and impurity as matters of routine. Within the Priestly source of the Pentateuch, for example, it is understood that Israelites will become impure during the course of their lives, and that such impurities can be dealt with. Contact with corpses (Numbers 19), with the carcasses of unclean animals (particularly in real or potential connection with food, Leviticus 11), with sexually related discharges (Leviticus 12, 15), with certain conditions of the skin (or objects susceptible of similar eruptions, Leviticus 13-14), and with several cultic means of removing uncleanness (Leviticus 16:26-28; Numbers 19:21, 22) may all be remedied, and blame does not seem ordinarily to attach to the impurity involved with such contact.[43] Washing, sacrifice, the passage of time, and disposal, in prescribed combinations, are understood to restore the required purity. But matters become more grave, and transgressions may even bring about a cutting off from the community and from life (cf. the use of the verb כָּרַת), when volition is or may be involved. Instances include a delay of a required purification (Leviticus 5:2, 3; Numbers 19:13, 20),

---

[43] Cf. David P. Wright, *The Disposal of Impurity. Elimination Rites in the Bible and in Hittite and Mesopotamian Literatures*: Society of Biblical Literature Dissertation Series 101 (Atlanta: Scholars, 1987), as well as ''Unclean and Clean (OT),'' *Anchor Bible Dictionary* 6 (ed. D.N. Freedman; New York: Doubleday, 1992) 729-741.

sins involving public duty or fraud (Leviticus 4-6), and specified sexual and cultic perversions (Leviticus 18-20).[44]

When certain of Jesus' programmatic activities are placed within the context of purity defined in such a manner, as a nexus of issues impinging upon the status of death, food, sexuality and cult, a coherent pattern emerges. The Gospels, of course, cannot be assumed to reflect deeds and statements of Jesus directly, and yet their reference to him within public events is most sensible when purity is taken as a framing concern. That concern was not operative within most of the communities which produced the Gospels, but it was crucial at an early stage of the movement centered on Jesus. Examples of passages which manifest a concern for purity at such an early stage[45] would include stories in which Jesus has contact with women who are explicitly or implicitly characterized as impure (cf. Matthew 9:20-22//Mark 5:25-34//Luke 8:43-48; Matthew 15:21-28// Mark 7:24-30; Luke 7:36-50; 8:2; John 4:7-30),[46] the cleansings of "lepers," where Jesus takes up the authority assigned to priests in Leviticus 14:2-9 to declare someone clean who has suffered from an impure eruption (Matthew 8:2-4//Mark 1:40-44//Luke 5:12-14; Luke 17:11-19),[47] reports involving his contact with the dead (Matthew 9:18-19, 23-26//Mark 5:21-24, 35-43//Luke 8:40-42, 49-56; Luke 7:11-17; John 11:1-44),[48] and the pervasive claim of his authority over "unclean spirits."[49] Jesus' relationship to the cult in Jerusalem, of course, was notoriously problematic and resulted in his execution, but discussion of that aspect is reserved for the next chapter. The paradigmatic categories of purity (death, food, sexuality and cult) are, then, involved within the programmatic representation of Jesus in the Gospels. In what follows, the issues of accept-

---

44 I depart from Wright's scheme, in categorizing sexual and cultic infractions together, as in Leviticus, rather than separately. Moreover, homicide is here omitted, as constituting a special case.

45 A fuller discussion of some of what follows is available in "The Sacrificial Program of Jesus," *The Temple of Jesus*, 113-136. In addition, passages which may be associated with the present theme are discussed there.

46 Cf. Luke 4:26; 7:11-17; 13:10-17.

47 Cf. Matthew 10:8; 11:5//Luke 7:22; 26:6//Mark 14:3; Luke 4:27.

48 Cf. Matthew 10:8; 11:5//Luke 7:22, and the notable emphasis in John 12:1, 2 that Lazarus enjoyed fellowship with Jesus and his companions during the meal at Bethany prior to the festal entry into Jerusalem.

49 Cf. Matthew 10:1//Mark 6:7; 12:43-45//Luke 11:24-26; Mark 1:23-28//Luke 4:33-37; Mark 3:11, 30; 5:2-20//Luke 8:26-29; 7:25; 9:14-29//Luke 9:37-43a; Luke 6:18.

able food and fellowship over food will be treated. But they may only be understood on the basis of a clear apprehension of their importance within the wider nexus of issues of purity.

The link between the acceptability of food and cleanness is explicitly made in Matthew 15:11; Mark 7:15, where Jesus asserts, It is not what goes into a man which defiles him, but what comes out of a man defiles him. By their various means, Matthew (15:20) and Mark (7:19) convey that statement as an insistence that foods generally are not to be considered impure, and that meaning comports well with the sociology of the Christian movement, once it had made the transition from a Pharisaic campaign of purity, through an apocalyptic phase, to a Graeco-Roman cult of a savior.[50] But the meaning of the saying is not limited to food, and in fact does not make too much sense when it is so limited: on such an understanding, Matthew's wording (15:11) would have people justified by what goes out of their stomachs![51]

The fundamental issue is rather the *direction* from which purity might proceed. Jesus' claim is that observances of purity do not create the reality, but that human acts and words might extend the sphere of the pure. Purity is the condition in which an Israelite lives *as* an Israelite, not an achievement of practice or observation. What he produces is pure by definition; the issue of foods produced outside the people and the land of Israel, the target of the Matthean and Markan redactions of the saying, is beside of point of Jesus' likely concern.

Two distortions of Jesus' position in the present connection need

---

[50] Thomas *l.* 14 assumes a similar background of development, cf. Roger P. Booth, *Jesus and the Laws of Purity. Tradition and Legal History in Mark* 7: Journal for the Study of the New Testament Supplements Series 13 (Sheffield: JSOT, 1989) 227 n. 4; Elian Cuvillier, "Tradition et rédaction en Marc 7:1-23," *Novum Testamentum* 34 (1992) 169-192.

[51] For a cogent attempt to accept the meaning of the saying as applied to the general purity of food, cf. Booth, *op. cit.* The problem in his analysis, however, is that he does not sufficiently allow for the shift involved in the understanding of purity as the movement of Jesus evolved from its earliest phase to the greater pluralism of the Mediterranean environment at a later stage. He persistently construes Mark 7:15 in terms of 7:5, where the Pharisees' focus is alimentary purity (cf. pp. 64, 67, 74, 118, 122, 203, 205, 209, 213, 214). On his own logic, that construal is odd. Booth accepts that vv. 1-5 constitute a much broader attack on the notion of purity than Jesus ever mounted (pp. 23-114, 80, 81), and that the custom of hand washing assumed was not widespread in Jesus' milieu (p. 203), even on his own reading of Mishnah as a source of Judaism in the first century (*sic!* p. 128).

to be avoided. The first distortion is that Jesus was concerned only with "moral," as distinct from "cultic" matters (cf. the interpretation of the saying in Matthew 15:15-20; Mark 7:17-23).[52] That portrayal suited the packaging of the Gospels for a Graeco-Roman audience, and continues to serve the interests of religious apologists today, but it is far from the historical matrix of Jesus' thinking. The other distortion was also caused by the change in the social constitution of those who cherished the memory of Jesus, and represents his teaching as a dichotomy between what is within and what is without a person. Indeed, it is striking that Luke preserves, not a parallel to the saying under discussion, but a saying in a similar vein from its version of a collection of Jesus' sayings ("Q"): "Now you Pharisees cleanse the outside of the cup and of the dish, but inside you are full of extortion and wickedness" (11:39).[53] But the Lukan saying betrays its packaging both in the attack upon Pharisaism, which became popular during the period of the early Church, and in the acknowledgement which follows (vv. 40, 41) that Jesus' position involved the extension of purity from the inside outwards, not any denial of the possibility of "external" purity.[54] To say that God made both the "outside" and the "inside," and to assert that alms giving makes the whole clean, is far from a rejection of ritual practice, but amounts to the strongest assertion that the "moral" and the "cultic" realms are both contiguous and continuous.

The point of such sayings as Matthew 15:11, Mark 7:15, and Luke 11:40, 41 is that Israelites are properly understood as pure,

---

[52] Unfortunately, Booth falls into that distortion in his conclusion (pp. 213, 214, 219). He himself is aware of the contemporary texts, such as *De specialibus legibus* III, 63, 208, 209, which demonstrate the continuity of the two categories within Judaism.

[53] The absence of the saying from Matthew demonstrates that "Q" was far from the stable, written source it is often taken to be. The Markan material is included in 6:45-8:26, for which Luke does not present a coherent parallel. Proponents of Markan, literary priority must posit that "Luke" (understood as an individual) possessed a defective copy of Mark, but it is more straightforward to see in such divergences local variations of catechesis. What Luke omits is either of a summary nature, or addresses the issue of contacts between the preaching of Jesus and non-Jewish culture, which is the burden of Acts.

[54] The development of the gospel from a strain within the pluralistic fabric of early Judaism to a Hellenistic confession is today commonly agreed to have taken place, and some degree of anti-Semitism was a result (cf. John T. Townsend, "The New Testament, the Early Church, and Anti-Semitism," *From Ancient Israel to Modern Judaism: Intellect in Quest of Understanding* I: Brown Judaic Studies 159 [eds J. Neusner, E.S. Frerichs, N.M. Sarna; Atlanta: Scholars, 1989] 171-186.)

and that what extends from a person, what he is and does and has, manifests that purity. Paul was to write some twenty-five years later (and for his own purposes), "Do you not know that your body is a temple of the holy spirit within you, which you have from God?" (1 Corinthians 6:19a, b). Paul may be alluding to a particular saying of Jesus (cf. John 2:21) or to what he takes to be a theme of Jesus; in either case, he refers his readers to what he assumes to be elementary knowledge of the gospel. That Jesus and especially Paul (who identified himself as a Pharisee, cf. Philippians 3:5) speak from such a perspective is not unusual. It is said that Hillel took a similar point of view, and expressed it in a more heterodox manner. He defended an Israelite's right to bathe in Roman installations on the grounds that, if Gentiles deem it an honor to wash the idols of their gods, Israelites should similarly deem it an honor (indeed, a duty) to wash their bodies, the image of God (Leviticus Rabbah 34.3). In other words, bathing does not make one pure, but celebrates the fact of purity; in their quite different ways, Hillel and Paul demonstrate that representatives of the Pharisaic movement—contrary to its repute in the Gospels—conceived of purity as a condition which Israelites could be assumed to enjoy, and out of which they should act. Fundamentally, Jesus' concern appears similarly to have been with cleanness as a matter of production, rather than of consumption.

Jesus' perspective in regard to purity is reflected within a passage which is also common to the Synoptics, but which is particularly articulated in the source of sayings, "Q." In the commission to his twelve followers (or, in Luke, seventy followers) to preach and heal, Jesus specifically commands them to remain in whatever house they are received within a given village, until they depart (Matthew 10:11-14; Mark 6:10; Luke 9:4; 10:5-7). That commandment by itself is a notable development compared with a Pharisaic construction of purity, because it presupposes that what the disciples eat, within any house which might receive them, is clean. Jesus' itineracy and that of his disciples, treated in much recent literature as if it were an obviously Graeco-Roman practice, was a parabolic gesture, a vigorous statement of the general purity of food in Israel. The mishnaic source underscores that statement by having the disciples pronounce their peace upon the house in question (Matthew 10:12, 13; Luke 10:5, 6), and Luke's Jesus particularly insists that the disciples should eat what is set before them in whatever town they might enter (10:7, 8). The pronouncement of peace and the in-

junction not to go from house to house within a given community
(cf. Luke 10:7), but to stay put until the visit is over, had obvious
utility within the missionary concerns of the mishnaic source. But
the particular focus upon purity, all but obscured in "Q" with missionary directives, appears to have been Jesus'.

A last peculiarity of the commission in "Q," which has long
seemed incomprehensible, finds its sense under our analysis. Although Mark's Jesus has the disciples without bread, bag, money,
or a change of cloths, he does permit them a staff and sandals (6:8,
9). In the source of sayings, however, just those obviously necessary
items are singled out for exclusion (cf. Matthew 10:9, 10; Luke 9:3;
10:4). The traditional attempt to explain differences within the lists
as the result of missionary practices within the early Church is
reasonable superficially, but that attempt only diverts attention
from the obvious fact that the commission in "Q" makes extremely
poor sense as a missionary instrument. Why tell people not to take
what on any journey they, practically speaking, might need? Another contexts suggests itself. According to a Pharisaic teaching, pilgrims were to enter the Temple without the food, the sandals, the
staffs, the garments, the bags, and the money (cf. m. Berakhoth 9:5;
b. Yebamoth 6b) which would normally accompany a journey. The
sacred space was to be treated much as Moses was commanded to
treat the vicinity of the burning bush (see Exodus 3:5). But if we understand the commission to treat every village they might enter as
clean, as pure territory such as that from which sacrifice might be
offered,[55] the perplexing structure of the commission makes emi-
nent sense. "Q" makes Jesus' commission into a missionary discourse; within his ministry, it was designed to be an enacted parable
of Israel's purity.

New Wine in the Kingdom

A radical acceptance of the produce of all Israel as pure is therefore
cognate with Jesus' practice of an inclusive definition of those who
might join his fellowship, both at meals and on journeys, as children

---

[55] Of course, within the Pharisaic ethos, purity was held to be consistent with
sacrifice, without any assumption that such purity would actually occasion sacrifice
each time it was achieved.

of Abraham.[56] Indeed, the emblematic statement which provides the rationale of Jesus' program is the image of all Israel joining Abraham, Isaac, and Jacob in festal eating within the kingdom of God (Matthew 8:11, 12//Luke 13:28, 29).[57] The paradigmatic link between the kingdom and fellowship at meals is widely accepted as an established feature of what Jesus taught,[58] and with ample warrant (cf. Matthew 22:1-14//Luke 14:15-24; Matthew 20:21//Mark 10:37).

Meals in Jesus' fellowship became practical parables whose meaning was as evocative as his verbal parables (which have consumed much more scholarly interest). To join in his meals consciously was, in effect, to anticipate the kingdom in a certain manner, the manner delineated by Jesus. Each meal was a proleptic celebration of God's kingdom; the promise of the next was also an assurance of the kingdom. There is, then, a certain inevitability in the saying, I will not again drink of the fruit of the vine, until I drink it new in the kingdom of God (cf. Matthew 26:29//Mark 14:25 and Luke 22:16, 18). Quite outside the context of what came to be known as "the last supper," the practice of fellowship at meals within Jesus' movement in its formative period forged a link with the kingdom, such that the promise of God's final disclosure on behalf of his people was as ardently and carelessly anticipated as the next dinner. The saying, in effect, asserts the resolve only to drink of the fruit of the vine, in conscious anticipation of the kingdom, within the fellowship of restored purity which Jesus' meals established. Its meaning may be compared to the request for daily bread within the Lord's Prayer, which follows the petition regarding the kingdom (Matthew 6:11// Luke 11:3). In both cases, God's ultimate revelation is associated with the anticipation of an act of humble eating, one in the private context of prayer and the other in the communal context of a meal. Within Jesus' movement, the bread which sustains us and the wine which rejoices us are taken as a foretaste and a warrant of the kingdom which transforms us.

The interpretation of the promise of the kingdom's new wine has

---

[56] That appears to be the policy which is reflected, albeit indirectly, in Matthew 3:9//Luke 3:8; Luke 13:16; 16:19-31; 19:9.

[57] Cf. *God in Strength. Jesus' Announcement of the Kingdom*: Studien zum Neuen Testament und seiner Umwelt 1 (Freistadt: Plochl, 1979) 179-201.

[58] Cf. Otfried Hofius, *Jesu Tischgemeinschaft mit den Sündern* (Calwer: Stuttgart, 1967).

been governed by the assumption that the construction is designed
to convey a rigidly temporal meaning. The meaning is taken to be,
I shall fast until the kingdom comes, and then I shall drink. That is
a possible sense, and one can see for example in Luke 2:26 that such
a promise might be current: Simeon is not to die until he has seen
the messiah. The actual form of construction used, however, is that
he is not to die *before* that event (μὴ ἰδεῖν θάνατον πρὶν ἂν ἴδῃ τὸν
χριστὸν κυρίου), and it is a unique occurrence within the New
Testament.[59] Simeon is to die after he sees the messiah whom the
narrative assumes is Jesus. Taken apart from the Lukan narrative,
within the context of a truly eschatological expectation (as in 4 Ezra
7:28), seeing messiah might be equated with ruling with him
forever. If so, then Simeon is assured he will never die. The promise
not to drink wine until the kingdom comes, construed temporally in
the manner of the promise to Simeon, might involve a pledge of ab-
stention until then (as in the Lukan chronology), or a complete
renunciation of wine for all eternity (as the analogy with 4 Ezra 7:28
could suggest). The strictly temporal sense might be narrative or eschatological. Neither meaning, as we shall now see, comports well
with the position of Jesus.

The narrative meaning forces us to presuppose that Jesus is self-
consciously eating a last supper prior to his death, and refusing to
drink until the feast of the kingdom. Even if one grants (1) that Jesus' saying was only uttered at the last supper, and at no earlier
meal, and (2) that he proceeded on the basis of a personal insight
that he was about to die, the narrative reading remains implausible.
Who would claim that Jesus knew precisely how many meals he
would celebate in his fellowship prior to his execution? Although
that degree of foresight is not generally ascribed to Jesus today, it
is necessary for the narrative hypthesis. Jesus must say these words
at his *last* supper, and he must know it is his last, since otherwise any
act of eating with others—even if he abstained from wine—would
have pushed the supper out of last position. The problems of the narrative reading do not end there. In addition to being implausible,
it is simply contradicted by the Synoptic narrative itself. According
to Matthew 27:34 and Mark 15:23, Jesus was given wine immedi-

---

[59] See Joseph A. Fitzmyer, *The Gospel According to Luke (I-IX)*: The Anchor Bible
(Garden City: Doubleday, 1981) 422, 427.

ately prior to the crucifixion,[60] in accordance with a humane custom in Jerusalem.[61] Even on the assumption that a sip of wine would not break the promise, the contradiction is fatal to the usual reading and its many suppositions: after all, if Jesus knew he was to be executed and how many meals he would have before he died, he ought to have been familiar with the practice of giving prisoners drugged wine prior to capital punishment. The offer of vinegar to him on the cross (Matthew 27:48//Mark 15:36//Luke 23:36) only compounds the difficulty.

The saying might be taken temporally, but in an eschatological sense, to mean that Jesus resolved never to drink wine *simpliciter*. The plausibility of such a temporal reading is even less defensible than the narrative proposal. The wine given to Jesus at the crucifixion remains a contradiction, and in addition the festal imagery of eating and drinking—a topos of divine disclosure within early Judaism which is as vivid as Isaiah 25:6-8 and as primordial as Genesis 14:18-20—would be denied. Because the usage of the festal imagery of the kingdom was central to Jesus' message, the eschatological reading of his promise not to drink wine may safely be rejected. Consideration of the proposal, however, has not been unproductive. It emerged out of reflections upon Luke 2:26: taken apart from the narrative chronology of Luke, the promise that one would not die before seeing the messiah might imply that one would never die. The timeless nature of the messianic age would, in effect, override the temporal construction of the grammar.

What made it possible for the temporal construction to be overridden by reference to a timeless condition is that the syntax was not rigidly connected to a notion of time to begin with. In Genesis 28:15b, God at the place which will be called Bethel promises Jacob, "that I will not abandon you until I have done that of which I have spoken to you" (כִּי לֹא אֶעֱזָבְךָ עַד אֲשֶׁר אִם-עָשִׂיתִי אֵת אֲשֶׁר דִּבַּרְתִּי לָךְ). Evidently, that is not a promise to discharge a commitment, and then depart: the sense is rather that God will neither abandon nor

---

[60] Both Gospels add that he did not accept to drink it fully, in order not to present him as breaking his resolution. Luke avoids the difficulty by omitting the reference.

[61] See b. Sanhedrin 43a and Joachim Jermias *Jerusalem in the Time of Jesus* (tr. F.H. and C.H. Cave; London: SCM, 1969) 95. The Talmudic passage refers to providing wine with frankincense to one who is led out to execution (cf. Proverbs 31:6). Noble women in Jerusalem are held customarily to donate the drink.

fail Jacob at any time.[62] The force of the promise lies in the construction following "until" (עַד): God is warranting by the force of
his presence that he will fulfill what he promised. The point is conveyed by envisaging the completion spoken of in the perfect tense.[63]
As the examples in Appendix 2 indicate, constructions of the syntactical type "x will not occur, until y does," employing οὐ μή . . . ἕως
[ἄν] in Greek and reflecting עַד . . . לֹא in Hebrew or Aramaic, are
often asseverative by nature. The promise to Simeon is that he *is* to
see the messiah, not that he will die, and the emphasis falls so heavily
upon what is promised that whatever leads up to it should not be
taken to be of more than conditional importance. Just as God's per-
forming what he swore to Jacob cannot involve his abandoning
Jacob in any sense, so Simeon's vision of the messiah implies that
his own death will not be definitive.

Read along the same lines, the point of Jesus' saying is the image
of consuming new wine in the kingdom (cf. Matthew 9:16,17//Mark
2:21, 22//Luke 5:36-39), rather than not drinking any wine in the
present. It is designed principally to assure the hearer that the wine
of the kingdom is soon to be enjoyed. The saying belongs to a
definite syntactical type, which derives from the Semitic construction already mentioned, utilizing "not" (לֹא) and "until" (עַד).
Jesus' warrants of this type, which employ the emphatic negative
οὐ μή (for לֹא) and ἕως [ἄν] (for עַד), generally envisage that the condition initially posited will endure (see Appendix 2). For example,
he warns that, if you go to prison, you will not get out until you have
paid the last penny (Matthew 5:25, 26; Luke 12:58, 59). The point,
of course, is not that payment will secure release; rather, he warns
that Roman justice will impoverish those who appeal to it, with no
easy escape for those who are entangled in it. By analogy, Jesus' emphasis in the saying about drinking wine new in the kingdom would
be on that eschatological feast which is to include his followers, and
a corollary sense of the saying would be that Jesus will drink wine
only within the fellowship of those meals which celebrate the kingdom.

---

[62] See Appendix 2 and Klaus Beyer, *Semitische Syntax im Neuen Testament*: Studien zur Umwelt des Neuen Testaments 1 (Göttingen: Vandenhoeck und Ruprecht,
1962) 132, 133 (n. 1) and Chilton, *God in Strength*, pp. 268-272, where the analysis
is applied to Mark 9:1, as in "The Transfiguration: Dominical Assurance and
Apostolic Vision," *New Testament Studies* 27 (1980) 115-124.

[63] So E. Kautzsch, *Gesenius' Hebrew Grammar* (tr. A.E. Cowley; Oxford: Clarendon, 1974) 313.

Within the Synoptics, the ordering of the promise inside the artificial framework of the Passion means that Jesus' assertion is taken as a vow. Matthew (27:34) and Mark (15:23) have him refuse a drink given him prior to crucifixion, but then accept another on the cross (Matthew 27:48//Mark 15:38). For all that the presentation is flawed, as we have already seen, the construal of his promise of the new wine as a vow is understandable. A similar form of what must be taken as a vow is evidenced in Acts 23:12, 21. In both cases in Acts, however, ἕως οὗ is used instead of ἕως...ὅταν (Mark 14:25; Matthew 26:29). Matthew and Mark therefore manifest a tendency of interpretation, without actually making Jesus' saying into a simple vow which he actually kept. Luke is another matter. The saying in 22:16 reads ἕως ὅτου, and v. 18 has ἕως οὗ: identification with the form of the vow in Acts is achieved. But the distinction of Luke from Matthew and Mark is not only a matter of linguistic presentation. Luke also omits reference to the giving of what Mark calls myrrhed wine (15:23, ἐσμυρισμένον οἶνον) and what Matthew calls wine with gall (27:34, οἶνον μετὰ χολῆς μεμιγμένον), so that the issue of Jesus' breaking his vow does not arise. Similarly, Luke has soldiers offer Jesus vinegar, not a bystander, because the Matthean and Markan incident concerning Elijah is not represented. The vinegar for Luke is simply another form of mockery (23:36), and the soldiers only offer the drink, while in Matthew (27:48) and Mark (15:36) the drink is actually given. In aggregate, the Synoptics present the promise of new wine as a hero's vow of abstinence, and that results in either inconsistencies (so Matthew and Mark) or considerable recasting of the traditional materals (so Luke).

The heroic presentation of Jesus within the Synoptics will concern us further in chapter 5. The present concern is only to observe that the construal of the promise of new wine in the kingdom as a vow is a consequence of its ordering within events which have been so telescoped as to make their sequence and sense less than plausible. The vow of heroic abstinence, which is barely kept in Luke and is apparently broken in Matthew and Mark, is a consequence of the Synoptic ordering, not of Jesus' anticipation of the kingdom in the purity of his meals. For him, every act of fellowship in expectation of the divine rule was an assurance that the kingdom he prayed for would come. Matthew 26:29; Mark 14:25 represents a statement Jesus might have made during any celebration of mealtime fellowship in celebration of God's kingdom. Ordering them into a "last supper'' is an artificial development which imputes to the words an altogether different meaning.

The Lukan form of the saying (22:18) has been doubled (v. 16) to include the bread as well as wine, and in that order, to accord with the observation of Jesus' acts as liturgy. That the development is secondary is implicit in its liturgical character, and the usage of 22:18 brings the saying into the category of a vow in grammatical terms (as comparison with Acts 23:12, 21 has shown). Both the doubling and the liguistic form are developments within the Lukan tradition alone.

The Markan and Matthean traditions were no less creative. In them both, another consequence of a rigidly temporal understanding of the saying is carried to its logical conclusion. The kingdom is conceived of as coming as a result of the crucifixion. The promise that new wine would be drunk on ''that day'' (ἕως τῆς ἡμέρας ἐκείνος) in Mark 14:25 represents a coordination of imagery of the kingdom with the hope of the apocalyptic assize of the son of man. The ''day'' of the son of man is a principal feature within the expectation of Mark (see 13:32); the Markan form of the promise of new wine in the kingdom therefore unites two major keys of eschatology, the one predicated upon the kingdom and the other upon the son of man. Matthew 26:29 includes the same device as well as a parallel to Mark 13:32 (in Matthew 24:36; 25:13; see also 7:22; 10:15; 11:22, 24; 12:36; 24:42, 50) and two others which heighten the sense of an expectation of a coming age unlike the present: Jesus states that he will not drink ''from now'' (ἀπ᾽ ἄρτι) from ''this fruit of the vine.''[64]

Once the elements which are the products of development after the generative stage of the saying are identified, the saying itself is easily rendered into Aramaic:

לָא עוֹד אִשְׁתֵּי מִפְּרִי גָפְנָא עַד דִּי אִשְׁתֵּיה חֲדַתָּא בְּמַלְכַתָא אֱלָהָא.

An introductory formula such as בְּקָשְׁתָּא אֲמַרְנָא לְכוֹן (''In truth, I say to you'') may have been used at an Aramaic stage in the transmission of the saying, or ἀμὴν λέγω ὑμῖν may have been introduced at a latter stage.[65] In either case, the intention of the saying within

---

[64] Similarly, the promise to drink it ''with you'' (26:29) may be taken to reflect the language of apocalyptic reward.

[65] Cf. Chilton, '' 'Amen': an Approach through Syriac Gospels,'' *Zeitschrift für die neutestamentliche Wissenschaft* 69 (1978) 203-211 and *Targumic Approaches to the*

its originating context was to assure Jesus' followers that each meal taken in fellowship was a warrant of the festal kingdom which was shortly to come, and Jesus himself undertook to consume wine in no way but within such fellowship.

Gospels. Essays in the Mutual Definition of Judaism and Christianity: Studies in Judaism (Lanham and London: University Press of America, 1986) 15-23. Cf. the appendix of Aramaic retroversions in the present volume.

CHAPTER TWO

THE SURROGATE OF SACRIFICE

Jesus' Theory of Purity

Jesus' practice of meals celebrated the kingdom in anticipation by enacting the kingdom's purity. That character of purity in anticipation of the kingdom has influenced the presentation of "the last supper," as we have already seen. But Jesus' construction of purity put him at odds with some perspectives within early Judaism. He accepted as clean—as fit for social contact and participation in sacrifice—individuals and groups which were unclean according to the criteria of other teachers. His practice of fellowship at meals, which has already been considered in chapter 1, finds its rationale within his understanding of what makes for purity. A diverse group of stories, taken in aggregate, appear to attest his theory: he held that purity was a function of Israel offering its own while willing to forgive and be forgiven.

The purity of what Israel produced, and offered directly in sacrifice, is asserted in the paradigmatic story of the "leper" (Matthew 8:1-4//Mark 1:40-45//Luke 5:12-16). In the story, a leper approaches Jesus, and for no stated reason, asserts that Jesus is able to cleanse him. Jesus assents, pronouncing the man clean, and ordering him (a) to show himself to a priest, and (b) to offer the sacrifice prescribed by Moses for cleansing. The only literary sense the pericope has within the texts as we have them is christological. By a variety of devices, all of which are quite obvious (cf. Matthew 8:17; Mark 1:45; Luke 5:15, 16) the link is made between the cleansing of the leper, Jesus' fame as a healer, and his true identity. But that christological meaning is obviously not the originating sense of the story, whose terms of reference are explicitly given with the direction concerning the offering prescribed by Moses (cf. Leviticus 13, 14).

The assumption of Leviticus 13, 14, and therefore of the story in the Synoptics, is that "leprosy," which might more literally be rendered "outbreak" (צָרַעַת) comes and goes, and that its presence and absence can be detected. In Leviticus 13, where the issue is "outbreak" in humans (as distinct from cloth and houses), it is clear that the great concern, and the cause of uncleanness, is broken flesh (13:15). The suspicion of "outbreak" arises when there is a change in the pigmentation of the skin and accompanying hair, but a total change signals a return to cleanness (vv. 12, 13), since the fundamental concern is broken flesh, to which no human correctly has access. Accordingly, sufferers are banned (vv. 45, 46).

In the event one is declared clean by a priest, two quite distinct offerings are enjoined in Leviticus 14. The first is a local sacrifice, and may take place wherever there is running water. The priest kills a bird in a earthen vessel over the water, and dips a living bird in its blood together with cedar, scarlet, and hyssop. He then sprinkles the sufferer from "outbreak" with the living bird, and releases it (14:1-8). Purification follows (cf. v. 9), after which the sufferer needs to offer two male lambs, a ewe, cereal, and oil; together they constitute a sacrifice for guilt, a sacrifice for sin, a burnt sacrifice, and a cereal sacrifice, all with the sufferer particularly in view (14:10-20). Exceptional provisions are made for instances of poverty (vv. 21-32), but the requirement of ownership remains onerous.

Within the setting envisaged in Leviticus, the Synoptic story concerning Jesus therefore refers to a specific moment. The sufferer from "outbreak" attributes to Jesus the ability to adjudicate the status of his skin, and Jesus accepts the responsibility of telling him he may proceed directly to the sacrificial moment which is to occur *after* cleanness has been declared.[1] Although Jesus is not portrayed as taking over any sacrificial function, he is explicitly assigned—within the terms of reference the story itself establishes—the authority to pronounce on matters of purity. Pharisees evidently were similarly involved, as an entire tractate of the Mishnah (Negaim) attests,[2]

---

[1] In the Egerton Papyrus, the man explains that he became "leprous" by association with "lepers." That version of the story may not be assumed to be earlier than the Synoptics', because the Egerton Papyrus as a whole appears to present a hybrid of Johannine and Synoptic materials, as well as traditions of other provenience. Nonetheless, the fundamentally social aspect of "leprosy" is clearly marked in the Egerton Papyrus, which may be taken at least as a useful commentary. Jesus ("the Lord") also tells the man to show himself to the priests (not just one) in the Egerton Papyrus, which points the man (and the story) even more emphatically towards the Temple, and away from the local sacrifice prescribed in Leviticus.

[2] Cf. Jacob Neusner, *The History of the Mishnaic Law of Purities*. Part Six. *Negaim, Mishnah-Tosefta* (Leiden: Brill, 1975); Part Seven. *Negaim. Sifra* (1975); Part Eight. *Negaim. Literary and Historical Problems* (1975); Part Twenty-two. *The Mishnaic System of Uncleanness. Its Context and History* (1977), all in the series "Studies in Judaism in

but the Synoptic tradition had apparently lost explicit reference to the principal issue involved by the time the story was construed in the texts which are to hand. Indeed, by that time, Jesus was widely held to have been above issues of "mere" purity, so that the story of the cleansing of the sufferer from "outbreak" became a cipher of christology. Within the context which generated the concern of the story, however, the sense of Jesus' position is that the sacrifice of the "leper" is acceptable, and should be offered on the strength of his own declaration of purity. One Israelite could declare another clean.

A negative but even more forceful insistence upon the direct offering of Israel's produce by those who status as Israelites made them clean is conveyed by a famous story within the Synoptics (Mark 12:41-44; Luke 21:1-4). The story places Jesus opposite the "treasury" or "contribution box" (Mark 12:41; Luke 21:1),[3] watching people throw money in. The place at issue was not the treasury of cultic wealth (cf. Shekalim 3:1), which was within the priestly court of the sanctuary;[4] a woman would not have been permitted entry. She must be imagined as making her contribution somewhere in the southern part of the outer court or the women's court. According to Mishnah, receptacles in the shape of horns were set up there (Shekalim 2:1; 6:1).[5] Because the contribution involved was not immediately directed to the acquisition of sacrificial animals and utensils, there was no need first to exchange currency against the Tyrean shekel, as in the case of the tax of a half shekel (which will concern us below). Jesus remarks that a poor widow's contribution of two tiny coppers (λεπτά) was greater than the more substantial gifts clanging into the till, because she had not given from superfluity, but was effectively turning her life (βίος) over (Mark 12:43, 44; Luke 21:3, 4). The discourse concerning the destruction of the

---

Late Antiquity" (6). The concerns characteristically focus on whether one is to declare free of "leprosy" (לפטור), to certify as "leprosy" (להחליט), or to quarantine (הסגיר) until matters became clearer (cf. Negaim 1:3).

[3] The latter rendering is preferred in Walter Bauer, *A Greek-English Lexicon of the New Testament and Other Early Christian Literature* (translation and edition by F. Arndt, F.W. Gingrich, F.W. Danker; Chicago: University of Chicago Press, 1979) 149.

[4] So Joachim Gnilka, *Das Evangelium nach Markus* 2: Evangelisch-Katholischer Kommentar zum Neuen Testament (Köln and Neukirchen-Vluyn: Benziger and Neukirchener, 1979) 176, 177.

[5] So William L. Lane, *The Gospel according to Mark*: The New London Commentary (London: Marshall, Morgan & Scott, 1974) 442.

Temple, a late composition in light of the events of A.D. 70, follows in both of the Gospels in which the pericope appears.

"The widow's mite" has a firm place in Christian homiletics, where it has a certain obvious utility. But, although Jesus certainly does not criticize the woman, it is doubtful whether the intent of the story as it stands is simply to commend what she does, and even more doubtful that the point is that such a framework of giving is defended. Indeed, it is more plausible to see the vignette as a criticism of the system which would require or encourage someone to give as much away as the woman does.[6] Those who take the story as a criticism of systematic proportions, however, do so on the assumption that Jesus' concern was for the economic inequity involved in poverty and wealth. The difficulty of such a perspective is that Jesus does not seem to have promulgated a coherent economic agenda as such, and also—in a well attested as well as famous passage—that he encouraged the giving of alms, even to the point of becoming poor oneself (Matthew 19:16-30; Mark 10:17-31; Luke 18:18-30, cf. Matthew 6:2-4). If we assume some consistency in Jesus' teaching, the notion that he bamed the widow in some sense is most implausible. The widow's generosity does not seem to fall under any stricture of Jesus' against such giving *per se*.

Another well attested pericope has Jesus object to the giving of money, not as such, but to the benefit of the Temple, rather than one's parents (Matthew 15:3-6; Mark 7:9-13); that is the context in which he promulgates his distinctive view of cleanness, as that which proceeds from within (Matthew 15:11; Mark 7:15). In its present formulation, the passage no doubt reflects the global rejection of Judaism and its cult which became normative in the Church after the destruction of the Temple, but the particular teaching concerning ritual giving (κορβᾶν, a representation of the Aramaic term קָרְבָּנָא) reflects Jesus' stance, that what is owed to one's parents cannot be sheltered by declaring it dedicated to the Temple. The crucial maneuver in such a gambit of sheltering is that one might continue to use the property after its dedication to the Temple, while what

---

[6] So Joseph A. Fitzmyer, *The Gospel According to Luke (X-XXIV)*: The Anchor Bible 28 A (Garden City: Doubleday, 1985) 1321, citing A.G. Wright, "The Widow's Mites: Praise or Lament?—A Matter of Context," *Catholic Biblical Quarterly* 44 (1982) 256-265.

was given to a person would be transferred forthwith.[7] A more pointed statement of the appropriate direction of financial giving than Jesus' could not be desired, but there is no objection to cultic donation as such.

The understanding of Jesus' theory of purity, however, makes it possible to comprehend the vignette concerning the widow in its more plausible, negative sense, without imposing an economic ideology from another time upon Jesus, or attempting to construe it as a criticism of the widow's action. Jesus' occupation of the Temple was directed (as we shall see) against animals which did not genuinely belong, in his estimation, to those who were to offer them, because they were procured by means of a merely financial transaction in the Temple. His commendation of the widow was similarly designed to object to the notion of worship as essentially a financial contribution. Just as he wanted animals which were truly owned by Israel to be offered, he disapproved of a Temple which made the collection of money as such a matter of piety. His point in the occupation of the Temple was that a simply financial transaction was not sufficient to establish ownership of what was offered. The commendation of the widow was also designed to criticize the transformation of the cult into a monetary transaction, but from a different angle. In attempting to emulate the alleged piety of others, the woman was giving her life away; a system of sacrificial animals can make allowances for poverty (as in Leviticus 5:7f.; 14:21f.), while the practice of financial donations is inevitably impoverishing.[8] It is, of course, not necessary to assent to Jesus' criticism in order to understand it: he apparently belonged to a class which valued objects over money, and which understood money to be essentially alienated from the category of what was pure, and acceptable to God. You might reasonably make friends from unrighteous mammon (Luke 16:9),[9] but God cannot be satisfied with it.

---

[7] Cf. Nedarim 1:2; 5:6; 8:7; 9:1; Zeev W. Falk, "Notes and Observations on Talmudic Vows," *Harvard Theological Review* 59 (1966) 309-312; Ernst Bammel, "Gottes ΔΙΑΘΗΚΗ (Gal. III.17-17) und das jüdische Rechtsdenken," *New Testament Studies* 6 (1959/1960) 313-319; K.H. Rengstorf, "κορβᾶν, κορβανᾶς," *Theological Dictionary of the New Testament* III (ed. G. Kittel, tr. G.W. Bromiley; Grand Rapids: Eerdmans, 1978) 860-866.

[8] Cf. Frederic W. Madden, *Coins of the Jews* (London: Trübner, 1881) 69-71.

[9] Cf. Chilton, *A Galilean Rabbi and His Bible. Jesus' own interpretation of Isaiah* (London: SPCK, 1984) 117-123.

Matthew is written from a context in which the giving of money, in the form of a particular tax, is a fraught question. The years after the defeat of the Jewish revolutionaries by Rome and the destruction of the Temple were especially difficult for any community which remained in contact with Judaism, as Matthew's quite evidently did (see, for example, Matthew 23:1-12). Part of the provision of Vespasian and Titus was for the *fiscus ioudaicus*: the half shekel which had been paid into the Temple was now to be paid to Rome, and by women and children, as well as men.[10] The issue of the tax in Matthew accordingly took attention away from any other form of giving: accordingly, the widow disappears, but a rich *haggadah* concerning the half shekel (17:24-27) makes its appearance.

The *haggadah* is especially successful within Matthew, for appearing to be what it is not. It has attracted attention as a miracle story, in that it closes with Jesus' instruction to Peter, to fish for the tax of a half shekel, and pay the coin he finds in a fish for himself and Jesus (17:27). The command comports well with the convention of paying a *stater* for two persons, reckoned at the value of a half shekel for each,[11] but there is nothing in the story itself which suggests that Peter actually went fishing, caught a fish, found a *stater* in it, and paid the tax. The assumption that the commandment to fish for the tax resulted in a miraculous catch is indeed encouraged by Matthew, in that the literary context in which it is conveyed stereotypically associates commands of Jesus with miraculous events (cf. 17:14-21). But by definition, as a uniquely Matthean story, the *haggadah* must have circulated independently of the Synoptic construal of Jesus prior to its incorporation within the Matthean form of the gospel. There, too, the supposition may have been that Jesus' command resulted in a miraculous event, but the gist of the saying attributed to Jesus is inescapable: he tells Peter/Simon that "sons" are free of

---

[10] The principal citations are Josephus, *Jewish War* VII.6.6, 218; Dio, *Historia* 65.7; Suetonius, *Domitianus* 12. A standard discussion is available in E. Mary Smallwood, *The Jews under Roman Rule*: Studies in Judaism in Late Antiquity 20 (Leiden: Brill, 1976) 371-373. See Chilton, "A Coin of Three Realms (Matthew 17.24-27)," *The Bible in Three Dimensions. Essays in celebration of forty years of Biblical Studies in the University of Sheffield*: Journal for the Study of the Old Testament Supplement Series 87 (eds D.J.A. Clines, S.E. Fowl, S.E. Porter; Sheffield: Sheffield Academic Press, 1990) 269-282, 271-276.

[11] See A. Plummer, *An Exegetical Commentary on the Gospel according to S. Matthew* (New York: Scribner, 1910) 244-247; Smallwood, 124, 125; Chilton, "A Coin," 272.

the requirement to pay tax or tribute (17:25, 26). Despite Peter's assumption in his answer to the question of those who collected the tax (17:24, 25), Jesus' view appears to have been that the tax was not a valid requirement.

There is nothing surprising in Jesus' principled opposition to the requirement of such a tax. The institution itself was based upon Exodus 30:11-16, but the occasion of paying a half shekel there is a census. The notion of an annual tax is based upon Nehemiah 10:33, 34 (which specifies one third of a shekel), and reflects the reality that there was no longer a monarchy which would defray the costs of the service of the Temple.[12] As William Horbury has pointed out, the tax is not mentioned in certain texts which do mention offerings in the Temple (Tobit 1:6-8, the Letter of Aristeas, Jubilees), and 4Q159 explicitly insists that Exodus 30:13 refers to a single payment during a person's life.[13] Texts from a later period suggest that non-payment of the half shekel may well have been a problem.[14] That teachers such as Jesus did not recognize the collection as a requirement fits the overall picture of Judaism during the period of the Second Temple quite well.

The destruction of that Temple changed the picture radically. Judaism, left to its own devices, might simply dispense with the collection of the half shekel (as in m. Sheqalim 8:8), but the institution of the *fiscus ioudaicus* would make a refusal to pay disasterous. The assumption that the *haggadah* closes with a miracle saves Jesus from encouraging a tax-revolt against Rome, an important feature of the rebellion of A.D. 66. The same period which saw an attempt within the Church to reach an accommodation with Rome also saw an enhanced interest in stories of miracles.[15] Essentially, Matthew 17:24-27 represents Jesus' opposition to payments towards the Temple as a regular tax: he opposed such institutions of financial piety, for reasons which have already been uncovered in our reading of the pericope concerning the poor widow. His opposition was an

---

[12] The essential purpose of the tax is also reflected in m. Sheqalim 8:8, where the half shekel is held not to be required in the absence of the Temple.

[13] See William Horbury, "The Temple Tax," *Jesus and the Politics of His Day* (ed. E. Bammel and C.F.D. Moule; Cambridge: Cambridge University Press, 1984) 265-286, 277-279.

[14] See Sheqalim 1:4; Mekhilta Baḥodesh 1 (Exodus 19:1), and Chilton, "A Coin," 273, especially n. 6.

[15] See Günther Bornkamm, Gerhard Barth, Heinz Joachim Held (tr. P. Scott), *Tradition and Interpretation in Matthew* (London: SCM, 1963).

embarrassment within the Matthean community, where a refusal to pay the half shekel could be construed as *laesa maiestas*, with the result that a parable of refusal was turned into a miracle: the impossible at the level of proverbial discourse became the paradigmatic at the level of halakhic discourse. Everyone in the Church was to pay the very tax which Jesus taught did not need to be paid, on the grounds that he actually achieved the impossible condition of payment which he laid out before Peter.

Jesus' objection to the payment of the half shekel is coherent with his statement concerning the poor widow. In each case, the point at issue is that money is not the appropriate currency of sacrifice: Israel is to offer pure things, not monetary instruments, however they might be laundered. Once an Israelite, as in the case of the "leper," is seen to be clean by virtue of his identity, his approach to the Temple should be by means of his own offerings.

Matthew particularly emphasizes forgiveness as one of Jesus' programmatic concerns. The power to forgive is comparable to the power to declare someone clean. In both cases, what is accomplished is an acceptance of another person into the company of Israel.

The promise of the keys of the kingdom of heaven (Matthew 16:17-19) demonstrates the cultic implications of such acceptance within the earliest phases of Jesus' movement. The imagery of the keys is harnessed to speak of the power of the Church to forgive particular transgressions (16:19b,c; cf. 18:18, 23-35), and that may be regarded as the sense of the keys given Peter within the Matthean redaction. But the prehistory of the passage suggests another context. The keys of v. 19 are reminiscent of Isaiah 22:22, where Eliakim is given power of access into the Temple: the Targum of Isaiah makes the cultic implications of that power unmistakable. Eliakim is there given the key of what is specifically called the sanctuary, and he is provided with priestly vesture in v. 21 and with a priestly entourage in v. 24.[16] What Jesus promises Simon/Peter is the authority to determine who might and who might not be acceptable within the Temple; the subsequent shift to the liturgical forgive-

---

[16] Cf. "Shebna, Eliakim, and the Promise to Peter," *Targumic Approaches to the Gospels. Essays in the Mutual Definition of Judaism and Christianity*: Studies in Judaism (Lanham and London: University Press of America, 1986), 63-80 and *The Social World of Formative Christianity and Judaism* (eds J. Neusner, P. Borgen, E.S. Frerichs, R. Horsley; Philadelphia: Fortress, 1989) 311-326; *The Isaiah Targum*: The Aramaic Bible 11 (Edinburgh: Clark, 1987) 45.

ness of sins occurred under the influence of preoccupations of the
Matthean community. For Jesus, sin is "bound" or "loosed" because sacrificial practice may be changed in the Temple, the point
closest to heaven,[17] on his authority.

In the first Gospel alone we encounter the advice that, "if you are
offering your gift at the altar, and there remember that your brother
has something against you, leave your gift there before the altar and
depart: first be reconciled with your brother, and then come and
offer your gift" (Matthew 5:23, 24). That council is sandwiched between a more general warning against anger (vv. 21, 22), the leitmo-
tif of the passage, and a gnomon from the proverbial or mishnaic
source we call "Q," concerning one's behavior in a legal matter (vv.
25, 26, cf. Luke 12:57-59). The material which condemns anger fits
well within the antitheses in Matthew between Jesus' teaching and
the commandments of the Hebrew scriptures (cf. vv. 21-48), and the
theme of forgiving in advance of judgment at the divine tribunal is
characteristic of the Matthean recension of the gospel (cf. Matthew
18:15-35).

Matthew 5:23, 24 puts a particular twist on that theme: the setting
is specifically that of cultic worship, and the issue to hand is more
one of being forgiven than of forgiving. In both of those distinctive
aspects, the *halakhah* commends itself more as a source than a
product of the Matthean concern with forgiveness. The context of
the Temple is obviously not likely to have been invented over the
course of time within the Church, and Matthew moves steadily
away from the purely interpersonal understanding of forgiveness
which the *halakhah* presupposes, and towards the communal authority to forgive (again, cf. 18:15-18) which the disciples are reckoned
rightly to exercise (cf. 18:19, 20).[18] In its present form, the saying
is unrealistic in its supposition that people offer their own gifts at the
altar, and are in a position to halt proceedings out of subjective considerations. The sense of unreality becomes egregious in the specific
reference to the altar of incense (θυσιαστήριον), to which only priests

---

[17] Cf. Georg Fohrer, "Σιών, Ἰερουσαλήμ..., : *Theological Dictionary of the New
Testament* VII (eds G. Kittel, G. Friedrich, tr. G.W. Bromiley; Grand Rapids:
Eerdmans, 1971) 292-319.

[18] By the time of Matthew, the Syrian Church saw its own worship in the reference to the Temple in 5:23, 24; cf. "Forgiving at and Swearing by the Temple,"
Forum 7 (1991) 45-50.

had access.[19] But the link between forgiveness, purity and accept-able sacrifice is characteristic of Jesus; that connection may lie at the point of origin of the text as it can be read today.

The question naturally emerges: if Jesus taught that what was produced from Israel was to be taken as pure, how did he conceive of forgiveness, and particularly being forgiven, as a necessary prelude to sacrifice? It may be accepted that the thematic interest of Matthew exaggerates the importance of being forgiven, but must it be supposed that the issue is quite beside the point of purity? The peculiarly Lukan story of the woman who anointed Jesus' feet (7:36-50) would suggest otherwise. Here, the sinful woman's prox-imity to Jesus is justified on the basis of the love she shows him, on the principal that great love is a function of much forgiveness (v. 47). That vignette, and its attendant maxim, have provoked much debate,[20] but the governing assumption has been that the commanding issue is forgiveness in the abstract. In fact, the narra-tive specifies the concern of the Pharisee as the woman's physical contact with Jesus (7:37-39). Fundamentally, therefore, the ques-tion of purity is the concern of the story, and Jesus proceeds not only to justify the woman's contact with him, but to cite it in detail (vv. 44-46). Those who dine with Jesus rightly conclude that his en-dorsement of contact amounts to the forgiveness of sin (v. 49): that is what saves her (v. 50). Being forgiven and being pure are both coordinates of what it is to be an Israelite.

Similarly, the Lukan Jesus has a Samaritan, who is paradigmati-cally unclean, touch an Israelite, and portrays him as justified by his love (10:29-37); much as in the case of the woman in chapter 7, love is held to be a product of forgiveness, which also effects purity. At the same time, a priest and a Levite are implicitly criticized for exer-cising due caution in approaching what after all might have been a corpse (vv. 30-32; cf. Leviticus 21:1-4). Justification is predicated of a tax collector who humbly asks for mercy (18:9-14), while salvation is promised to one who is righteous (19:1-10, cf. 7:50). In all such cases in Luke, the key into which the issue has been cast is that of

---

[19] For further discussion of the meaning of the passage within Matthew, see Chilton, "Forgiving at and Swearing by the Temple," *Forum* 7.1/2 (1991) 45-50.
[20] Cf. C.F.D. Moule, " '. . .As we forgive. . .'—A Note on the Distinction be-tween Deserts and Capacity in the Understanding of Forgiveness," *Donum Gentili-cium. New Testament Studies in Honour of David Daube* (eds E. Bammel, C.K. Barrett, W.D. Davies; Oxford: Clarendon, 1978) 68-77.

forgiveness, or justification, or salvation, the undoubted focus of the received form of the texts. But the generative issue is Jesus' programmatic contact with what is conventionally taken to be unclean, and his assertion that forgiveness makes it clean. Just that dispute lies at the heart of his choice of a tax collector as one of his select band of followers, and his programmatic fellowship with such "sinners" at table (cf. Matthew 9:9-13; 11:19; Mark 2:13-17; Luke 5:27-32; 7:34; 15:1, 2).

A characteristic feature of the teaching of forgiveness within the program of Jesus is that it is understood to be effected apart from cultic means, much as the "leper" is pronounced clean in advance of any sacrifice (cf. Matthew 8:2-4; Mark 1:40-44; Luke 5:12-14). Forgiveness is the condition in which sacrifice is rightly offered, rather than the condition of which sacrifice is a remedy. As compared to the book of Leviticus, for example, that presupposition is surprising, in that the normal understanding was that sins of various sorts could only be understood as forgiven after the priest had offered a sacrifice on behalf of the worshiper, and after repentance (cf. Leviticus 4:22-5:16; 16:15, 16).[21]

Jesus takes it that Israelites are to be prepared immediately to offer pure sacrifice, and for that reason he commanded them to pray to be forgiven on a more regular basis than was usual in his time (cf. Matthew 6:12, 14, 15; Mark 11:25; Luke 11:4). Of course, once Jesus' program is appreciated within its sacrificial context, the association of his pronouncements of purity and his requirement of forgiveness and being forgiven is seen to be natural: cleanness and freedom from sin together are the aim in Leviticus, an aim which Jesus claims has been realized.

The conviction that a forgiven Israel was to offer of its own produce in the Temple was not immediately reconcilable with practices which would remove offerings from Israel prior to sacrifice. (One such removal was the occasion of Jesus' "cleansing" of the

---

21 In a *Jesus and Judaism*, E.P. Sanders has argued that Jesus' revolution lay in pronouncing forgiveness apart from repentance. I have elsewhere shown why that thesis in untenable (cf. "Jesus and the Repentance of E.P. Sanders," *Tyndale Bulletin* 39 [1988] 1-18), but it is notable that Sanders cites the very passages in Leviticus which are crucial to a cultic understanding of Jesus' *halakhah*. Sanders's treatment is too bound by the assumptions of Protestantism, in which Jesus is to be distinguished conceptually from Judaism, to be open to the horizon of Jesus' strictly cultic revolution.

Temple, as we shall see.) But a policy of such removal from Israel's direct control was encouraged in the Temple, where the donation of money increasingly became a surrogate of sacrifice. One paid one's half shekel or gave one's mite, and the smooth functioning of the priesthood made the gift a cultic act. Jesus seems to have objected to requirements, or even strong encouragements, of financial donations in place of sacrifice. Money alienated the act of offering from the Israel God had chosen to provide the offerings themselves. Similarly, the requirements of cultic reconciliation prior to sacrifice—taught by at least some authorities—alienated Israel from its divinely appointed function. Jesus rather saw reconciliation as effected within the act of sacrifice.

Jesus' Occupation of the Temple

Jesus' perspective on purity, with its insistence upon the actual possession of its own commodities by Israel immediately prior to sacrifice, could not indefinitely be enacted solely within the provinces. Fundamentally, his teaching touched upon how the cult in Jerusalem should function. In constructing a view of purity which logically and inevitably involved cultic reform, he was comparable to his Pharisaic or rabbinic contemporaries, and his practical interests—as theirs—focused unavoidably on the Temple.

In *The Temple of Jesus*,[22] I argued that the center of the story of Jesus' occupation of the outer court (Matthew 21:12-16; Mark 11:15-18; Luke 19:45-48; John 2:14-22; *Thomas l.* 64) was his forcible ejection of animals for market and their traders. Readers may turn to that discussion for a treatment of the pericope in particular:[23] the present concern is to place Jesus' meals with his disciples in the context of that action.[24]

His concern with sacrificial animals is not unusual when viewed from the perspective of Pharisaic discussion during the first century. Hillel is reported to have taught that offerings (as in the case of his own burnt sacrifice, עוֹלָה) should be brought to the Temple, where

---

[22] Chapter 6, ''Jesus' Occupation of the Temple,'' 91-111.

[23] After the publication of the book, an important article by Peter Richardson appeared. It is here discussed in Appendix 3.

[24] For a response to the recent suggestion that the collection of the Tyrian shekel in the Temple was the object of Jesus' action, see Appendix 3, ''Jesus' Purpose in Jerusalem: Peter Richardson's Contribution regarding the Half Shekel.''

the owners would lay hands on them, and then give them over to priests for slaughter. His perennial and stereotypical disputants, the house of Shammai, resist, insisting that the animals might be handed over directly. One of the house of Shammai, however, was so struck by the rectitude of Hillel's position, that he had some 3,000 animals brought to the Temple, and gave them to those who were willing to lay hands on them in advance of sacrifice. In effect, the position of Hillel involved generalizing the rule concerning a sacrifice of sharings in Leviticus 7:29, 30, that one should bring it with one's own hands, to include sacrifices as a whole.[25]

In one sense, the tradition concerning Hillel envisages the opposite movement from what is represented in the tradition concerning Jesus: animals are introduced, rather than their traders expelled. But the purpose of the action by Hillel's partisan (Baba ben Buṭa) is to enforce a certain understanding of correct offering, in the event one which accords with a standard feature of sacrifice in many cultures: the imposition of hands. The gesture is frequently explicated as an attempt to identify with the victim of sacrifice, but I have argued that the focus is rather upon appropriation. Hillel's *halakhah*, in effect, insists upon the participation of the offerer by virtue of his ownership of what is offered,[26] while ''the house of Shammai'' is portrayed as sanctioning sacrifice as a more self-contained action.

From a period slightly later than that of Jesus, Mishnah (Kerithoth 1:7) relates the following story:

---

[25] In Beẓah 20a, b, Hillel pretends the animal is a female, for a sacrifice of sharings (לזבחי שלמין), in order to get it by the disciples of Shammai. The passage manifests indecision whether the dispute concerns the laying on of hands itself, or the requirement for the laying on of hands immediately prior to slaughter. In any case, the dispute appears to be more vigorous than the perennial discussion, whether one should lay hands on a festal offering (cf. Ḥagigah 2:2). Baba b. Buṭa is named in the Talmud (and Tosephta Ḥagigah 2.11) as the heroic Shammaite who supported the *halakhah* of Hillel, but the number of sheep is specified elsewhere (cf. Yerushalmi Ḥagigah 2.3; Yerushalmi Beẓah 2.4; Jacob Neusner, *The Peripatetic Saying. The Problem of the Thrice-Told Tale in Talmudic Literature*: Brown Judaic Studies 89 [Chico: Scholars, 1985] 119-122). For further discussion of the practice among later rabbis (most notably Yose the Galilean and Aqiba), cf. Adolf Büchler, *Studies in Sin and Atonement* (New York: Ktav, 1967) 416-418. Büchler shows with reference to Philo (*De specialibus legibus* I, 198) that the practice was current during the first century (p. 416, n. 2).

[26] That sense of the laying on of hands is demonstrated within Hittite ritual by David P. Wright, *The Disposal of Impurity* (Atlanta: Scholars, 1987) 54, 55.

Once in Jerusalem a pair of doves cost a golden denar. Rabban Simeon b. Gamaliel said: By this Place! I will not rest this night before they cost but a [silver] denar. He went into the court and taught: If a woman suffered five miscarriages that were not in doubt or five issues that were not in doubt, she need bring but one offering, and she may then eat of the sacrifices; and the rest is not required of her. And the same day the price of a pair of doves stood at a quarter denar each.

Although the story requires more effort to understand than the one concerning Hillel, it rewards the attention required. The assumption of the whole tale is that a pair of doves might be offered by a woman, one as a burnt sacrifice and one as a sacrifice for sin, in order to be purified after childbirth. The second of the two would be offered routinely, while the first—in the case of poverty—might take the place of a yearling lamb (Leviticus 12:6-8) in cases of poverty. The story also assumes that miscarriages and unusual issues of blood akin to miscarriages should be treated under the category of childbirth, from the point of view of purity. That presupposition is characteristically Pharisaic, in the application of agreed definitions of uncleanness and cleanness to cognate conditions. The issue of when the woman might be considered entitled to eat of offerings is also a typical concern of the movement, since the Pharisees defined purity as fitness to take part in sacrifice, and in meals which—in their teaching—were related to the holiness of the Temple (cf. chapter 1).

Simeon's anger, which causes him to swear by the Temple (cf. Matthew 23:16-22), is therefore motivated to some extent by economic considerations, and his response is, like Jesus', to teach in the court of the Temple, to which point such offerings would be brought. But his action there is far less direct than Hillel's or Jesus'. Instead of importing more birds, or releasing those bought at an extortionate price, he promulgates a *halakhah* designed to reduce the trade in doves, no matter what their price. If a woman may await several miscarriages or flows of blood, and then offer a single pair of doves, and be considered pure enough to eat of sacrifices, the potential revenue from sales of doves would obviously decline. In effect, Simeon counters inflationary prices with sacrificial monetarism. The political lesson was quickly appreciated (on the very day, if we believe the story) and prices went lower even than Simeon had intended. Presumably, there was no reason for him to continue promulgating his view in the court of the Temple, and both he and the traders were content to stand down.

Hillel, Simeon, and Jesus are all portrayed as interested in how[27] animals are offered to the extent that they intervene[28] in the court of the Temple in order to influence the ordinary course of worship. None of the three needs to be understood as acting upon any symbolic agenda other than his conception of acceptable sacrifice, or as appearing to his contemporaries to be anything other than a typical Pharisee, impassioned with purity in the Temple to the point of forceful intervention. Moreover, none of their positions may be understood as a concern with the physical acceptability of the animals at issue: in all three cases, the question of purity is, What is to be done with what is taken to be clean? The pragmatic aspect of sacrifice here, as ever, involves gestures, as well as objects. Indeed, it is even possible that Jesus can best be understood within the context of a particular dispute in which the Pharisees took part, a controversy over where action was to occur. In that the dispute was intimately involved with the issue of how animals were to be procured, it manifests a focus upon purity which is akin to that attributed to Hillel and Simeon.

The exterior court was unquestionably well suited for trade, since it was surrounded by porticos on the inside, in conformity with Herod's architectural preferences. But the probable assumption of Rabbinic literature and Josephus is that the market for the sale of sacrificial beasts was not located in the Temple at all, but in a place called Ḥanuth (meaning "market" in Aramaic) on the Mount of Olives, across the Kidron Valley.[29] Victor Eppstein has argued that Rabbinic literature attests the innovation to which Jesus objected.[30] It is said that, some forty years before the destruction of the Temple, the principal council of Jerusalem was removed from the place in the

---

[27] In the case of Simeon, the issue is the price of the offerings initially, and then as a corollary the frequency of such offerings.

[28] In the case of Hillel, of course, a surrogate intervenes.

[29] By association, the site was sacred; money found among the dealers and not in the Temple itself, for example, was to be considered as tithe (Shekalim 7:2). According to Josephus, one of the rocks he associates with the Mount of Olives was called "Dovecote" (*Jewish War* V, 504). It might be added that Philo assumes that excrement, inevitably associated with the marketing of animals, is not be be brought into the Temple (cf. *De specialibus legibus* I, 74).

[30] "The historicity of the Gospel account of the Cleansing of the Temple," *Zeitschrift für die neutestamentliche Wissenschaft* 55 (1964) 42-58. An alternative point of view, which posits the probability of trade in or near the Temple, was championed by Joachim Jeremias (tr. F.H. and C.H. Cave), *Jerusalem in the Time of Jesus* (London: SCM, 1969) 49.

Temple called the Chamber of Hewn Stone to Ḥanuth.[31] Eppstein argues that Caiaphas both expelled the Sanhedrin and introduced the traders into the Temple, "an exceptional and shocking license introduced in the Spring of 30 C.E. by the vindictive Caiaphas" (p. 55).

Eppstein's argument is marred by its portrayal of Caiaphas as a villain, and it is by no means certain that he formally expelled the Sanhedrin, or even that a formal expulsion is at issue. On the other hand, the reference to the council's removal does suggest that, during the high priesthood of Caiaphas, there were disputes concerning physical arrangements concerning the Temple, and Caiaphas' good relationship with Pilate, under whom he served for ten years,[32] and with whose departure he was removed, would suggest that he was not held in high esteem by those Jews who resisted Pilate.[33] Given that he enjoyed the support of the Romans, and that he was involved in disputes concerning the location (and presumably also the jurisdiction) of the council, the allegation of the Gospels that trade was permitted in the Temple during his tenure appears tenable.[34]

From the point of view of Pharisaism generally, trade in the

---

[31] Cf. Abodah Zarah 8b; Shabbath 15a; Sanhedrin 41a. The wording of Sanhedrin is representative:

ארבעים שנה קודם חורבן הבית גלתה סנהדרין וישבה לה בחנות.

Eppstein's reading is supported, independently it would seem, in Benjamin Mazar (tr. G. Cornfeld), *The Mountain of the Lord* (Garden City: Doubleday, 1975) 126, although Mazar expresses due skepticism in regard to the exact placement of the shops before and after Caiaphas' reforms.

[32] He had been appointed high priest c. A.D. 18 by Valerius Gratus (cf. *Antiquities* XVIII, 33-35).

[33] Caiaphas was removed by Vitellius in A.D. 36/37, who also dismissed Pilate and—at the same time—released the high priestly vestments from custody in the Antonia (*Antiquities* XVIII, 88-95). Evidently, Caiaphas had acquiesced in that arrangement, and had accepted the close control of the Roman administration which it implied. See Gerd Theissen (tr. L.M. Maloney), *The Gospels in Context. Social and Political History in the Synoptic Tradition* (Minneapolis: Fortress, 1991) 137-140, 171-174.

[34] It is conceivable that the Gospels present us with a fiction which is designed to portray worship in the Temple as distorted by commercialism. But the Johannine account of the occupation does not make commercialism the issue as much as "zeal" (2:17), and in any case the tables of the money-changers, not the traders in animals, would make the best primary target in any ideological assault on the Temple on the grounds of alleged exploitation (to judge from recent commentaries).

southern side of the outer court might well have been anathema.
Purses were not permitted in the Temple according to the Pharisees'
teaching (m. Berakhoth 9:5; b. Yebamoth 6b). Sufficient money
might be brought to put directly into the large containers for
alms,[35] to purchase seals redeemable for libations,[36] and/or to exchange against Tyrean coinage in order to pay the annual half-
shekel,[37] but the introduction of trade into the Temple rendered the
ideal of not bringing into the Temple more than would be consumed
there impracticable. (References in Matthew 21:12 and Mark 11:15
to people selling and buying animals within the court may even imply that serial transactions were involved.) Incidentally, the installation of traders in the porticos might also involve the removal of those
teachers, Pharisaic and otherwise, who taught and observed in the
Temple itself.[38]

From the point of view of the smooth conduct of sacrifice, of
course, the innovation was sensible. One could know at the moment
of purchase that one's sacrifice was acceptable, and not run the risk
of harm befalling the animal on its way to be slaughtered. It is therefore unnecessary to impute malicious motives, "vindictive" or
otherwise, to Caiaphas in order to understand what was going on,
although it may be assumed that additional profit for the Temple
was also involved. But when we look at the installation of the traders
from the point of view of Hillelite Pharisaism, for example, Jesus'
objection becomes understandable. Hillel had taught that one's
sacrifice had to be shown to be one's own, by the imposition of
hands; part of the necessary preparation was not just of people to the
south and beasts to the north, but the connection between the two
by appropriation.[39] Caiaphas' innovation was sensible on the understanding that sacrifice was a matter of offering pure, un-

---

[35] Cf. Shekalim 6:1, 5; 7:1 (and 5:6).
[36] Cf. Shekalim 5:4.
[37] Cf. Shekalim 1:3; 2:1.
[38] Cf. Sanhedrin 11:2; Pesaḥim 26a.
[39] It may also be of interest that in Shekalim 4:7, Eliezer and Joshua enter a dispute concerning what should be done with cattle which are among goods dedicated
to the Temple. Eliezer holds that the males should be sold to those who wanted
עלות, and the females to those who wanted זבחי שלמין. But Joshua teaches that the
males should *themselves* be offered, and the females sold for זבחי שלמין, with the proceeds designated for the purchase of עלות. The unbreakable affinity between
animals owned and dedicated for sacrifice, and the act of sacrifice itself, is upheld
by Joshua, and is somewhat analogous to Jesus' position.

blemished animals *simpliciter*. But it failed in Pharisaic terms, not only in its introduction of the necessity for commerce into the Temple, but in its breach of the link between worshiper and offering in the sacrificial action. The animals were correct in Caiaphas' system, and the priests regular, but the understanding of the offering as by the chosen people appeared—to some at least—sadly lacking. The essential component of Jesus' occupation of the Temple is perfectly explicable within the context of contemporary Pharisaism,[40] in which purity was more than a question of animals for sacrifice being intact. For Jesus, the issue of sacrifice also—and crucially—concerned the action of Israel, as in the teachings of Hillel and Simeon. His attitude was all the more vehement, insofar as it was shaped by the ethos of peasants' life in Galilee.[41]

Jesus' Final Meals

In his recent study of the Passion in Mark, Matti Myllykoski argues that, in the earliest narrative, there was an immediate connection between Jesus' occupation of the Temple and his denunciation before the high priest.[42] But an immediate connection between the occupation and Jesus' arrest is precisely what the sources do not relate. Intermediately, Jesus' meals intrude as further possible occasions of high priestly offense.

When what is called "the last supper" is placed in the context of Jesus' program of purity, and his practice of social eating, three consequences follow. Those consequences are all the more pointed, when the more precise context occasioned by the failed occupation of the Temple is also appreciated.

First, the literary motif of a single meal is exploded: in all probability, Jesus ate several times, self-consciously and socially with his disciples, after he entered Jerusalem (cf. Matthew 26:6-13//Mark

---

[40] Of course, were we better informed of the concerns of other movements within Judaism at the time, we might discover that the Pharisees were far from unique in their direct attempts, by demonstration and example, to change arrangements in the Temple.

[41] See Sean Freyne, *Galilee, Jesus and the Gospels. Literary Approaches and Historical Investigations* (Philadelphia: Fortress, 1988) 261, 262; Theissen, 25-59.

[42] *Die letzten Tage Jesu. Markus und Johannes, ihre Traditionen und die historische Frage*, I: Suomalaisen Tiedeakatemian Toimituksia Annales Academiae Scientiarum Fennicae B.256 (Suomalainen Tiedeakatemia, 1991) 49, 59, 62, 63, 78, 121, 191.

14:3-9//John 12:1-8, cf. Luke 7:36-50). The focus on the *single* meal immediately prior to Jesus' death is a function of the ritual dramatization which characterizes the Gospels, and their theology of solidarity with the archetypical martyr (see chapter 5). Some supper must have been Jesus' last, but the texts as received give the impression it was his only supper. The meaning of his commensality after the failed occupation of the Temple, and any gesture attributable to him within those meals, is therefore first of all to be thought through within Jesus' understanding of purity. The Gospels' portrayal of a heroic martyr who enacts the symbolic representation of his own departure within a farewell discourse reflects the agenda of a later day.

Second, within the secondary literature, Jesus' meals—most especially his "last supper"—have persistently been equated with particular rituals or practices of Judaism. The principal candidates have been the Seder at Passover, the *kiddush* which sanctified the Sabbath or a feast with a preliminary cup of wine, and the meal of Pharisaic colleagues (*haverim*) who put into practice their agreement in regard to purity in a fellowship known as *haburah*.[43] No doubt, such meals instance the sort of meaning commensality might be held to convey. The emergence of paschal themes within meals near Passover, as of themes related to the giving of the law near Pentecost, and of themes related to the sojourn of Israel in the wilderness near Sukkoth, would have been natural within the fellowship of Jesus. Likewise, his meals at any period within his ministry might have been looked upon by a thoughtful participant as a kind of *kiddush* for the kingdom, and they did enact Jesus' version of purity, although with a surprisingly inclusive vision of collegiality. But the distinctive meaning of Jesus' meals will never be identified by equating his practice with conventional usage without remainder. His practice was sufficiently characteristic to constitute a definable context and meaning of its own.

But third and most crucially: in that Jesus' practice of social eating was related to his program of purity, and because that program had entered a critical phase with his occupation of the Temple, a dis-

---

[43] See Gregory Dix, *The Shape of the Liturgy* (Westminster: Dacre, 1954) 50-78 for a detailed exposition of Jesus' meals as meetings of a *haburah*. Cf. m. Hagigah 2:6, 7, and (for exclusive practices which might attend being a *haber*) m. Demai 2:3; 6:6, 8, 9, 12; Bikkurim 3:12; Gittin 5:9; Tohoroth 7:4; 8:5.

tinctive shift in the ideology of the meal after his occupation is to be anticipated. Such a shift is clearly marked in the Gospels, by the position of Judas' ''betrayal'' of Jesus. Although there is signal variety in presentation, there is also an interesting accord that Judas determined to inform on Jesus immediately before (John 13:2) or immediately after a meal (Matthew 26:14-16//Mark 14:10, 11).[44] Even more tellingly, Judas is said actually to be designated as the betrayer at table (Matthew 26:21-25//Mark 14:18-21//Luke 22:21-23; John 13:21-30). The ambiguities of the designation are notorious, with the result that Judas has become a favorite figure of revisionist readings of Jesus' death. But the issue of his motivation is imponderable, given the sources as they exist; what does emerge, however, is that a feature of Jesus' meals after his occupation of the Temple may have been the occasion of Judas' ''betrayal.'' Indeed, the sense of those meals was the only substantial news Judas (or anyone else) would have had to report; whatever Judas and the other disciples may have thought of the meals at that stage, the priestly authorities' knowledge of the new ideology evidently caused them to act. ''Judas'' is the name given to the informant, and his informing is taken to be a betrayal, but given the semi-public nature of Jesus' meals from the outset of his activity, news of the interpretation he was putting on commensality with him was probably not difficult to come by for anyone in Jerusalem.

At the time of his arrest, Jesus is portrayed as calling attention to the irony that he is taken into custody in secret, when he had been preaching in public within the Temple (Matthew 26:55//Mark 14:48//Luke 22:52, 53; cf. John 18:20). That observation is telling for what it passes over in silence: the authorities may be acting on the basis of knowledge they acquired after the occupation of the Temple. The occupation was a challenge to their authority, but the act was within the idiom of the sort of disputes with Pharisees which had erupted before. Jesus, much as Hillel before him, insisted that what is offered should be, and should be seen to be, one's property. But after that confrontation, it appears that Jesus' meals with his followers assumed a character they did not have before, a character

---

[44] Only Luke 22:3-6 breaks the pattern, but that is probably because the earlier story of an anointing (7:36-50) has replaced the story of the anointing in Bethany which Matthew and Mark convey.

such that the priests who opposed him could act to denounce him to the Romans.

The position of Jesus' opponents was extremely delicate. He was taking a line in respect of purity and the provision of animals which had precedents, and which would ultimately prevail, at least insofar as Ḥanuth was recognized as the normal place for vending animals both before and after Caiaphas' innovation. In order to find a way to refute him decisively (if only for the short term), it was necessary to find an occasion other than his position in regard to purity. The Gospels would have us believe that christology was the issue (cf. Matthew 26:57-68//Mark 14:53-65//Luke 22:54-71//John 18:13-24), in accord with their construction of faith in Jesus, but that reading is anachronistic. More plausibly, the character of Jesus' meals with his followers had become sufficiently offensive to warrant action against him.

The only distinctive features of those meals after the occupation of the Temple are the so-called words of institution. When Jesus says "This is my blood" (Matthew 26:28//Mark 14:24 cf. Luke 22:20 and 1 Corinthians 11:25) and "This is my body" (Matthew 26:26//Mark 14:22//Luke 22:19//1 Corinthians 11:24), a fresh meaning is injected into the proceedings, quite apart from the standard reference to purity and the kingdom which had long characterized his practice. Schweitzer was correct that the christological sense of those words, as indicating solidarity with the martyr in his faithful obedience, needed to be set aside as a criterion of the original significance of the meal.[45] But to set aside the words themselves is hasty. It is perfectly possible to offer an exegesis of them within the frame of reference of sacrifice. Jesus would be saying that, alienated from the Temple of which his occupation had apparently failed, wine alone was his "blood," the definitive fluid of sacrifice, and bread alone was his "body," in the sense of his sacrificial victim.[46]

---

[45] Cf. Schweitzer (tr. A.J. Mattill), *The Problem of the Lord's Supper according to the Scholarly Research of the Nineteenth Century and the Historical Accounts. I. The Lord's Supper in Relationship to the Life of Jesus and the History of the Early Church* (Macon: Mercer University Press, 1982).

[46] Cf. Jeremias (tr. N. Perrin), *The Eucharistic Words of Jesus* (London: SCM, 1964), 198-201, 223, who argues that "flesh and blood" in Aramaic is the pairing which "body" and "blood" in the Gospels represent; he helpfully cites Genesis 9:4; Leviticus 17:11, 14; Deuteronomy 12:23; Ezekiel 39:17-20; Hebrews 13:11; Pesaḥim 7:5; Parah 4:3; Makhshirin 6:5; Zebaḥim 4:4; 13:8; Kerithoth 6:1; Meilah 1:2.

The usage of "body" in such a way appears strained, from the point of view of the traditional, biographical construction of "the last supper" as Jesus' conveyance of his personal body and blood. That meaning was indeed developed, but at a later stage. But within the cycle of a final round of social meals after the end of the Temple's occupation, it is more reasonable to construe the wine/"blood" of the meal as surrogate for animal blood, and the bread/"body" of the meal as surrogate for the flesh of sacrifice. In linguistic terms, such a sacrificial construction is straightforward, since "body" (σῶμα) in the Septuagint sometimes represents "flesh" (בָּשָׂר) in the Masoretic Text. Σῶμα within the New Testament actually refers to an offering in sacrifice at Hebrews 10:5 (cf. v. 10); 13:11, and the term appears in the plural with that sense in the Septuagint at Genesis 15:11.[47] Why, then, has the possibility of a sacrificial exegesis of the words of institution not been pursued?

In his article on σῶμα in the New Testament, Eduard Schweizer argues that such usages are somehow "Hellenistic," and that in the words of institution "originally σῶμα, like αἷμα, denoted the whole person of Jesus, σῶμα as the I in its totality, αἷμα as the I in the act of dying."[48] That interpretation is only possible because it is argued that "body" and "blood" are not "typical in sacrificial language," and that the motif of solidarity with the primordial martyr is the original meaning of the last supper. Schweizer's approach runs afoul of the fundamental insight of Albert Schweitzer, that theologies of that sort are the product, not the presupposition, of the Church.

Schweizer is, however, entirely correct in the assertion that Jesus' reference to his "body" and his "blood" is far from transparently sacrificial. Indeed, it should also be stressed that the form of sacrificial construal Schweizer denies, that Jesus is himself a sacrificial victim, replacing the cult of the Temple, does not come into question at the present stage. That was a doctrine which required a self-

---

[47] At that point, σῶμα renders פֶּגֶר, but it may also render נָשַׁם, גוּפָה, גּו, בָשָׂר, עוּר, נֶפֶשׁ, גְּבֵלָה, טַף, חַיִל, and שְׁאָר. The range of terms which appear in the passages concerned in the Targumim is similarly wide, so that the attempt of Dalman, to specify גוּפָא in Aramaic as the antecedent of σῶμα in the words of institution, appears implausible, as Jeremias, p. 200, rightly insisted. See also Léon-Dufour, 141-142.

[48] "σῶμα κτλ. D. The New Testament," *Theological Dictionary of the New Testament* VII (ed. G. Freidrich, tr. G.W. Bromiley; Grand Rapids: Eerdmans, 1979) 1057-1081, 1058, 1059.

conscious theology, and the destruction of the actual Temple, in order to emerge. But ''blood'' and ''body'' may be read sacrificially, as referring to the offerings one brings to God, without being identified with Jesus' death. In order to avoid confusion with the reading of the supper which makes Jesus the replacement of the Temple, the reading which takes the wine and bread as surrogates of sacrifice will here be called the cultic (rather than the sacrificial) exegesis of the words of institution.

An apparent oddity in the text of Luke enables us to see Jesus' development of his fellowship at meals during the stage of his confrontation with the authorities. The Lukan presentation matches Matthew and Mark in having Jesus refer to his body and blood in that order (22:19, 20), but beforehand he gives thanks over a cup of wine and makes his promise concerning the fruit of the vine and the kingdom (22:17, 18). At the foundational stage of his practice which has been identified in chapter 1, Jesus made sharing meals into parables of the kingdom, and the promise over the wine is the enduring testimony of his own understanding of what such fellowship meant. The emphasis upon wine in the context of celebration is evocative of the *kiddush*, the prayer over a cup of wine said on the occasion of sanctifying a sabbath or festival at its outset.[49] Later developments placed the emphasis upon the bread, a symbol of Jesus as paschal victim, but Luke preserves a reminiscence that the blessing over the cup preceded. At the time of his recasting his meals as a surrogate for sacrifice in the Temple, Jesus would also naturally have referred to the new ''blood'' first: that order would also concur with a sacrificial symbolism, of first pouring out blood at the altar, and then offering the butchered victim. That observation constitutes the point of departure for two recent articles by Bernhard Lang.[50] He suggests, quite simply, that '' '*This is my body*' and '*this is my blood*' *can be understood as formulas of presentation*,'' such as Jesus encouraged lay Israelites to use in the Temple at the time they sacrificed.[51]

---

[49] See m. Berakhoth 8:1 and Pesaḥim 10:2; A.J.B. Higgins, *The Lord's Supper in the New Testament*: Studies in Biblical Theology 6 (London: SCM, 1960) 14-16.

[50] ''Der Becher als Bundeszeichen: 'Bund' und 'neuer Bund' in den neutestamentlichen Abendmahlstexten,'' *Der neue Bund im Alten. Studien zur Bundestheologie der beiden Testamente* (ed. E. Zenger; Freiburg: Herder, 1993) 199-212; ''The Roots of the Eucharist in Jesus' Praxis,'' *Society of Biblical Literature 1992 Seminar Papers* (ed. E.H. Lovering; Atlanta: Scholars, 1992) 467-472.

[51] Lang, ''Roots,'' 468-470.

Because the Synoptics and Paul reflect the dislocated order of the theologies which dominated at a later period (see chapters 3 and 4), they have Jesus refer to his "body," and only then to his "blood." Luke follows that pattern (22:19, 20), but another thanksgiving over the cup precedes (22:17). The appearance of multiple cups of wine also suited the later association with Passover.[52] The strength of the later (and strict) association of "the last supper" with the Passover and a fixed order of bread and wine is demonstrated by the deletion of the first Lukan cup in some manuscripts. The text with v. 17, however, is to be preferred,[53] and it is to be taken as part of the Lukan plan to do better justice to the order of events within the Church's catechetical teaching (1:3). In v. 18, the saying about not drinking wine is located after the thanksgiving in v. 17; those scribes who took v. 18 as a temporally literal promise not to drink would have had difficulty understanding why Jesus drank so soon after v. 18.[54] That failure of understanding was another occasion of textual adjustment: v. 18 was therefore deleted in some witnesses. But the placement is correct, and it confirms, as we have argued in chapter 1, that the saying is a promise of the kingdom's association with Jesus' meals, not a vow of abstinence.

The context which makes the cultic reading the most plausible is Jesus' own activity. He has just occupied the Temple, where he made the issue of purity paramount. That incursion is no temperamental outburst, but the culmination of a program which had stressed forgiveness and genuine ownership of what was offered as requirements of acceptable sacrifice in the Temple. But once Jesus' halakhah clearly is not to be accepted in the Temple, the character of his meals with his disciples changes. Earlier, they have been enactments of the purity which was demanded within sacrifice. Now, that social purity, and especially the food and drink consumed, are the sacrifice. God, Jesus teaches, is better pleased with that "blood" and "body" than with what is offered incorrectly on Mount Zion.

The meal still anticipates the kingdom, on the assumption that the Temple will be the seat of God's ultimate rule, but Jesus at the end of his ministry as surely withdraws from ordinary cultic practice as

---

[52] Cf. Higgins, 17.

[53] Cf. Joachim Jeremias (tr. A. Ehrhardt), *The Eucharistic Words of Jesus* (New York: Macmillan, 1955) 87-106.

[54] That is also a difficulty for Jeremias, cf. pp. 165-172.

the sectarians of Qumran did. The issue of the withdrawal is purity, rather than priestly succession and calendar, but the breech is all the more dramatic for Jesus' proximity to the Temple. Moreover, and crucially, Jesus begins to refer to what he offers in the meals which enact the purity he strove for as his "blood" and "body." Where the Essenes longed for the time when they would control the offering of sacrifice, they did so outside of Jerusalem, and in the meantime many of them took part in the regular worship of the Temple.[55] Their intramural theory was far more confrontative than their extramural practice. By contrast, Jesus' theory of purity, although it affirmed the centrality of the cult as it was then conducted, resulted in a demand for practice which put him in opposition to the authorities of the Temple over the question of the location of the vendors; those authorities were correctly informed that the teacher who had demanded a new view of purity in the Temple was acting in a way which set up an alternative cult, a surrogate of sacrifice, and he was found guilty of blasphemy.[56]

The Gospels, of course, make the gravamen of the charge against Jesus that he predicted the destruction of the Temple and claimed to be the messiah (cf. Matthew 26:57-68//Mark 14:53-65//Luke 22:54-71; cf. John 18:13-24). Those are the issues of a later day. Jesus and the authorities in the Temple began disputing the pragmatics of sacrifice, how the purity of what was offered was to be assured. Throughout their dispute, their assumption was that purity, culminating in sacrifice, was its own affective reward and the promise of divine favor. But when the dispute resulted in the defeat of Jesus within the precincts of the Temple, his social eating took on a new and scandalous element: the claim that God preferred a pure meal to impure sacrifice in the Temple. Any such claim struck at the conception of the unique efficacy of the cult on Mount Zion. The

---

[55] See Michael A. Knibb, *The Qumran Community*: Cambridge Commentaries on Writings of the Jewish and Christian World 200 BC to AD 200 (Cambridge: Cambridge University Press, 1987) 52, 53.

[56] Such an interpretation obviates defining the "blasphemy" either as formal, as in Sanhedrin 7:5, or as a matter of christology, cf. Rudolf Pesch, *Das Markusevangelium II. Teil*: Herders Theologischer Kommentar zum Neuen Testament (Freiburg: Herder, 1980) 440. Josephus can refer as blasphemy to attacks on Jews (*Against Apion* I, 59, 223), on Moses (*Antiquities* III, 307; *Apion* I, 279), or on patriarchal law (*Apion* II, 143); cf. Herman Wolfgang Beyer, "βλασφημέω ..." *Theological Dictionary of the New Testament* I (ed. G. Kittel, tr. G.W. Bromiley; Grand Rapids: Eerdmans, 1978) 621-625.

dispute concerning the pragmatics of purity turned out to strike at an axiom within the ideology of Israel's sacrifice. Eschatological purity had become more important than place, and the authorities of the Temple could never accept any such inversion of their ideological priorities.

After Jesus' occupation of the Temple, and his failure to reform cultic worship, he presented his "blood" and "body" as the replacement of conventional sacrifice. Matthew 26:26-28//Mark 14:22-24//Luke 22:19, 20 (with v. 17 in respect of the correct order)//1 Corinthians 11:24, 25 reflect that development clearly, although in an indirect and elaborated form. At the level of dominical practice, however, the sense of the gesture is plain: pure wine and bread, shared in a community created by mutual forgiveness, is a better sacrifice than the priesthood of the Temple is willing to permit.

The sense of the gesture is confrontative, but does not involve the formal blasphemy which a later interpretation of the saying would require: this is my personal blood which is shed, this is my living flesh for you. Here, too, as in the case of the saying regarding the new wine of the kingdom, the underlying Aramaic which may be supposed is straightforward:[57]

דֵין דְמִי דִי שְׁפִיךְ   this is my blood which is poured out
דֵין בִּסְרִי הוֹא   this is my flesh here.

As Berhard Lang has pointed out,[58] the most original form of the wording is represented by Justin (*Apology* I.66):

τοῦτό ἐστι τὸ σῶμά μου   this is my body
τοῦτό ἐστι τὸ αἷμά μου   this is my blood.

Justin preserves the essential meaning of the words and the gestures, that wine and bread are now, in cultic terms, sacrificial blood and

---

[57] Cf. Joseph A. Fitzmyer, *The Gospel According to Luke (X-XXIV)*: The Anchor Bible (Garden City: Doubleday, 1985) 1394, where the retroversion conflates the dominical meaning with the Petrine emphasis on the theme of the covenant (cf. chapter 3). For that matter, Fitzmyer accepts the Jacobean chronology too readily (cf. chapter 4). Finally, Fitzmyer also retroverts "which is given for you" from Luke 22:19; that is clearly a phrase from a late development in eucharistic theology, and even christology (cf. Perrin, "The Use of παραδιδόναι in Connection with the Passion of Jesus in the New Testament," *Der Ruf Jesu und die Antwort der Gemeinde* [eds E. Lohse, C. Burchard, B. Schaller; Göttingen: Vandenhoeck und Ruprecht, 1970] 204-212).
[58] Lang, "Roots," 468.

flesh. But Justin's wording (itself probably traditional) accepts the
order of a later day, and omits the term "poured out" (שְׁפִיךְ in
Aramaic, ἐκχυννόμενον in the Greek of Matthew 26:28//Mark
14:24//Luke 22:20), which comports perfectly with the generative
sense of the wine as being sacrificial blood. The line of demarcation
between the generative sense of the wine as sacrificial blood which
is shed, on the one hand, and the later explanation of that meaning,
on the other hand, cannot be drawn with any certainty. Justin's
wording (although not his order) might therefore be regarded as
more primitive than the Aramaic retroversion suggested above, and
the addition of "poured out" might be taken as explanatory. The
explanation would nonetheless accord with the dominical sense of
the meal, and on any reading is more primitive than the commandment to "do this for my remembrance," which precedes Jesus'
reference to his body in Justin's version. Justin's inclusion of the
notion of remembrance should be taken as an index of the late form
of some of the traditions which he preserves (see chapter 5).

Elements within Luke 22:14-20 constitute the latest commentary
on the meal within its dominical meaning.[59] V. 15 establishes a
pre-Paschal chronology, in that Jesus expresses an unfulfilled desire
to eat of the Passover;[60] v. 17 demonstrates that the order of the

---

[59] The elements within Luke 22:14-20 which comport well with the dominical
meaning of the meal are conveyed as sayings of Jesus, and may be assigned to "Q."
Nonetheless, the analysis of 22:18 in chapter 1 has suggested that the presentation
of the sayings has been redacted so as to conform to the heroic presentation of Jesus
within the Synoptic catechesis, and the Lukan redaction has clearly deployed the
material of "Q" here in order to comport with the later, Paschal chronology of the
early Church (cf. chapter 4). Fitzmyer, p. 1386, assigns the material to the source
he calls "L," but that judgement is mechanical. "L" as used by Fitzmyer stands
for whatever in Luke is surplus to Mark, but missing from Matthew. Insofar as
"L" is a source, however, its narrative is haggadic (or legendary) and its speech
is proemic (or discursive) in style, while the sayings here gathered are halakhic (or
occasional). In generic terms, assignment to "Q" is preferable.

[60] So Léon-Dufour, p. 195. He conceives of vv. 15-18 as reflecting a testamental tradition of the meal, along the lines of the *Testament of Naphtali* (see pp. 266-
284), in which bread and wine are the occasion (and, as Léon-Dufour would have
it, the symbols) of a discourse of farewell. His hypothesis involves imagining first
that the testamental tradition was overlaid with a cultic tradition, in which the
"body" and "blood" of Jesus are paramount, and then that the testamental tradition was rediscovered by Luke and John. It is simpler to suppose that the testamental motif of a farewell over a meal has been picked up at the literary stages in the
exposition of the significance of Jesus' meal which Luke and John represent.
Moreover, the testamental tradition which Léon-Dufour imagines is so filled with
the prophetic symbolism of Jesus' "body" and "blood," the contemporaneous

meal involved reference to "blood" before reference to "body." V. 17 also, in its reference to dividing what is sacrificed,[61] suggests the sort of sacrifice which Jesus saw the meal as standing surrogate for.

Leviticus 3 describes the ritual of the "sacrifice of sharings," which Gary Anderson has described as a kind of "festive meal" in a cultic context.[62] The notion that a sacrifice might involve worshipers in a meal is a commonplace in ethnographic studies,[63] and it is specifically attested in patriarchal and Mosaic narratives. Jacob formalizes his treaty with Laban on that basis (Genesis 31:51-54), and Jethro celebrates both the LORD's greatness and the presence of Aaron and the elders thereby (Exodus 18:9-12). In 1 Samuel 1:3-5, that Elkanah should distribute sacrificial portions in his own household is recounted as a matter of course. Within the Priestly source, however, burnt sacrifice and cereal sacrifice gained in importance at the expense of the sacrifice of sharings. But that demotion could not obscure the enduring place of the sacrifice of sharings within the tradition. At the time of the sacrifice to solemnize the covenant, Moses, Aaron, Nadab, Abihu and the seventy elders are particularly said to behold God, eat and drink, and that festive communion is specifically associated with the sacrifices of sharings referred to in the text (Exodus 24:4-11).

The paradigmatic function of the sacrifice of sharings within cultic discussion during the first century is suggested by the story concerning Hillel's teaching which has already been cited. The sacrifice of sharings is appealed to by Hillel as a means of establishing his *halakhah* in respect of the burnt sacrifice within the Temple.[64] Neither Jesus nor Hillel would have formally invoked the sacrifice of sharings as his paradigm, but it was natural for both of them to

---

existence of something like what he calls the cultic tradition would seem to be presupposed. After all, Naphtali in the *Testament* mostly talks: the meal is simply the dramatic setting.

[61] Cf. 2Q New Jerusalem fragment 4.10, 11, where bread is to be divided (יתפלג) among priests.

[62] Gary A. Anderson, *Sacrifices and Offerings in Ancient Israel. Studies in their Social and Political Importance*: Harvard Semitic Monographs 41 (Atlanta: Scholars, 1987), 51-53. For a further discussion of the זבח שלמים, including how it should be rendered in English, see "Sacrifice in 'Classic' Israel, *The Temple of Jesus*, 45-67, 57-60.

[63] For reference to human consumption of the sacrifice of sharings, see Leviticus 7:11-18, 28-36; 19:5-8; Philo, *De specialibus legibus* I, 212.

[64] Cf. Beẓah 20a, b, discussed above.

revert to that type of common offering in the discussion of sacrifice generally.

Xavier Léon-Dufour has attempted to be even more precise in the identification of eucharist with a particular type of sacrifice.[65] Among various types of sacrifice of sharings, he calls our attention to the sacrifice of sharings for thanksgiving (עַל־תּוֹדָה, Leviticus 7:11-15). It might also be called (v. 12) ''sacrifice of thanksgiving,'' זֶבַח הַתּוֹדָה. In the Septuagint, the phrase is rendered θυσία τῆς αἰνέσεως, ''sacrifice of praise.'' Léon-Dufour, following a recent investigation,[66] observes that passages such as Psalm 50:14, in its call to offer God a sacrifice of thanksgiving, show the tight connection between offering praise and the act of worship itself. He defines the sacrifice of thanksgiving as a sacrifice of sharings in which one offered, ate, and sang God's praises for his mercies, both present and to come.

It would comport precisely with the present analysis to identify Jesus' practice at meals after the occupation of the Temple as an attempt to establish a surrogate for the sacrifice of thanksgiving. But the dimension of praise which is a characteristic feature of eucharistic texts of Christianity need not be a function of the sacrifice of thanksgiving and its prayers in particular. The celebration of the kingdom, acknowledgement of the risen presence of Jesus, proleptic joy at the Lord's return are all more immediate sources of the expression of Christian praise in eucharistic worship. In any case, the reason for which the sacrifice of thanksgiving could emerge and flourish as a form which produced a literature is that the sacrifice of sharings, the type of offering to which is pertains, exerted a paradigmatic influence on the worship of Israel and the thought of early Judaism. When a Hillel or a Jesus thought in terms of sacrifice, the sacrifice of sharings would spring readily to mind.

---

[65] See Xavier Léon-Dufour, *Le partage du pain eucharistique selon le Nouveau Testament* (Paris: Editions du Seuil, 1982) 54-58, 206-209. In his analysis of typologies of meaning, Léon-Dufour represents a movement in the direction of the present approach.

[66] He repeatedly cites C. Giraudo, *La structura letteraria della Preghiera eucaristica. Saggio sulla genesi letteraria di una forma. Toda veterotestamentaria, B'raka giudaica, Anafora cristiana*: Analecta biblica 92 (Rome: Pontifical Biblical Institute, 1981).

CHAPTER THREE

THE COVENANTAL SACRIFICE OF SHARINGS

The Temple of Jesus and the Temple of Peter

Given that Jesus was executed in Jerusalem as a consequence of a dispute concerning the Temple, a considerable change must have occurred to enable his followers to organize in Jerusalem and to worship in that same Temple. The picture provided in Acts is clear and consistent: under the leadership of Peter and a group of twelve, the followers of Jesus lived commonly, broke bread together regularly in their homes, and participated in the cult (see Acts 1:12-26; 2:46; 3:1-26; 4:1-37).

It is acknowledged widely that the picture of a smooth transition, entirely within the ambit of Jerusalem, and from deadly persecution to relative acceptance, is an example of Lukan idealization. The matter of appearances of Jesus as risen in Galilee is left out entirely.[1] But even Luke relates stories in which the mention of Jesus' name within the precincts of the Temple leads to arrest and interrogation at the hands of priestly authorities (see Acts 4:1-22; 5:12-42), so that the pivotal question of the compatibility between Jesus' movement and ordinary practice of the cult is marked.

The transition from a movement of protest against certain practices in the Temple to a residential community whose activities included worship and teaching within the Temple is perhaps the most important in a century which saw a series of stunning transformations in the social constituency of those who followed Jesus. The absence of direct evidence of how the group around Peter emerged is daunting. The Lukan picture in Acts is dominated by the concerns of a Gentile Christianity of a later day, and the Synoptic Gospels attest only indirectly the traditions framed and transmitted by the Petrine group.

Certain preliminary conclusions, by way of orientation, may

---

[1] That is the point of departure for the analysis of F.J. Foakes Jackson and Kirsopp Lake, "The Disciples in Jerusalem and the Rise of Gentile Christianity," *The Beginnings of Christianity* I (Grand Rapids: Baker, 1979) 300-320.

nonetheless be drawn from what we can know with a fair degree of
certainty. First, the Temple on any reading emerges as a defining
concern. The formation of the Petrine group undercuts any supposition that Jesus had led a campaign of general opposition to the
Temple, and substantiates the argument that Jesus' dispute with the
cultic authorities was over particular issues, such as are identified in
chapter 2. Second, the Petrine stage of the movement is marked as
the moment at which a definable pattern of social arrangement
characterized the movement. Institutions of leadership, residence,
property, eating, and worship became apparent in a way they were
not before, when Jesus himself had engaged in a program which
took him and some others away from their homes, but left the
majority of his hearers living where they were. Third and finally, the
importance accorded to "breaking bread at home" (Acts 2:46; cf.
20:7, 11; 27:35) suggests that the Petrine stage of the movement was
crucial in the establishment of eucharistic practice.

    The eucharistic practice of the Petrine circle is accessible only in-
directly, by means of the Synoptic Gospels. In order to identify the
Petrine elements within their presentations of Jesus' last meal, certain preliminary questions need to be addressed. In what follows, we
shall consider how arrangements within the Temple changed in
order to permit of worship by Jesus' followers, and also how the
movement itself accommodated to the new situation. That consideration will form the perspective from which we will then consider the
traditions of the Petrine circle within the Synoptic Gospels, and—in
particular—the Petrine eucharist.

    With the constitution of the group around Jesus as a socially
definable movement within Judaism, the Petrine circle put its mark
on Christianity forever after. In what follows, we will see how the
fellowship meals of Jesus were transformed. They had been occasions on which eating together had been taken as a pledge of the festivity of the kingdom of God, and then Jesus had approved the communal wine and bread as more acceptable to God than regular
sacrifice. The Petrine circle literally domesticated such meals, hold-
ing them at home and deliberately taking part in the worship of the
Temple. At the same time, Peter's group accommodated the meal
of fellowship to the general, ancient, and widespread practice of
blessing what was consumed at meals (see m. Berakhoth 6:5-8 and
b. Berakhoth 42a-45a), beginning with bread (see b. Berakhoth
46a). In addition to recollecting what Jesus came into the habit of

saying during his meals of fellowship, the Petrine eucharist also made explicit reference to the covenant. In so doing, the group reinforced both its loyalty to the Temple and its devotion to Jesus as a teacher of purity comparable to Moses. The breaking of bread took place at home in the Petrine circle, but the meaning of those meals was so specific, their elements and gestures so routine, that what had been an occasion of fellowship and a parable of eschatological purity within the activity of Jesus had now become a ritual.

That the dispute involving Jesus' occupation of the Temple concerned physical arrangements therein is supported by the story of the Sanhedrin's removal, as Victor Eppstein demonstrated and is developed in chapter 2. Another text of Rabbinic literature suggests that the period of Jesus' activity was also one which saw intense dispute concerning the efficacy of the Temple (b. Yoma 39b, cf. Yerushalmi Sota 6:13):[2]

> Forty years before the destruction of the house, the lot did not come up in the right hand, the crimson strap failed to turn white, and the western light would not burn, and the gates of the Temple opened on their own . . .

The precise meaning of the portents will be discussed in the paragraphs which follow, because in aggregate they suggest that the time around A.D. 30 was remembered for debates over what God himself made of arrangements within the sacrificial cult.

The omens are placed in a particular setting: the day of atonement. That is the day on which, in the story which precedes, Simeon the righteous enters the holy of holies, and the omens themselves concern the lot for the LORD and the lot for Azazel, the crimson straps used for the goats, and the lights in the sanctuary. Although Leviticus 16 provides a general sense of the setting envisaged, Mishnah gives a much clearer indication of the contextual meaning of the omens. The precise moment in which the lot for the LORD came up is designated in Yoma 4:1 (cf. 3:9): the high priest, at the instigation of the *sagan* (the "captain" of the Temple), raises the hand in which the LORD's lot has come up, so that whether it is the

---

[2] The text is straightforward:

אַרְבָּעִים שָׁנָה קוֹדֶם חוּרְבַּן הַבַּיִת לֹא הָיָה גוֹרָל עוֹלֶה בִּימִין וְלֹא הָיָה לְשָׁן שֶׁל זְהוֹרִית
מַלְבִּין וְלֹא הָיָה נֵר מַעֲרָבִי דוֹלֵק וְהָיוּ דְּלָתוֹת הַהֵיכָל נִפְתָּחוֹת מֵאֲלֵיהֶן.

Both are cited by Craig Evans in an unpublished paper entitled, "Jesus and Predictions of the Destruction of the Herodian Temple in the Pseudepigrapha."

right or the left in a given year could be a matter of common
knowledge. The period on that basis is characterized as literally
sinister by the omen, in that the lot which determined which goat
was the LORD's came up in the high priest's left hand.

Following usual practice, a crimson strap (or "tongue," as a literal translation would have it) is tied both on the goat to be sent out,
and on the goat which has just been chosen to be slaughtered (Yoma
4:2). According to Ishmael in Yoma 6:8, there was a crimson strap
also tied to the door of the sanctuary, and when the goat for Azazel
reached the wilderness, it turned white. The meaning of the change
is spelled out in terms of Isaiah 1:18, and accords with the opinion
in Yoma 39b (attributed to Isaac b. Ṭablai) that the Temple is called
Lebanon (לְבָנוֹן) because it makes sins white (לָבָן). The portent indicated otherwise.

The omens, in effect, cast doubt on God's acceptance of the goat
for himself (the lot in the left hand), and on the removal of sin effected by the ritual of the goat for Azazel. The mention of the light may
at first appear gratuitous, but the kindling of the lights is specifically
made a high-priestly duty in the week before Yom Kippur in Yoma
1:2. Moreover, the light which is most westerly is the light nearest
the holy of holies, and that is the direction in which both the high
priest himself and his own bull are to face as he lays his two hands
upon it and makes confession (Yoma 3:8). The extinguished light
brings in question the dwelling of the Shekhinah within the Temple,
and the efficacy of what is done there. The reference to the door
which opens mysteriously only serves to underline the suspicion that
the house of God is such in name only.

The signs are taken in Yoma 39b to mean that the Temple would
be destroyed by fire; Zechariah 11:1 is cited in a statement attributed to Yoḥanan ben Zakkai. The attribution to Yoḥanan, of
course, may be anachronistic, and the assignment to him of prophetic powers is presumably legendary, much as in his alleged acclama-
tion of Vespasian as a king, which is suspiciously like Josephus'
similar feat.[3] Moreover, the reference to "forty years before the
destruction of the Temple" is at least as much a *topos* (for a generation) as it is chronology.[4] Nonetheless, the Rabbinic memory of the

---

[3] Cf. Giṭṭin 56 a, b; *Jewish War* III, 399-408; IV, 622-629; *A Galilean Rabbi*,
pp. 19, 20.

[4] Cf. M.H. Pope, "Number, Numbering, Numbers," *The Interpreter's Dictionary of the Bible* 3 (New York: Abingdon, 1962) 561-567, 565.

removal of the Sanhedrin, discussed in the previous section, may be associated with the present reference to omens of the inefficacy of the Temple.

The conviction that, some forty years before its destruction, the Temple was the site of disputes so fierce that its integrity as the enduring locus of worship came to be doubted may be related both to Jesus' occupation and to the notice of the torn curtain at the time of his death, another portent of destruction as it is presented in the Gospels (Matthew 27:51a; Mark 15:38; Luke 23:45). Of course, both the Gospels and Rabbinica speak with the advantage of hindsight where it concerns the burning of the Temple under Titus (and its subsequent demolition under Hadrian, in the case of Rabbinica and the Apocryphal Gospels). What is pertinent here is not that such portents as they refer to happened or, if they did, that they were interpreted correctly, but rather that collectively they represent a common acknowledgement—in the two collections of sources—that the integrity of the Temple was actively disputed approximately one generation before its destruction. The mention of a στάσις in Mark 15:7, in order to explain the crime and consequent arrest of Barabbas, is an indication that the controversy prompted by Jesus' occupation of the Temple degenerated into violent contention. The fundamental nature of the challenges to the Temple's efficacy adduced in Yoma 39b suggests why a protest such as Jesus' could turn bloody: one generation before the destruction of the Temple, the most serious doubts concerning the conduct of the cult were being raised, and any dispute might unleash forces of protest which the disputants themselves were not party to.

Jesus' fateful words, "This is my blood," "This is my body," brought him into conflict with the cultic authorities, in that his claim represented his communal meals as fitter occasions of God's presence than sacrifice in the Temple. His execution joins the torn curtain in the Gospels, as well as the removal of the Sanhedrin and the dispute concerning the efficacy of the Temple on the day of atonement in Rabbinica, in attesting the difficulties which faced Caiaphas in the last years of his tenure as high priest. But the tumultuous events of c. A.D. 30, including Jesus' execution, resulted eventually in the return of the vendors with their animals to Ḥanuth, their place as generally assumed in Rabbinica.[5] That resolution

---

[5] Cf. *The Temple of Jesus*, 107-108.

might conceivably have taken as long to achieve as A.D. 36/37, when Vitellius removed Caiaphas,[6] but it evidently was achieved, and accorded with a broad consensus among those who interested themselves in the conduct of worship in the Temple.

In any case, when we meet Jesus' followers in Acts, including the "pillars" (Peter, James, and John, as explained below), they are portrayed as both assembling in the Temple daily and breaking bread at home (Acts 2:46). Jesus' protest was ultimately effective, then, in that his followers could worship in a Temple where commercial arrangements were no longer offensive to them. But the protest in itself had focused religious forces in such a way that a movement emerged which would not only survive the destruction of the Temple, but rejoice in its destruction. But those developments are as recent as "the little apocalypse:" the circle led by Peter, James, and John made no such a claim of cultic transcendence.

To some extent, then, what permitted the transition from protest against to accommodation with the prevailing arrangements in the Temple was that those arrangements themselves had changed. Even more importantly, the Temple of Jesus was the site of profound disputes in a way that the Temple of Peter was not. Vitellius' removal of both Pilate and Caiaphas, and his return of high-priestly vestments to the custody of the high priest (*Antiquities* XVIII, 90-95) are all indications that the period after Caiaphas saw a return to arrangements which would appeal to widely agreed notions of purity and piety. Had Jesus entered the great court of the Temple ten years after he in fact did so, he would not have encountered the innovations of Caiaphas, and the atmosphere in which any protest occurred would have been far less charged.

In any event, shortly after the occupation of the Temple by Jesus and his followers, the movement in Jerusalem (as well as in Galilee and Syria) looked to Peter for leadership. If the arrangements in the Temple had changed markedly, the movement had been transformed. Even allowing for Lukan idealization, the devotion of the Petrine circle to the Temple and their residence in Jerusalem stand

---

[6] Cf. *Antiquities* XVIII, 90-95. At the same time, high-priestly vestments were removed from custody in the Antonia. Caiaphas' apparent acquiescence in that arrangement may be seen as cognate with his policy in regard to the Sanhedrin and the vendors. In all three cases, Caiaphas would be enhancing his position as the sole legitimate ethnarch in relation to the Romans.

in stark contrast to Jesus' challenging stance towards cultic norms as well as to his itineracy. Whatever Peter's group made of Jesus' *halakhah* concerning purity, they found it possible to square it with residence in Jerusalem and regular participation in the worship of the Temple. It is conceivable, as has been suggested above, that Jesus also could have resided in Jerusalem without coming to grief at the hands of Caiaphas' successors. But residence in Jerusalem was not a part of his intention, and his own conception of purity was better suited to the world of peasants than to the exigencies of cities.

Acts also places Peter in Samaria (8:14-25), Lydda (9:32-35), Joppa (9:36-43), and Caesarea (10:1-48; 12:19). Paul refers, as if as a matter of course, to Peter's presence personally in Antioch (see Galatians 2:11-14), and by the time of the pseudepigraphic 1 Peter (written around A.D. 90) he is pictured as writing from Rome (see 1 Peter 4:13) with Silvanus (4:12) to churches in the north of Asia Minor (1:1, 2). If, then, Jerusalem was a center for Peter in the way it was not for Jesus, it was certainly no limit of operations. Rather, the Temple appears to have featured as the hub of a much wider network of contacts,[7] which linked Jews from abroad and even Gentiles (see Acts 10:1-48 and especially 11:1-18, 15:1-11 with Galatians 2:1-14) in common recognition of a new, eschatological purity defined by the teaching of Jesus. The Petrine circle took part in worship within the Temple, embracing it in a way Jesus had not, and at the same time viewed Jesus as the source of a teaching which envisaged the participation in worship of those far outside Jerusalem.

The Petrine Circle and its Eucharist

Peter, James, and John were recognized by Paul as "pillars" of the community in Jerusalem; they had achieved that status by the time Paul wrote to the Galatians, probably around A.D. 53 (see 2:1-10). Paul claims to have met with Peter (whom he refers to under his Aramaic cognomen, Cephas [כֵּיפָא]) and James, Jesus' brother, at an earlier date, some three years after he began preaching (Galatians 1:18-20). He pointedly remarks that he did not meet with any

---

[7] As evocative studies of contacts between Jerusalem and other cities, see Wayne A. Meeks and Robert L. Wilken, *Jews and Christians in Antioch in the First Four Centuries of the Common Era* (Missoula: Scholars, 1978), and Raymond E. Brown and John P. Meier, *Antioch and Rome. New Testament Cradles of Catholic Christianity* (New York: Paulist, 1983).

other apostle at that time, that is c. A.D. 35. Peter, then, is Paul's
chief contact in Jerusalem initially; after some fourteen years, at the
meeting described in Galatians 2:1-10, he appears again, but is listed
as one of three "pillars," after James (2:9).[8]

During the intervening years, James, the son of Zebedee and the
brother of John, had been executed, under Herod Agrippa I (cf. Acts
12:2). The martyrdom is associated in Acts with Herod's negotiation of peace with Tyre and Sidon (Acts 12:20-23), and may be dated
c. A.D. 44.[9] The "James" to whom Paul refers in Galatians 2:9, in
connection with a meeting which took place c. A. D. 49, is therefore
the brother of Jesus. Paul also names James before Cephas and
John, although in the reference to meetings in Jerusalem c. A.D. 35
Cephas is given precedence before James (Galatians 1:18, 19).

During the same period between Paul's visits to Jerusalem (and
out of considerations of the same policy which resulted in James'
death) Agrippa is said to have imprisoned Peter (Acts 12:1-5). Mention of Peter's imprisonment and escape (cf. vv. 6-19) occasions
reference in Acts 12 to two factors of great importance in the development of the tradition which would emerge as the Synoptic
Gospels: Peter is linked particularly with those gathered in the house
of Mary, the mother of John Mark (vv. 12-17), and he tells his hearers to report his release to "James and the brothers" (v. 20). In the
Petrine ministry, John Mark would figure crucially; he would also
feature in Paul's activity (cf. Acts 12:25). But the reference by Peter
to "James and the brothers" also reflects a transition of authority
within the residential community in Jerusalem: the old triumvirate
of Peter, James (the son of Zebedee), and John was replaced by
James (the Lord's brother), Peter, and John, and in that order
(Galatians 2:9). Paul remarks, not without sarcasm, that the latter
three "seemed" to be "pillars" (v. 9, οἱ δοκοῦντες στῦλοι εἶναι, cf.
v. 6), as if that honor might rightly belong to others in his estimation.

The three earlier "pillars"—Peter, James, and John—were responsible for the next development in eucharistic teaching. That de-

---

[8] See Karl P. Donfried, "Peter," *The Anchor Bible Dictionary* 5 (eds D.N. Freedman and others; New York: Doubleday, 1992) 251-263.

[9] Cf. Eugen Ruckstuhl, "Jakobus (Herrenbruder)," *Theologische Realenzyklopädie* (Berlin: de Gruyter, 1987) 485-488. The dating derives from *Antiquities* XIX,
343-52, which differs from the passage in Acts, although it is not inconsistent with
it. Josephus does not mentioned Herod's meeting with ambassadors of Tyre and
Sidon, for example.

velopment can best be appreciated on the basis of their own claim
to authority prior to the emergence of Jesus' brother as the preemi-
nent figure in Jerusalem. The three are singled out as having exclusively been with Jesus on crucial occasions (Mark 5:37//Luke 8:51;
Mark 14:33//Matthew 26:37); in that apostles are appointed to be
with him, as well to be sent out by him (Mark 3:13, 14; 6:7;
Matthew 10:1, 5-7; Luke 6:12, 13; 9:1-2), their claim to teaching
with authority is strengthened by reference to such occasions.

A scene which implicitly involves the authorization of the three
"pillars" within the Synoptic tradition is the "Transfiguration"
(Matthew 17:1-9//Mark 9:2-10//Luke 9:28-36). Stories concerning
heavenly voices are well known in Rabbinica;[10] a frequently encountered view is that, with the removal of the holy spirit and the
end of prophecy, only an echo (בַּת קוֹל, "daughter of a voice") or
resonance from the heavenly court, expressed God's perspective. In
Tosephta Soṭah 13:3, just that statement is explicitly made. An example follows. When the sages were gathered at the house of Guria
in Jericho, they heard a בַּת קוֹל, "There is here a man who is pre-
destined for the holy spirit, except that his generation is not worthy
of it."[11] The sages then looked at Hillel, whom they took as the object of the praise. The Transfiguration obviously includes more motifs than are involved in most stories which refer to divine voices,
and yet a certain generic affinity is manifest with the story about
Hillel. As in the case of Hillel in the house of Guria, the basic structure of the Transfiguration first locates Jesus physically and socially,
and then makes him the object of the בַּת קוֹל's praise, as his companions appreciate. Only the companions, whether in the house of
Guria or on the mount of the Transfiguration, can attest the message of the divine voice, so that the stories warrant their testimony
at the same time as Hillel and Jesus are singled out.

But if the generic structure of the Transfiguration is to be found

---

[10] Cf. L. Blau, "Bath Ḳol," *The Jewish Encyclopedia* (ed. I. Singer; New York:
Funk and Wagnalls, 1903) 588-592; S.L. Lieberman, *Hellenism in Jewish Palestine.
Studies in the Literary Transmission, Beliefs and Manners in Palestine in the I Century
B.C.E.—IV Century C.E.*: Texts and Studies 18 (New York: Jewish Theological
Seminary of America, 1962) 194-199.

[11] Cf. J. Neusner, *The Peripatetic Saying. The Problem of the Thrice-Told Tale in the
Canon of Talmudic Literature*: Brown Judaic Studies 89 (Atlanta: Scholars Press,
1985) 114, 115; Chilton, *Profiles of a Rabbi. Synoptic Opportunities in Reading About
Jesus*: Brown Judaic Studies 177 (Atlanta: Scholars Press, 1989), "Bath Qol—The
Cases of Jesus and Hillel," 77-89.

in stories concerning divine voices, its narrative structure, in the run and nature of the events recounted, is reminiscent of Moses' approach and assent of Sinai with his companions (Exodus 24). At the close of the story, Moses is said to ascend the mountain, when God's glory covered it as a cloud (v. 15). The covering lasts six days (v. 16), which is the amount of time between the Transfiguration and the previous discourse (concerning Jesus' and his disciples' vocation to suffer) in both Matthew (17:1) and Mark (9:2). After that time, the LORD calls to Moses from the cloud (24:16b), and Moses enters the glory of the cloud, which is compared to a devouring fire (vv. 17, 18). Earlier in the chapter, Moses is commanded to select three worshipers, Aaron, Nadab, and Abihu, together with seventy elders, in order to confirm the covenant (vv. 1-8). The result is that just these people (v. 9) are explicitly said to have seen ''the God of Israel'' in his court (v. 10), and to have celebrated their vision by eating and drinking (v. 11b). The motifs of master, three disciples, mountain, cloud, vision, and audition, are held in common between Exodus 24 and the Transfiguration.[12]

It has already been mentioned that the reference to six days in the Matthean and Markan stories, but not the Lukan story, coheres with Exodus 24. Luke puts a distance of eight rather than six days between the previous discourse and the Transfiguration, a fact which has baffled commentators. Placed within the context of rabbinic interpretation of Exodus 24, however, the numerical variation is meaningful. In the Targum Pseudo-Jonathan (Exodus 24:10, 11), it is particularly Nadab and Abihu who see ''the glory of the God of Israel.'' Because ''man will not see God and live'' (Exodus 33:20), they are punished; but the blow falls on the eighth day. Other distinctive elements (that is, elements not held entirely in common among the Synoptics) within the Gospels' versions of the Transfiguration may also be associated, if not strictly with Exodus 24, than with the complex of material to which it belongs. So, for example, Matthew 17:2 uniquely refers to Jesus' face shining as the sun, which is reminiscent of Moses' aspect as a result of his talking with God, as described in Exodus 34:29-35. In more general terms, the Markan reference to the whiteness of Jesus' garments, ''such as a fuller upon the earth is not able to whiten'' (9:3),[13] establishes by

---

[12] Cf. Chilton, ''The Transfiguration: Dominical Assurance and Apostolic Vision,'' *New Testament Studies* 27 (1980) 115-124.

[13] The remark is commonly treated as extraneous, but it may represent an

its own means the heavenly context which is more elaborately developed in Exodus 24 (particularly, by vv. 16-18).

Luke also has Moses and Elijah discussing Jesus' "departure" (ἔξοδος) in 9:31; quite evidently, Exodus 24 provides no firm limit to developments within the Transfiguration, since the terms "exodus" and "Elijah" have associations all their own. Elijah's immortality is already suggested in 2 Kings 2:9-12, and is well established within early and rabbinic Judaism.[14] The statement in Deuteronomy 34:7, that Moses in fact died, did not prevent Josephus from describing Moses as disappearing (ἀφανίζεται) in the course of conversation with Eleazar and Joshua (*Antiquities* IV, 326). In that Josephus speaks of Elijah and Enoch with the cognate adjective (ἀφανεῖς), his understanding that Moses was immortal is intimated by his choice of words. Such associations are at work throughout the Synoptic presentation, perhaps as powerfully as the more obvious associations with Elijah's experience on a theophanic mountain (1 Kings 19:1-18). Similarly, the term σκήνη ("tent," "booth," or "lean-to") although it does not appear within the Septuagint in Exodus 24, features both as a natural place of abode during this period in Exodus 18:7, and as a particular place of God's dwelling (25:8, 9; and frequently from 26:1).

Elements of Exodus 24, then, are assembled within the Transfiguration, but the chapter in no sense limits the range of associations within the Synoptic story. Crucial matter within Exodus 24 (cf. vv. 12-14, particularly the references to the tablets of stone and to Joshua) has no analog whatever. In fact, Exodus 24 in the Hebrew Bible is but a preamble to the divine instructions which commence properly in chapter 25 of the book. What happens on the mountain designates Moses, in narrative and visionary terms, as the single spokesman of divine revelation (24:18); others in the chapter are presented, only to be excluded at the pivotal moment of divine disclosure. They join in the celebration of the divine vision, but they

---

awareness that the Transfiguration is of Petrine, not Jacobean, provenience. James' martyrdom included beating with a fuller's club, and the moment is treated as a seal of James' noble character (cf. Eusebius, *Ecclesiastical History* II.1, 5 [citing Clement's *Hypotyposes*] and II.23, 1-19 [citing Hegesippus]). The comment in Mark may be seen to trump the Jacobean claim.

[14] Cf. Chilton, *God in Strength*, 268-270; Christopher Begg, "'Josephus' Portrayal of the Disappearances of Enoch, Elijah and Moses': Some Observations," *Journal of Biblical Literature* 109 (1990) 691-693.

do not hear what Moses hears. By contrast, the climax of the Trans-figuration is precisely the moment when the voice addresses, not Jesus alone, but the three disciples. The generic structure involving the בַּת קוֹל turns out to be the focus of interest after all, so that the role of Peter, James, and John as witnesses proves to be structurally important.

Peter, James, and John are also presented within the story of Jesus' prayer in Gethsemane. There, too, they are privileged in their participation, but their understanding of the events is partial; they are at a loss in their response to revelation.[15] Myllykoski has rightly maintained that the story of Gethsemane was associated in the tradition prior to Mark with reference to the "last supper," an account of which precedes.[16] Within the Petrine cycle, as we may designate stories of the "pillars," the Transfiguration initiated the complex leading up to Jesus' death, and the meal—taken in associa-tion with the prayer in Gethsemane—brought it to fruition. Peter, James, and John are the privileged witnesses and the principal guarantors of the meaning of Jesus' death in his own (and God's own) understanding.

Just as Exodus 24 lies at the heart of the Transfiguration, so it proves a key to understanding Jesus' meal within the Petrine cycle. Jesus' "blood" is now understood to be "of the covenant"[17] and

---

[15] See Mark 9:6 with 14:37-42; Matthew 17:6, 7 with 26:40-46; Luke 9:32, 33 with 22:45-46, and—for a discussion of shared elements between the two peri-copae—A.C. Kenny, "The Transfiguration and the Agony in the Garden," *Ca-tholic Biblical Quarterly* 19 (1957) 444-452. On p. 444, he cites the setting on a moun-tain, a change in Jesus' appearance, the role of Peter (with James and John), the setting at night (cf. Luke 9:37a), and an acute consciousness of color. The last two elements may be disregarded. *Pace* Kenny, the reference of Luke 9:37a to the fol-lowing day is not naturally taken to imply that the events which precede the refer-ence occurred at night. The reference to the bloody sweat in Luke 22:43, 44 (which is apparently also on Kenny's mind in respect of his second element, when he refers to "a spiritual experience which changed his physical appearance in a unique man-ner") is probably an intrusion into the text of the Gospel, and has no obvious relevance to a sensitivity to color. (In any case, the bloody sweat may have more to do with haggadic portraits such as Hebrews 5:7 represents than with Petrine tra-dition.) But Kenny proceeds usefully to discuss similarities between the pericopae, verbal and thematic, in the three Synoptics.

[16] Cf. Myllykoski, p. 148.

[17] The phrasing which involves a "new covenant," in Luke 22:20 and 1 Corin-thians 11:25, is to be treated separately, along with the phrases εἰς ἄφεσιν ἁμαρτιῶν (Matthew 26:28), ὑπὲρ πολλῶν (Mark 14:24), and ὑπὲρ ὑμῶν (Luke 22:20). In his analysis of the words of institution, Xavier Léon-Dufour (*Le partage du pain eucharis-tique selon le Nouveau Testament* [Paris: Editions du Seuil, 1982] 118-121) offers an al-

"poured out" (Matthew 26:28; Mark 14:24). Both elements are reminiscent of Exodus 24:6-8, where Moses declares that the blood of the sacrifices is "the blood of the covenant," and throws half of it on the altar, and half on the people. The phrase "blood of the covenant" (τὸ αἷμα τῆς διαθήκης) is common to the passage in Exodus (v. 8) and the pericopae in the Gospels; the use of "my" in Matthew and Mark, which is present from the earlier formulation (cf. chapter 2), makes the phrase as a whole clumsy, because the "blood" is now over-determined in its meaning. As Léon-Dufour observes, the reference to the covenant, the only such reference in sayings of Jesus within the Gospels, appears to be intrusive.[18] In order to describe the blood as "poured out," Matthew and Mark use the perfect passive participle of the verb ἐκχέω; the related verbs ἐγχέω and προσχέω appear in the Septuagint at Exodus 24:6 (the latter for זָרַק in the Masoretic Text, cf. v. 8).[19] The Petrine cycle understood Jesus' last meal with his disciples within the context of his final purpose, and associated the meal with a unique sacrifice at the inauguration of the Mosaic covenant.

In cultic terms, the scene in Exodus 24 is an adaptation of the

---

ternative explanation. He holds that the Markan form of the tradition assimilated the words over the cup to the words over the bread, and that Luke and Paul represent a more primitive, Antiochene tradition. Whether Markan or Antiochene, at issue are aetiological narratives of a cult (pp. 100, 188). As will emerge in chapter 5, I agree with the purpose of the traditions, and the importance of Antioch; but in my reading the Lukan and Pauline wording reflects later developments.

[18] See Xavier Léon-Dufour, *Le partage du pain eucharistique selon le Nouveau Testament* (Paris: Editions du Seuil, 1982) 101, 104, 170, 199-203.

[19] By comparison, attempts to link the meal with Isaiah 53 on the grounds of the usage of ἐκχέω appear strained (as, for example, in the case of Léon-Dufour, pp. 178-181). After all, in the Septuagint at Isaiah 53:12, the servant is said to hand over his life to death (παρεδόθη εἰς θάνατον ἡ ψυχὴ αὐτοῦ), and that rendering comports well with the Targum and the Vulgate. There is therefore no question in Isaiah 53:12 of the same sort of immediate resonance of the phrase in Exodus 24:6 with the words of institution. That, in turn, is not surprising, because the Hebrew form rendered by παρεδόθη (הֶעֱרָה) might as easily mean that the servant laid his life open to death as that he poured it out to death. The meaning of the verb is not straightforward, certainly not as compared to זָרַק and ἐκχέω. An articificial resonance between Isaiah 53:12 and Matthew 26:28//Mark 14:24 has been created in some English translations. The Geneva Bible and the King James Version render the former with "poured out" and the latter with "shed," while the American Revised Version, the Revised Standard Version, and the New Revised Standard Version render the former and the latter with "poured out." The New English Bible retains "shed" in the saying over the cup, and innovates with "exposed himself to death" at Isaiah 53:12.

"sacrifice of sharings," the זֶבַח שְׁלָמִים (cf. v. 5 and Leviticus 3:1), the implicit paradigm within Jesus' practice of fellowship in Jerusalem, after his occupation of the Temple (again, see chapter 2). In Exodus 24, as is usually the case, those who offer the animal share in the consumption, either directly or through a priestly representative (cf. v. 11 and Leviticus 7:11-21, 28-36; 19:5-8). Only the mention of the covenant and the peculiar tossing of the blood makes the scene exceptional, although blood was tossed routinely (albeit not on worshipers) within the institution of the זֶבַח שְׁלָמִים (cf. Leviticus 3:13; 7:14, where the common verbal pair זָרַק/προσχέω appears). The sacrifice of sharings was still practised within the first century, as is reflected in the story about Hillel's teaching of the laying on of hands which has already been mentioned. Hillel attempts to get his burnt sacrifice past the disciples of Shammai on the grounds that it is a female for a sacrifice of sharings.[20]

The construal of the "last supper" as a sacrifice of sharings with specifically covenantal meaning suited the practice of daily worship in the Temple together with fellowship at meals, the emblematic pattern of the Petrine circle in Jerusalem (see Acts 2:46, cf. v. 42). The dominical paradigm of the ordinary sacrifice of sharings, however implicit, ran the risk—if simply repeated by Jesus' followers—of being taken as a challenge to the regular practice of sacrificial offering, which was how the authorities in the Temple had understood Jesus' own meals after his occupation of the outer court. The Petrine modulation of the paradigm to assimilate the meal of Jesus' followers to Exodus 24 enabled regular worship to proceed, while insisting upon the normative value of what Jesus had done. The portrayal of Jesus in Mosaic terms, which was a feature of the Petrine cycle (cf. the Transfiguration and the story of Gethsemane) was perpetuated by the new wording: Jesus' definition of purity, a principle feature of his teaching (cf. chapter 1), was associated with ordinary worship in the Temple, which could proceed without interruption.

At the same time, the Petrine circle enacted Jesus' inclusive program of purity by widening—both geographically and socially—the circle of Israelites and their supporters (above all, see Acts 10) who might be included within the fellowship. Israelites who lived abroad and those who worshiped the God of Israel (see Acts 10:2) could join

---

[20] Beza 20a, b; Yerushalmi Ḥagigah 2:3; Yerushalmi Beẓa 2:4; Tosephta Ḥagigah 2:11, as discussed in chapter 2.

those who prayed in the manner of Jesus, broke bread within the purity effected by forgiveness, and either directly or indirectly (that is, by belonging to the group) offered sacrifice in Jerusalem.

Petrine practice of eucharist was responsible for the repetitive, ritual character of the meal. Jesus' statements were remembered, and at the same time interpreted, in a way which gave them consistent meaning within the attempt to widen participation in the cult of the Temple on the basis of Jesus' teaching, and especially in the light of his death and resurrection. The witnesses of Gethsemane were also the witnesses of the Transfiguration: a new Moses showed the way of purity. Because he was a new Moses, he himself was a deathless witness. An irreducibly vital aspect of the Petrine eucharist is the insistence upon the joy of knowing Jesus as risen from the dead by means of the breaking of bread.

In his seminal study, Oscar Cullmann relates the "overflowing joy" (ἀγαλλίασις) of Acts 2:42, 46 to the recognition of Jesus as risen in the setting of meals (see Luke 24:13-32, 36-43; John 21:1-14): "*The certainty of the Resurrection* was the essential religious motive of the primitive Lord's Supper."[21] Acts 10:41 has Peter warrant his own stature (with others') as a witness by his reference to his having eaten and drunk with Jesus after he was raised from the dead, and Cullmann concludes "that the joy manifested by the early Christians during the 'breaking of bread' has its source, not in the fact that the assembled disciples eat the body and drink the blood of their crucified Master, but in the consciousness they have of eating *with* the *Risen* Christ...."[22] As the famous passage from Acts as a whole (that is 10:34-43) suggests, the Petrine circle stressed its own authority in respect of its fellowship with Jesus both from the beginning (vv. 36-39) and after the resurrection (vv. 40, 41), in order to insist upon Jesus' identity as the final judge attested by the prophets (vv. 42, 43).

The related issues which frame Peter's speech in Acts 10 concern who may be regarded as clean and acceptable to God (vv. 1-35) and how forgiveness may be obtained by means of belief in the name of

---

[21] Oscar Cullmann, "The Lord's Supper and the Death of Christ," *Essays on the Lord's Supper*: Ecumenical Studies in Worship 1 (with F.J. Leenhardt, tr. J.G. Davies; Richmond: John Knox, 1958), 5-23, 9-12. Cf. "La signification de la Sainte-Cène dans le christianisme primitif," *Revue d'Histoire et de Philosophie religieuse* (1936).

[22] Cullmann, 16, cf. 11.

Jesus (v. 43-48). Although the idiom of Acts is its own, it accurately
reflects the motivating attempt of the Petrine circle to practice Jesus'
purity in the home, even the home of a centurion, in a manner consistent with worship in the Temple.

Petrine practice was responsible, within its ritual regularity, for
the stereotypical order of bread before wine within the eucharist.
The meal was understood as a domestic "breaking bread", when
the master of a house would begin a meal on festive occasions (see
b. Berakhoth 46a). Such a breaking of bread was a particular
development within the general, ancient, and widespread practice
of blessing what was consumed at meals (see m. Berakhoth 6:5-8 and
b. Berakhoth 42a-45a). Accommodation of eucharistic practice to
the model of a *berakhah* avoided any impression of direct competition
with sacrifice in the Temple. At the same time, the fellowship of such
meals could be governed by the *halakhah* of a teacher whose resurrection made him comparable to Moses, and the ultimate master of the
occasion.

The practice of fellowship at meals as ritual "body" and
"blood," a communion in the manner of the covenantal sacrifice of
sharings, may help to explain why the activity was conducted "for
my memorial" (εἰς τὴν ἐμὴν ἀνάμνησιν) according to one version of
Petrine tradition (Luke 22:19; 1 Corinthians 11:24, 25). In the case
of a sacrifice which might be consumed by priests,[23] the portion
reserved for immolation on the altar was the "memorial" (אַזְכָּרָה,
cf. Leviticus 2:2, 9, 16, 5:12; 6:8; Numbers 5:26; τὸ μνημόσυνον in
the Septuagint). The incense sprinkled on the bread of the presentation is designated in the same way in Leviticus 24:7, although it is
not immolated. Aaron and his sons are to eat it (v. 9), and its presentation every sabbath is taken as a covenant (v. 8), which the Petrine
language of eucharist may echo; at just this point (that is, at 24:7),
the Septuagint renders the term אַזְכָּרָה as ἀνάμνησις, the term used
in Luke and 1 Corinthians. The notion that the activity of consuming might be involved in a sacrificial "memorial" is therefore
precedented. Moreover, the agreement of Luke and 1 Corinthians

---

[23] The application of priestly language to followers of Jesus within Petrine tradition is attested, cf. Chilton, "Shebna, Eliakim, and the Promise to Peter," *Targumic Approaches to the Gospels. Essays in the Mutual Definition of Judaism and Christianity*:
Studies in Judaism (Lanham and London: University Press of America, 1986)
63-80 and *The Social World of Formative Christianity and Judaism* (eds J. Neusner,
P. Borgen, E.S. Frerichs, R. Horsley; Philadelphia: Fortress, 1989) 311-326.

in using the possessive adjective, rather than the more usual pronoun, is striking. Jesus is depicted as insisting the meals should be consumed "for *my* memorial," not merely in his memory. It is yet another incentive to frequent repetition of an action related to the cult, as in the case of ὁσάκις ἐὰν πίνητε (1 Corinthians 11:25).[24]

At its earliest stage, the Petrine cycle was in fact Cephan, a representation of the Mosaic Jesus for his followers in Jerusalem and Galilee after the crucifixion. The incorporation within the cycle of dominical sayings which appear to have originated in Aramaic (cf. chapters one and two) suggests that the Cephan source also was transmitted in that language. If so, it probably ran:[25]

$$\text{דֵין בְּסְרִי הוּא עֲבִידוּ דָא לְדָכְרָנִי}$$
$$\text{דֵין דַּמִי דִי קְיָמָא הוּא דִי שְׁפִיךְ.}$$

The retroversion would account for a notably clumsy Greek text on the basis of an Aramaic couplet characterized by assonance in the first line, alliteration in the second, and—most importantly—a symmetrical structure of four beats per line.

The very name "Peter," without explanatory reference to its Aramaic origin (of the sort Paul provides, see Galatians 1:18; 2:6-14), attests the early translation of the cycle into Greek, perhaps in association with the wider field of ministry for which Peter accepted responsibility (again, see Acts 10 and 11:1-18). It is interesting that, in Galatians 2:7, 8, Paul refers to the apostle as "Peter" (rather than as Cephas) just as he speaks of his being entrusted with the gospel "of the circumcision," a phrase without limitation to Palestine (much less Jerusalem), which implies that the content of the preaching, as well as the name of the preacher, was rendered in Greek. The Petrine cycle was in fact a narrative catechesis, which—to judge from those passages from the Gospels which refer to the three primitive "pillars"[26]—included reference to the initial call of the first

---

[24] The reasons for Paul's insistence upon a covenantal understanding of the meal remain to be discussed (in chapter 5), along with the fresh meaning brought to bear in the use of the phrase εἰς τὴν ἐμὴν ἀνάμνησιν within Hellenistic Christianity.

[25] For further discussion, see Appendix 4, "Aramaic Retroversions of Jesus' Sayings."

[26] More pericopae, of course, may originally have been included within the catechesis; the present purpose is simply to make a cumulative list of contents on the basis of the appearance of the names "Peter (or Simon), James, and John" within a pericope in any combination of the Synoptic Gospels. The association of

disciples, the healing of Jairus' daughter, the confession at Caesarea Philippi, the Transfiguration, the eucharist, and the struggle in Gethsemane.

Two features of that narrative line are particularly striking: it represents Jesus' activity as reaching to its northern most extent according to any extant Gospel, and it is christological in focus. Moreover, of course, it is crucial to recognize that the catechesis is narrative, generically suited for use among those not themselves familiar with the substance of Jesus' ministry. Peter (and not under the name "Cephas") appears to have hit upon the narrative representation of Jesus which would later be called a gospel. He did so in order to reach Jews and proselytes with the message that Peter, James, and John were commissioned by Jesus to heal and to attest his own identity, although they had barely grasped that identity during his life.[27]

The purpose of the Petrine teaching of the eucharist is indicated by the sense of διαθήκη (cf. Exodus 24) in Matthew 26:28; Mark 14:24; 1 Corinthians 11:25, and of ἀνάμνησις in Luke 22:19; 1 Corinthians 11:24, 25.[28] Because the meal of Jesus with his disciples is presented as a covenantal sacrifice, a type of sacrifice of sharings, the continuing validity of worship in the Temple is presupposed, while the Mosaic stature of Jesus is also conveyed. At the same time, Peter's hearers are invited to join in the pattern of meals current among Jesus' initial followers, and to practice the purity which would make them fit for worship in the Temple and for the fellowship of the kingdom.

those three with other disciples, when those others are taken as of equivalent stature, is not taken here to represent the cycle of Peter.

[27] Cf. the presentation of Peter's message in Acts 10:34-43.

[28] Peter's priestly role in Matthew 16:17-19 is consistent with the same theology, and with the *haggadah* of the Transfiguration (see also 2 Peter 1:16-21). The growth of such elements in Matthew reflects the continuing development of the Petrine cycle in Syria, even after A.D. 70.

CHAPTER FOUR

THE PASSOVER

The Artifice of the Seder

The Petrine circle transformed the meaning of the final meals of
Jesus with his disciples. The last supper, a specifiable moment within the story of the passion, was presented within the idiom of a
covenantal sacrifice of sharings, after the manner of Moses on Sinai.
In its own way, the Petrine transformation was as dramatic as the
earlier, dominical transformation, from meals as instances of a purity which anticipates the kingdom into meals whose purity compensates corruption within the Temple. The next stage of development
after that of the Petrine circle is, in conceptual terms, less momen-
tous, in that it also affiliates Jesus' meal with the cultic practice of
Israel, as in the Petrine tradition. But a different practice is the
focus, and that lateral move from one festal analogy to another,
while comparatively conservative, marked the texts as they are read
today far more deeply. Indeed, the development now to be considered all but obliterated the earlier stages of understanding.

The impact of the present transformation of the meal has been so
great that it is routinely granted by some scholars that "the last supper" was a Passover,[1] although the consensus is now opposed to
that position.[2] There is no doubt, of course, but that the supper
came to have paschal associations. Paul could call Christ "our Passover" (1 Corinthians 5:7), and, as Passover became the only feast
of Judaism which could be kept after the destruction of the Temple,
such an assertion could usefully sum up the distinctions between
Judaism and Christianity as they evolved into mutually exclusive
perspectives. The chronology of John, however, has Jesus die on the
day of preparation, prior to the feast (18:28b; 19:14a, 31), so that

---

[1] Cf. A.J.B. Higgins, *The Lord's Supper in the New Testament*: Studies in Biblical
Theology 6 (London: SCM, 1960), 14-23; J. Jeremias (tr. N. Perrin), *The Eucharistic Words of Jesus* (London: SCM, 1964), 41-62.

[2] Robert F. O'Toole, "Last Supper," *The Anchor Bible Dictionary* 4 (ed. D.N.
Freedman and others; New York: Doubleday, 1992) 234-241, 235-237 provides a
balanced appraisal.

his final meal cannot have been literally paschal (see 13:1). Jesus'
statement in Luke 22:15 can similarly be taken as an unfulfilled
desire to eat the Passover with his disciples,[3] and such a reading
would accord with the stated aim of the authorities, to have done
with Jesus prior to the feast (see Mark 14:1, 2//Matthew 26:1-5).

Gerd Theissen cites the resolve of the authorities as the principal
evidence that the tradition prior to Mark agreed with the Johannine
chronology. He goes on to observe that Simon of Cyrene would not
likely be coming into Jerusalem from the countryside on the day of
Passover itself (15:21), and that the day of preparation mentioned
in 15:42 may originally have been understood as for Passover, not
the sabbath.[4] Theissen goes on to offer an additional consideration
(p. 167):

> The motive for removing Jesus from the cross and burying him before
> sundown would probably have been to have this work done before the
> beginning of the feast day, which would not make sense if it were al-
> ready the day of Passover. Finally, the ''trial'' before the Sanhedrin
> presupposes that this was not a feast day, since no judicial proceedings
> could be held on that day.

Such considerations may be regarded as pressing the texts for more
accuracy than they can reasonably be expected to deliver. After all,
if what can be read today was produced through circles of tradents,
whose traditions were written for the general instruction of churches
culturally removed from setting of Jesus, we should not anticipate
an exacting concern for the institutions of Judaism. The notice of the
timing of Jesus' burial in Matthew 27:57//Mark 15:42 may be entirely incidental, rather than a fragment of a more primitive awareness of the chronology of Jesus' death.[5] And (as Theissen recognizes) the meeting which concluded that Jesus should be condemned
might better be described as political than judicial. But Theissen's
somewhat exaggerated arguments serve to draw attention to what is
perhaps the most implausible aspect in the story of Jesus' execution
as it has been received: the regular contact between the priestly

---

[3] Cf. F.C. Burkitt and A.E. Brooke, ''St Luke xxii 15, 16: What is the General
Meaning?'' *Journal of Theological Studies* 9 (1907-1908) 569-575.

[4] See Gerd Theissen (tr. L.M. Maloney), *The Gospels in Context. Social and Political History in the Synoptic Tradition* (Minneapolis: Fortress, 1991) 166, 167.

[5] In any case, Theissen's reading of Matthew 27:57-61//Mark 15:42-47//Luke
23:50-56 in effect harmonizes the pericope with John 19:31-37.

authorities and the Roman authorities during the period of the feast, in a manner which would have made that contact obvious to the sort of pious pilgrims who would have taken offense at it.

Recent scholarship has rightly seen that the identification of the last supper with Passover is theologically motivated. The Gospels correctly report that the authorities had every reason to deal with Jesus *before* the crowds of Passover arrived (Matthew 26:1-5//Mark 14:1-2//Luke 22:1-2). Jesus' final meals would therefore have taken place near the paschal season, but not during the feast. That would explain why the most basic elements of the Seder—lamb, unleavened bread, bitter herbs (see Exodus 12:8)—are notable in the narratives only for their absence. Jesus might well have expressed a desire to eat the Passover, such as Luke 22:15 attributes to him, but if so, that desire remained unfulfilled.

Joseph Fitzmyer attempts to discount the possibility of such a reading of Luke, by accepting Jeremias's contention that the "last supper" was understood as paschal from the beginning.[6] But as Fitzmyer himself observes (p. 1386), the saying is likely from a source, which he argues is "L," although we have found cause in chapter 2 to assign the saying to "Q." Although the saying is peculiar to Luke, the assignment to "L" is not recommended, in that it is not characterized by the narrative and discursive tendencies of proto-Luke which B.H. Streeter rightly used to characterize that source. Streeter in fact held that "L" and "Q" were already combined in "proto-Luke," prior to the addition of Markan material,[7] so that proto-Luke amounted to "a kind of half-way house between Collections of Sayings, like Q, and the biographical type of Gospel of which Mark was the originator" (p. 214). More particularly, he observed that the section including the last supper (from v. 14) was especially well integrated with Markan material (p. 222). That is, it does not belong to the purest run of proto-Luke, and even if some material within the section derived proximately from "proto-Luke," "Q" was probably the ultimate source.

Although Fitzmyer's reference to a source may be confirmed, then, vv. 15-17 are better assigned to the version of the source

---

[6] Joseph A. Fitzmyer, *The Gospel According to Luke [X-XXIV]*: The Anchor Bible 28 A (Garden City: Doubleday, 1985) 1389.

[7] See *The Four Gospels. A Study of Origins* (London: Macmillan, 1924), "Proto-Luke," pp. 199-222, especially pp. 208-214.

known to Luke called "Q," in that the discourse of "proto-Luke" tended to be structured as *haggadah* within the narrative structure Streeter identified. As presented prior to vv. 19, 20, vv. 15-17 refer directly to the desire to eat Passover and the command to drink wine as parallel to the identification of bread and wine in vv. 19, 20. Whatever the narrative context of the one tradition, is the narrative context of the other, by virtue of the splicing together of the two statements concerning eating and drinking (one derived from the Petrine cycle and one from "Q").[8] That context is not provided by any element intrinsic to the last supper of the Petrine cycle or the wistful reference to Passover in "Q." What makes the last supper into a Seder is the story of the arrangements which Jesus made for the Passover which precedes (Matthew 26:17-20//Mark 14:12-17// Luke 22:7-14): that introduction, which we must turn to next, is the engine of the paschal interpretation of the meal. Unless the paschal connection is held to dominate at each stage in the tradition, Fitzmyer's attempt to rule out the possibility that Luke 22:15 refers to an unfulfilled desire cannot be sustained.[9] It is a case of historical preconception dominating exegetical sensibility.

On the other hand, there is no question of any distortion in the usual reading of Matthew 26:17-20//Mark 14:12-17//Luke 22:7-14: the pericope explicitly and emphatically presents the last supper as paschal. Whatever the sense of the meal originally, there is no doubt a theological investment in the Synoptics as great as Paul's in presenting the meal in that light, just as the Johannine timing of Jesus' death when the paschal lambs were normally slain is highlighted as relevant (John 19:36 with Exodus 12:46).[10] The degree of concern to link the entire complex of material related to the death of Jesus with Passover is so great throughout the sources, that certainty regarding chronology is impossible. It is clear that the calen-

---

[8] The seam of the splice is v. 18, which has been transposed from the end of the passage in the Petrine cycle.

[9] His argument that the form of the verb should be pluperfect in order to amount to a condition contrary to fact (1395-6) ignores the facts (1) that however elegant the Lukan redaction may appear, traditional elements within the Gospel may be rough and (2) that even at the redactional level, the Gospel appears deliberately textured with reminiscences of Semitic and Septuagintal forms (Cf. *God in Strength. Jesus' Announcement of the Kingdom*, 123-177).

[10] Cf. Rudolf Schnackenburg (tr. D. Smith and G.A. Kon), *The Gospel according to St John*, volume three: Herder's Theological Commentary on the New Testament (London: Burns & Oates, 1982) 292.

dar of the early Church has vitiated the historical value of all the extant documents.

When the pericope specifies the timing of the last supper, its identification as a Seder appears problematic. Matthew 26:17//Mark 14:12//Luke 22:7 insist that Jesus' instructions to prepare to celebrate the feast in the city were given on the first day of unleavened bread, when the paschal lamb was to be slain. On any reckoning, that must be regarded as short notice, in that the lamb was to be selected on the tenth day of the month, for slaughter on the fourteenth day of the month (Exodus 12:3-6). Whatever arrangements needed to be made therefore required several days prior to the feast in strictly cultic terms. The exigencies of accommodation in Jerusalem—which is commonly recognized to have had an infrastructure grossly inadequate for the number of its pilgrims[11]—would no doubt have required even more notice. The paradox, then, is that the only pericope to insist upon a paschal chronology (see Matthew 26:19//Mark 14:16//Luke 22:13, with the unequivocal reference to the meal as the Passover [τὸ πάσχα]) does not make good sense in the light of that chronology.

The strain which the pericope places upon plausibility emerges in another, more technical consideration. Commentators have observed that the reference to "the first day of the unleavened bread" in Mark 14:12 and Matthew 26:17 is odd, since that would presumably be Nisan 15.[12] But the lambs were slain on Nisan 14, so that they could be eaten on the evening which marked the beginning of Nisan 15. Luke's Gospel appears both to recognize and to clean up the difficulty, by referring to "the day of the unleavened bread, in which it was necessary to sacrifice the Passover" (22:7). But with or without the Lukan explanation, a pericope which otherwise makes good sense of the considerable preparations involved in keeping Passover in Jerusalem then betrays its own credibility by confining

---

[11] See Jeremias, *Jerusalem in the Time of Jesus: An Investigation into Economic and Social Conditions during the New Testament Period* (London: SCM, 1969) 77-84. The temporal problems which the pericope created for itself in the reference to the day are well observed in Alan Hugh McNeile, *The Gospel According to St. Matthew* (London: Macmillan, 1957 [from 1915]) 377.

[12] See C.E.B. Cranfield, *The Gospel according to St Mark*: The Cambridge Greek Testament Commentary (Cambridge: Cambridge University Press, 1963) 420-422; William L. Lane, *The Gospel according to Mark*: The New London Commentary (London: Marshall, Morgan & Scott, 1974) 496, 497.

the action to a short and ill defined period of time. The substance of the story seems plausible; its chronology seems schematic.

The Synoptic Gospels nonetheless proceed with the chronology invoked by the pericope. The tensions involved with a narrative of Jesus' meal which is neither explicitly nor implicitly paschal are evident, but they are less striking, the greater the distance from the actual practices of Passover. The most severe tension is confronted in Luke, where the originally unfulfilled desire of 22:15 is now expressed in the setting of a Seder. Luke 22:16 puts 22:15 into a new key, by framing its meaning to accord with that of v. 18 (cf. Matthew 26:29//Mark 14:25), as if Jesus were swearing an oath, not to eat or drink of Passover until the fulfillment of the kingdom. But the Lukan gambit is only successful, if Jesus is supposed in the meal recounted by the narrative to be drinking fulfilled wine or eating fulfilled Passover in the kingdom. That assumption accords with the interpretation developed in chapter 1, as does the exegesis of the Lukan presentation as an oath. Luke provides a window into the considerable adjustments of meaning which were consequent upon transforming Jesus' meal from a surrogate of sacrifice enacted near (but before) Passover into a Seder in a strict sense.

The Exclusive Policy of James' Circle

What purpose is served by the strict identification of the last supper as a Seder in Matthew 26:17-20//Mark 14:12-17//Luke 22:7-14? Several changes in the understanding of the meal are effected by a single shift of liturgical setting, however implausible its precise chronology. First, of course, the meal becomes a unique occasion within the ritual year: it is a paschal supper, and only that. Second, it is possible to keep the Passover only because Jesus makes specific preparations in or near Jerusalem (see Matthew 26:18, 19//Mark 14:13-16// Luke 22:8-13), where it is assumed he is acquainted with at least one householder sufficiently sympathetic with his position to permit him to use a space for the celebration. The intentionality of Jesus' timing of the last supper as a Seder is conveyed by the narrative.

None of the Synoptics makes mention of the paschal lamb or its sacrifice, although they may be assumed to have been a part of the preparations which are envisaged, once the identification with the Seder is accepted. In any case, from the moment of Jesus' arrival (Matthew 26:20; Mark 14:17; Luke 22:14), there is no express reference to the Passover, except in Luke 22:15, 16, as part of a statement that Jesus will eat and drink of the paschal celebration only in the kingdom. Moreover, there is no reference to any of the constituent elements of a Seder: the roasted lamb with unleavened bread and bitter herbs (Exodus 12:8). They are left to be inferred, on the strength of the context created by Matthew 26:17-20//Mark 14:12-17//Luke 22:7-14.

The mention of singing in Matthew 26:30//Mark 14:26 (ὑμνή-σαντες) is sometimes taken as evidence of a paschal setting,[13] and it may belong to the presentation of the meal as a Seder. In order to construe the singing in that way, however, it must be assumed that the Hallel, a sung version of some form of Psalms 113-118, is at issue; even on that assumption, the Hallel was not specifically paschal, but amounted to a festal song which might be used on several occasions.[14] Whether or not the mention of singing is of apiece with the vignette concerning preparations for Passover, it adds nothing to the introductory setting which is the principal instrument of the paschal presentation. That presentation makes the last meal of Jesus into a Passover, truly repeatable only once a year, and then only with the sympathetic cooperation of other Jews of sufficient wealth to provide the conditions necessary for the celebration.

By a stroke of artificial context, then, the meal is more tightly linked to the liturgical year than it ever had been before, and its only possible occasion is in Jerusalem. The dominical and Petrine meals were repeatable anywhere and frequently. The present transformation of what is now a last Passover could only truly be enacted "between the evenings" (during the twilight of passage from one day to the next within the calendar of Judaism) of 14 and 15 Nisan,[15] and in the vicinity of the Temple, where the paschal lambs were slain. If Jesus' "last supper" were understood as strictly paschal, its re-enactment would be limited in three ways. Temporally, it would only take place at Passover; geographically, the only appropriate

---

[13] See W.L. Lane, *The Gospel according to Mark*: The New London Commentary (London: Marshall, Morgan & Scott, 1974) 509.

[14] See Francis L. Cohen, "Hallel," *The Jewish Encyclopedia* 6 (New York: Funk and Wagnalls, 1906) 176-178.

[15] See "The Poem of the Four Nights" in the so-called Palestinian Targumim at Exodus 12:42, and Roger Le Déaut, *La nuit pascale. Essai sur la signification de la Pâque juive à partir du Targum d'Exode XII 42*: Analecta Biblica 22 (Rome: Pontifical Biblical Institute, 1963).

venue would be Jerusalem; socially, participants would need to be Jews.

The last limitation appears the most dramatic, given the increasing importance of non-Jewish Christians during the course of the first century and later. By fully identifying Jesus' meal and Passover, the circle of potential participants in eucharist excluded the uncircumcised and was limited to those who were Jews or who accepted circumcision, since circumcision was a strict requirement for males who took part in a Seder (according to Exodus 12:48-49). Once Jesus' movement reached Gentiles, the matter of their participation in such a paschal supper would become problematic. Before we proceed to investigate a paschal limitation in the understanding of who might participate in eucharist, we need to consider whether difficulties of the sort which might be caused by such a policy of exclusion in fact arose.

Problems accommodating eucharist and Passover were in fact a feature of the early Church. A strict association of the meal and Passover lies at the heart of the Quartodeciman controversy.[16] Eusebius provides the fullest account of the controversy, as erupting towards the end of the second century (*Ecclesiastical History* V.23-24). The consequence of the policy of ending the fast prior to Easter on 14 Nisan was that the day of the resurrection would often be other than Sunday, and such a practice conflicted with apostolic tradition. But such is the tenacity of Quartodeciman practice, Eusebius reports, that councils were convened in Palestine, Rome, Pontus, Gaul, Osrhoene, and Corinth (V.23).

Eusebius' claim of a cheerfully unanimous rejection of Quartodecimanism is dubious, especially in the light of his own premise, that the controversy persisted in Asia. Polycrates is designated as the leader of bishops there in insisting upon the antiquity of their practice (V.24). Eusebius proceeds to cite Polycrates' position in some detail, he says on documentary evidence. Polycrates claims that keeping the day is connected to the rising of the luminaries to meet the coming Lord, and the gathering of the saints. Some of the saints

---

[16] See Thomas M. Finn, "Pasch, Paschal Controversy," *Encyclopedia of Early Christianity* (ed. E. Ferguson; New York: Garland, 1990) 695-696. Finn observes that the celebration of eucharist on the first day of Passover is attested in the paschal homily of Melito, and the occasion is firmly linked to baptism by the time of Tertullian's *On Baptism*.

are enumerated, including Philip, John, Polycarp, and Melito; it is furthermore claimed that they all kept "the day of the fourteenth of Passover according to the gospel," as does Polycrates himself in the tradition of his kin (συγγενεῖς).

Several features of Polycrates' apology invite our immediate attention, in that the strict association of Passover and Jesus' last meal, such as is achieved in Matthew 26:17-20//Mark 14:12-17// Luke 22:7-14, would largely account for his position. The observance is indeed Quartodeciman, and in its attachment to the fourteenth day of the month, it is paschal in a calendrical sense.[17] The calendrical observation is linked to the position of the luminaries, much as Passover was to be observed on the basis of the coincidence of a full moon and the vernal equinox.[18] The practice is said to derive from the gospel; a continuous tradition from the apostles is said to derive from that evangelical mandate; the tradition is kept alive, not only in Asia, but in precisely those churches in which the Judaic environment is attested in Acts and/or the Pauline letters.

The Quartodecimans do not provide the cause for the association with Passover, only the assertion that it is correct (indeed, that it is both evangelical and apostolic). Eusebius would have us believe that the controversy is simply a matter of when the fast ends and the feasting begins, and that may have been the case by his time (at least in his mind). But the heat of the controversy is such as to suggest that the identification of Jesus' last supper and Passover carried with it far more profound implications. Melito, for example, dwells on the correspondence between Jesus and the paschal lamb in a manner which appears to reflect the practice of Passover in his time.[19] The evident affinity between the Quartodecimans and Christian

---

[17] See Wolfgang Huber, *Passa und Osten: Untersuchungen zur Osterfeier der alten Kirche*: Beiheft zur Zeitschrift für die neutestamentliche Wissenschaft 35 (Berlin: Töpelmann, 1969) 8-15. Huber cites the *Epistula Apostolorum* 15 (cf. the *Didascalia* 21) to establish his argument, that the Quartodeciman Passover was concluded at three in the morning with a celebration of a love-feast and eucharist (p. 9). He also cites the restriction of m. Pesaḥim 10:9, that Passover was not to be celebrated beyond midnight, but he does not observe that in this case Mishnah might be responding to perceived abuses such as the supplementary celebrations of Christian Jews. It should be noted that Huber vigorously disputes the consensus that Melito was a Quartodeciman.

[18] See Baruch M. Bokser, "Unleavened Bread and Passover, Feasts of," *Anchor Bible Dictionary* 6 (ed. D.N. Freedman; New York: Doubleday, 1992) 755-765, 756.

[19] See Baruch M. Bokser, *The Origins of the Seder. The Passover Rite and Early Rabbinic Judaism* (Berkeley: University of California Press, 1984) 26-28.

Judaism[20] serves to confirm that, at an earlier stage, identifying eucharist with Passover and limiting participation within it to Jews were tendencies which went together.

The letter to the Galatians mentions just the elements cited here as observances, practices and beliefs which are to be avoided. Paul warns his readers against their observation of days, months, seasons, and years, and connects those practices to serving the "elements" στοιχεῖα (4:8-11). The question of the meaning of the term as employed by Paul is not entirely settled,[21] but it is the same word which clearly means "luminaries" in Eusebius' citation of Polycrates' position. Paul is also upset that "another gospel" should be competing with his among the Galatians (1:6-12; 2:7); he is nearly scathing in his reference to the apostolic authority of others in chapter 2 (vv. 6, 9, 11-14, as we have seen); he attacks those who would impose Judaic customs upon non-Jews in the name of Christ (2:14-21; 5:1-12, cf. 1:13, 14),[22] and Peter in particular (2:11-14); he identifies that threat with Cephas and James' followers in Antioch, who are said to have influenced Barnabas and "the other Jews"[23] (2:11-13). In aggregate, Paul is opposing practices involving the observation of a calendar which themselves claim evangelical and apostolic warrant, rooted in Christian Judaism.

The fundamental dispute in which Paul was engaged, and which would take up his attention for years after the particular argument which he relates, was far more profound than the simple question of dating Easter. His charge is that Cephas, Barnabas, and "the rest of the Jews" were unduly influenced by unnamed followers of James, with the result that they ceased to eat with the Gentiles, and separated from them (2:11-13). Quartodecimanism was a dispute regarding when to end the fast prior to the celebration of baptism

---

[20] The phrase is used here of communities where Judaism had established itself prior to Christianity, and where it provided a matrix for preaching the gospel. The result was that those already known as or associated with Jews were also seen as followers of Jesus. "Jewish Christianity," by contrast, is used here to refer to those non-Jews who accepted Christianity, and who self-consciously embraced customs of Judaism as a consequence of their conversion.

[21] Cf. Hans Dieter Betz, Galatians: Hermeneia (Philadelphia: Fortress, 1979) 204-205, with rich citation of discussion. He describes them as "demonic forces which constitute and control 'this evil aeon'...".

[22] For a treatment of ἰουδαΐζειν, cf. Betz, p. 112.

[23] Paul's own wording shows that it was Christian Jews, not Jewish Christians, who originated the practice he condemns.

and eucharist within the Christian institution of the paschal mysteries. The archaic tradition from which it derived was based upon the custom among Christian Jews of keeping Passover and recollecting Jesus' last eucharistic meal, a custom which by the definition of Exodus 12:43-49 would exclude the uncircumcised. Circumcision is, of course, just the line of demarcation which Paul in Galatians wishes to eradicate (cf. 2:3-5, 7-9, 12; 5:2, 3, 6, 11, 12; 6:13, 15).[24]

The maintenance of an exclusive fellowship at meals is associated with the named wing of the movement which plagued Paul. By the time Paul wrote to the Galatians, around A.D. 53, people from the circle of James had established themselves as watchmen of rigor in regard to purity at meals. Paul claims that, when Cephas was in Antioch, he was accustomed to eat with Gentiles, but when representatives of James arrived, he deferred to them and separated himself from his former association (2:12). Indeed, Paul has to admit that even Barnabas was convinced to follow the Jacobean policy (v. 13). Paul proceeds to deliver himself of a peroration on faith and works (vv. 14-21), as an alleged account of what he said to Peter. The policy of James may well have been more nuanced than Paul suggests in Galatians, but our considerations in chapter one would lead us to anticipate that anyone who was sympathetic to a Pharisaic construction of purity might be disinclined to extend fellowship at meals to Gentiles.

When Acts gives an account of the Jacobean policy towards Gentiles, James appears much more sympathetic, but nonetheless rigorous. The occasion of his statement of policy is said to be the suggestion that one must be circumcised in order to be saved (Acts 15:1), a suggestion which is associated with a form of Christian Pharisaism (v. 5). Peter is said to side with Paul, with the argument that Gentiles who receive the holy spirit should not have the burdens laid on them "which neither our fathers nor we were able to bear" (v. 10, within vv. 7-11). Peter sounds remarkably Pauline at this juncture: Paul uses a similar line of argument *against* Peter in Galatians 2:14-21, and Peter according to Acts 15:11 sums up by aver-

---

[24] Gentiles may have been associated with archaic Quartodecimans in their practice, in that Exodus 12:19 prescribes that leaven is to be removed from all those in Israel, including the "sojourner" (גֵּר, cf. v. 45, where the issue concerns a תוֹשָׁב, not a גֵּר). Moreover, a sojourner who is circumcised with his household may eat of the Passover (12:48, 49), as may a slave who has been circumcised (12:44).

ring that both Jews and Gentiles are to be saved "through the grace
of the Lord Jesus" (cf. Ephesians 2:5). Whatever the precise relationship between Acts 15 and Galatians 2, it is apparent that the
Lukan portrayal of Peter seeks an accommodation with a Pauline
perspective. James in Acts agrees that Gentiles who turn to God are
not be be encumbered (15:19), and yet he insists they be instructed
by letter to abstain "from the pollutions of idols, and from fornication, and from what is strangled, and from blood" (v. 20).

The grounds given for the Jacobean policy are that the law of
Moses is commonly acknowledged (Acts 15:21); the implication is
that to disregard such elemental considerations of purity as James
specifies would be to dishonor Moses. Judas Barsabbas and Silas are
then dispatched with Paul and Barnabas to deliver the letter in
Antioch along with their personal testimony (vv. 22-29), and are
said particularly to continue their instruction as prophets (vv. 32,
33). They refer to the regulations of purity as necessities (v. 28), and
no amount of Lukan gloss can conceal that what they insist upon is
a serious reversal of Paul's position (see 1 Corinthians 8). The dis-
patch of Judas and Silas implicitly undermines the standing of Paul
and Barnabas, and James' policy amounts to a constraint upon the
behavior of Gentiles who joined the movement.[25]

An extension of the Torah to the "last supper," as to a paschal
meal, would carry with it the consequence that "no uncircumcised
person shall eat of it" (Exodus 12:48). Insofar as eucharistic meals
were modeled on Jesus' final meal, exclusive fellowship would prevail then, as well, for two reasons. First, ordinary considerations of
purity would make separation from non-Jews incumbent upon Jews
(as in Galatians 2:11-13). Second, even those who might permit of
exceptional social intercourse with non-Jews could not circumvent
the strictures of the Seder. The exclusionary policy of James, as
reflected in Galatians 2 and Acts 15, finds its narrative rationale in
Matthew 26:17-20//Mark 14:12-17//Luke 22:7-14: only the circumcised celebrated the last Seder, and even then, only at Passover.

The Jacobean policy limited both participation in and the frequency of eucharistic celebrations. In both aspects, a restriction of

---

[25] The constraints are sometimes compared to the so-called Noachic commandments of b. Sanhedrin 56b; see Kirsopp Lake, "The Apostolic Council of Jerusalem," *The Acts of the Apostles* V (eds F.J. Foakes Jackson and K. Lake; Grand
Rapids: Baker, 1979) 195-212, 208.

the practice of the Petrine circle is evident. Another implication of
keeping the ''last supper'' as a Passover is that any confusion or conflict with daily ritual in the Temple is avoided. Even within the practice of a highly centralized cult, when the paschal lambs were slaughtered in the Temple, the assumption that they are to be consumed
in households remains. The character of a domestic meal which was
developed within Peter's circle is perpetuated by a paschal association, but the Petrine equation with a covenantal sacrifice of sharings
(cf. chapter three) and the dominical association with the blood and
flesh of offerings more generally (cf. chapter two) are obviated.
Eusebius (*History* II.23.1-9) cites Hegesippus to the effect that James
was especially devoted to the Temple, as well as to the practice of
prayer and purity. Care for purity is especially manifested in his
wearing linen and his refusal to use oil, and Acts 21:18-25 refers to
the achievement and demonstration of purity by means of sacrifice
in the Temple as an especial concern of those associated with
James.[26] His policy of associating eucharist and Passover would accord with a deliberate attempt to avoid confrontation with the
authorities of the Temple, as well as with an insistence upon the
Judaic identity of the new movement and upon Jerusalem as its
center. The narrowing of eucharistic celebration to the practice of
Passover would be consistent, then, with James' policy in regard to
purity, Gentiles, and the Torah. Moreover, his standing within the
Church, along with the supportive authority of ''prophets'' such as
Judas and Silas, would explain why the Synoptics are so emphatically stamped with a paschal interpretation of Jesus' meal.

The reach of the Jacobean circle, from the group in Jerusalem to
envoys such as Judas Barsabbas and Silas in Antioch, helps to explain the development of tradition associated with James. Matthew
26:17-20//Mark 14:12-17//Luke 22:7-14 represents a frustrating
mixture of plausible and implausible material. Incidental references
to the preparation of a Passover in Jerusalem seem to reflect local
knowledge. The disciples know that Jesus will celebrate Passover,
they have only to ask where, and Jesus instructs them how to go

---

[26] It is notable that, with the reference to abstaining from wine and refusing to
cut his fair, James in Hegesippus is identified as a Nazirite, and that a Nazirite vow
seems to be at issue in Acts 21. Cf. Kirsopp Lake and Henry J. Cadbury, *The Beginnings of Christianity. Part I, The Acts of the Apostles: Vol. IV English Translation and Commentary* (eds F.J. Foakes Jackson and K. Lake; Grand Rapids: Baker, 1979) 272,
273.

about making the contact necessary to complete preparations. It is
only the strictly chronological insistence that all those preparations
were accomplished on the fourteenth day of Nisan, and that the last
supper itself was a Seder, which strains credibility. The Jacobean
tradition began by associating Jesus' final meal with the Passover for
which he prepared (but did not observe). In the midst of conflict concerning the meaning of and appropriate participation in eucharist,
involving prophetic teachers such as Judas Barsabbas and Silas, the
cycle of tradition hardened into a chronological identification of that
supper with the Seder.

We may now evaluate the extent to which the interaction of
spheres of meaning (dominical, Petrine, and Jacobean), have influenced the Synoptic texts as they may be read today. The beginning of the Jacobean source of the eucharist is the notice of the Passover (Matthew 26:2;[27] Mark 14:1a; Luke 22:1). It represents a
transformation of the earlier chronology of the Petrine source, according to which the cultic authorities unequivocally determined to
dispose of Jesus *prior* to the feast (Matthew 26:3-5; Mark 14:1b, 2).
Luke 22:1, 2 represents an attempt at the harmonization of the Jacobean and Petrine chronologies, by making the reference to the beginning of Passover vague (v. 1), and eliminating mention of any
temporal constraint among the authorities (v. 2).[28]

Nothing within our analysis so far puts us in a position to understand the story of Jesus' anointing in Bethany (Matthew 26:6-13;
Mark 14:3-9, cf. Luke 7:36-50 and John 12:1-8). That is a pericope
whose placement is of crucial importance in the specifically narrative development of the setting of the "last supper," as is the next
pericope, the "betrayal" of Jesus by Judas (Matthew 26:14-16;
Mark 14:10, 11; Luke 22:3-6 cf. John 13:2, 26, 27). Although the
Jacobean source meticulously establishes the paschal setting of the
eucharist, neither it nor the Petrine source manifests what we shall
characterize in the next chapter as the heroic representation of Jesus
in the Synoptic transformation of the entire complex of material.
The stories of the anointing and the betrayal constitute signal moments within that transformation, but the concerns of the Jacobean
cycle lie elsewhere.

---

[27] Matthew 26:1 represents a typically Matthean casting of the material, cf.
7:28; 11:1; 13:53; 19:1.

[28] The concern to resolve such anomalies is typically Lukan, cf. 1:3.

The story of the preparation of the Passover (Matthew 26:17-20; Mark 14:12-17; Luke 22:7-14) is, on the other hand, an idealized representation from the Jacobean source of the sort of arrangement Jesus might have had with friends in Jerusalem. Jesus is portrayed as concerned with an exacting readiness to "eat" Passover (Matthew 26:17; Mark 14:12; Luke 22:8), so that the identification of the meal as paschal, despite the uncertainty of the source in its opening notice of chronology (owing to its dependence upon Petrine tradition), becomes straightforward. A paschal lamb is not mentioned at all, but the readiness of the room (Mark 14:14-16; Luke 22:11-13, cf. Matthew 26:18, 19) presupposes the presence of sympathetic followers in Jerusalem, who recognize Jesus as "teacher" (Matthew 26:18; Mark 14:14; Luke 22:11). That the disciples are able to prepare all that was necessary (Matthew 26:19; Mark 14:16; Luke 22:13) comes as a matter of course, and the apparent absence of the lamb (which has troubled some commentators) is only apparent, and no mystery: the assumption is that the disciples followed the pertinent customs.

The Jacobean source, as derived through Joseph Barsabbas and Silas, needed to take account of paschal practice in the Diaspora. Even prior to A.D. 70, all the Jews of Antioch were scarcely in a position to acquire lambs which had been slaughtered in the Temple.[29] The only other options were (1) to revert to the domestic conception of the paschal meal (as in Exodus 12) against the provisions of Deuteronomy 16:5-7, or (2) to suppress the consumption of the lamb itself, as in later, Rabbinic practice.[30] The Jacobean source, absent an explicit mention of the lamb, could proceed on the tacit understanding that, within its community, the paschal lamb

---

[29] The close relationship between Antioch and Jerusalem makes the acquisition of such lambs by some Jews conceivable, but any practice of that sort cannot have been general. Acquiring a lamb slaughtered in Jerusalem would not in any case have fulfilled the requirement to eat the passover there (cf. Deuteronomy 16:7). Moreover, the very relationship which made the acquisition of some lambs slaughtered in Jerusalem possible also would rule out the use of other lambs. Cf. W.A. Meeks and R.L. Wilken, *Jews and Christians in Antioch in the First Four Centuries of the Common Era* (Missoula: Scholars, 1978) and J.B. Segal, *The Hebrew Passover from the earliest times to A.D. 70*: London Oriental Series 12 (London: Oxford University Press, 1963) 248. Segal is also inclined against a paschal theory of the dominical eucharist (pp. 243-245).

[30] See Baruch M. Bokser, *The Origins of the Seder. The Passover Rite and Early Rabbinic Judaism* (Berkeley: University of California Press, 1984) 29-49, 101-106.

was either eaten (in the vicinity of Jerusalem, and elsewhere by a special cultic and commercial arrangement) or it was not (further afield). The device would particularly come into its own after the destruction of the Temple in A.D. 70 and A.D. 135, from which points, from the perspective of sacrifice, Jerusalem itself entered the Diaspora. The burden of the pericope is that Jesus joined with the "twelve" specifically, the signature group of the Jacobean source (cf. Mark 4:10-12[31]), for a commemoration of Passover, and that he followed the appropriate customs. The meal was therefore marked definitively—both before and after A.D. 70—as a last supper and a paschal meal.

The next passage, the designation of the betrayer (Matthew 26:21-25; Mark 14:18-21; Luke 22:21-23), is of apiece with the earlier reference to Judas in the Hellenistic narrative of the Synoptic transformation. The placement and impact of the pericope will concern us in the next chapter. The genius of the Jacobean presentation does not reside in narrative, except insofar as the Passover is established as the sense of the meal by narrative means. The Jacobean tradents (Judas Barsabbas, Silas, and their colleagues in places other than Antioch) were able simply to enfold within their paradigm earlier meanings; the pure warrant of the kingdom, the surrogate of sacrifice, and the covenantal sacrifice of sharings were all but effaced within the definitive context of Passover.

---

[31] Chilton, *A Galilean Rabbi and His Bible. Jesus' own interpretation of Isaiah* (London: SPCK, 1984), 90-97.

CHAPTER FIVE

THE HEROIC ḤAṬAʾAT:
PAULINE AND SYNOPTIC SYMPOSIA

Paul's Symposial Strategy

The success of the Jacobean program was virtually complete by the time the Synoptics came to be written, at least insofar as the program related to the transformation of the model of eucharist into Passover. But the Jacobean program as a whole did not go unchallenged in Antioch, as Paul's correspondence attests. Paul, we have already seen, reports his own resistance to James' program in regard to purity. A few years later (c. A.D. 55-56), in the course of writing to the Corinthians concerning appropriate behavior during the Lord's supper, he also develops a line of resistance to the Jacobean understanding of eucharist (1 Corinthians 11:17-34).

It is well known that Paul's overall concern in the passage is with the practical good order of the congregation during fellowship at meals (1 Corinthians 11:17-22, 33, 34). In light of that purpose, the solemn assurance towards the beginning of the passage, that he is passing on the tradition he received (1 Corinthians 11:23), has seemed somewhat out of place.[1] The insistence upon precision in regard to what Jesus did and said is not obviously in keeping with the simple purpose of maintaining decorum at the "dominical supper" (κυριακὸν δεῖπνον, v. 20). But in the context of the success of the Jacobean program, Paul's valiant effort to resist—largely a failure at the time—becomes explicable.

Paul is, in effect, insisting upon the older, Petrine view that the meal is of the type of a sacrifice of sharings: his inclusion of the terms "memorial" (ἀνάμνησις, 1 Corinthians 11:24, 25) and "covenant" (διαθήκη, Corinthians 11:25) reveals the source of his tradition (see

---

[1] Cf. Hans Conzelmann (tr. J.W. Leitch), *1 Corinthians*: Hermeneia (Philadelphia: Fortress, 1975) 195, who suggests that "Paul lays the foundation" in v. 23a. For discussion, and a suggestion which anticipates the present treatment, cf. Oscar Cullmann, "The Lord's Supper and the Death of Christ," *Essays on the Lord's Supper*: Ecumenical Studies in Worship 1 (with F.J. Leenhardt, tr. J.G. Davies; Richmond: John Knox, 1958), 17-20.

chapter 3). Paul's own reference in Galatians 1:18 to a period of fifteen days he visited with Cephas in Jerusalem confirms what his language in 1 Corinthians 11:23 attests: he indeed "received from the Lord" (1 Corinthians 11:23), through Cephas (Galatians 1:18), what he "handed over" (1 Corinthians 11:23) to his hearers, the Petrine model of eucharist. In writing to the Corinthians some seven years after the meeting in Jerusalem which agreed his sphere of interest in the relation to the "pillars" (Galatians 2:1-10),[2] Paul resisted the emerging influence of the annual Passover ritual upon eucharist which was a hallmark of the Jacobean tradition. In Pauline teaching, frequent repetition was a commandment: "do this, *as often as you drink*, for my memorial" (τοῦτο ποιεῖτε ὁσάκις ἐὰν πίνητε εἰς τὴν ἐμὴν ἀνάμνησιν, 1 Corinthians 11:25c).[3] The plain meaning of Paul's clause is softened by the habit of adding "it" in translations. But taken at face value, Paul's paradigm involves the recognition that any festive meal is an appropriate occasion of the "memorial."

Paul resists the Jacobean paradigm of eucharist in 1 Corinthians as much as he deplores the Jacobean program of purity in Galatians. He confirms the Petrine teaching, because that tradition permits of the accessibility and the repetition of eucharist.[4] He reminds his hearers of what he already had taught as authoritative, a teaching "from the Lord" and presumably warranted by the earliest "pillars:" in that sense, what he hands on is not his own, but derives from his highest authority, "the Lord" (11:23). The rhetoric of the

---

[2] The council is plausibly dated in A.D. 49 on the basis of Paul's contact with Priscilla and Aquila shortly thereafter, a meeting which presupposes the edit of Claudius by which Jews were expelled from Rome (cf. Acts 18:1-3). The inscription of Gallio (c. A.D. 52), the governor in Corinth at the time of Paul's visit, and the likely sequence from Galatians to Corinthians, makes a dating of the Corinthian correspondence around A.D. 55-56 plausible. Following the isolation of the period during which he wrote Galatians, which forced Paul to write entirely on his own authority, he managed to associate himself with Sosthenes (1 Corinthians 1:1), Timothy, and Silvanus (2 Corinthians 1:1, 19) by the next phase of his ministry. By the end of his life, of course, the Pauline network was more impressive (cf. Romans 16:1-23). For a plausible reconstruction of Paul's relationship to James, Peter, Barnabas, and the communities they represented, cf. Nicholas Taylor, *Paul, Antioch and Jerusalem. A Study in Relationship and Authority in Earliest Christianity*: Journal for the Study of the New Testament Supplements 66 (Sheffield: Sheffield Academic Press, 1992). For further considerations of the date of Claudius' expulsion of the Jews, with bibliography, cf. Chilton, "Romans 9-11 as Scriptural Interpretation and Dialogue with Judaism," *Ex Auditu* 4 (1988) 27-37, 36 n. 27.

[3] "*As often as you drink*" also reflects the original meaning of Jesus' saying about new wine, a promise to drink only in celebration of the kingdom (see chapter 1).

introduction would exclude any conscious attempt at creativity, and the Corinthian correspondence would hardly be the place for Paul to claim traditional authority, only then to introduce an idiosyncratic perspective (see 2 Corinthians 1:15-22). When there is evidence of development from the Petrine norm (as reflected in the texts discussed in chapter 3) within what Paul cites as traditional, such distinctions should not be seen as Pauline innovations, but as the shape the Petrine tradition had assumed within the Hellenistic mission of Paul.

Before those distinctions are identified, it should be observed that, in their own ways, the Synoptics also convey the Petrine perspective in a Hellenistic key, so that their comparability with the Pauline tradition is evident. Paul may alone give us the explicit reference to repetition within Jesus' words (1 Corinthians 11:25c), but that element is inherently important within the Petrine teaching as a whole. Paul also attests the notion of "memorial" (11:24, 25) which directly reflects the Petrine ideology of eucharist as a type of sacrifice of sharings; otherwise, only Luke attests the usage (22:19).

Paul in another respect, as in the case of the Synoptics, accepts the influence of the Petrine program upon Hellenistic Christianity generally: he refers to the bread first, and then the cup (11:23-25). As a result, only Luke's placement of 22:17, 18 and *Didache* 9:1-5 attest the older, dominical order. Paul's acceptance of the Petrine sequence served to distinguish eucharistic celebrations from the more alcoholic symposia of contemporary, Hellenistic fashion. It should be noted, however, that Paul elsewhere shows an awareness of the older order (cf. 1 Corinthians 10:16), and within chapter 11 itself, the cup is made to bear more significance than the bread, as will emerge.

In any case, in the course of accepting the Petrine order, Paul prefaced the identification of the wine in 1 Corinthians 11:25a with what seems a clumsy introduction:

"And similarly also the cup, after having supped. . ."
ὡσαύτως καὶ τὸ ποτήριον μετὰ τὸ δειπνῆσαι. . . .

---

[4] Xavier Léon-Dufour, *Le partage du pain eucharistique selon le Nouveau Testament* (Paris: Editions du Seuil, 1982) 118, 119 also acknowledges the possibility of Paul's familiarity with what he calls the Markan and I call the Petrine tradition. The form of words cited by Paul derives from Antioch, according to Léon-Dufour; the relationship between Pauline and Synoptic phrasing is discussed below.

The identification of the bread by Jesus is said simply to have taken place "in the night in which he was handed over" (v. 23b). The statement that the cup came "similarly" at first appears equally vague, but then the phrase "after having supped" seems to insist upon a particular moment. But if the actions indeed unfolded "similarly," both the bread and the cup were identified by Jesus "after having supped." The wording of Luke 22:20a, which employs the same phrase, is within a better defined narrative context, which distinguishes the cup after the meal from what precedes; Paul's presentation is less lucid. Whenever exactly Paul understood the bread to have been eaten in relation to other foods, his abstraction of the "dominical supper" from an actual meal by means of his rendering of the Petrine tradition is evident.

The effect of the introduction concerning the cup is to distinguish the drinking of wine from a single cup—and perhaps even the eating of bread—from any meal which might occasion the "dominical supper." Indiscriminate eating and drinking were practices which particularly concerned Paul (11:21, 22); by emphasizing the Petrine order, he could address local abuses at Corinth, and at the same time claim unity with the practice within the primitive Church warranted by Petrine authority. The price of Paul's formulation was to abstract the "supper" from the sorts of meals which had inspired it within the ministry of Jesus.[5]

Both the acceptance of the Petrine order and an abstraction of the eucharist from communal meals were attractive within Hellenistic Christianity. Eucharist became sensible and commendable within the practice of philosophical symposia. Such symposia were distinguished from others by a formal transition from meal to the symposium proper, or "drinking party,"[6] and an avoidance of less than

---

[5] Conzelmann, p. 199, observes that "the whole Eucharist had been transposed to follow the meal." Paul's presentation in regard to the bread is less clear than that finding would allow, but the tendency towards abstraction in the development of the tradition seems apparent.

[6] See Dennis E. Smith, "Table Fellowship as a Literary Motif in the Gospel of Luke," *Journal of Biblical Literature* 106 (1987) 613-638, 630 (citing Plato, *Symposium* 176A; Xenophon, *Symposium* 2.1; Athenaeus, *Deipnosophists* 11.462c-d). The passage from Xenophon also refers to more popular entertainments, involving a female flute-player, a female dancer/acrobat, and a young man who both played the zither and danced. The passage from Athenaeus shows how the usage of συμπόσιον differs from that of δεῖπνον, and 462f. attests the extent to which drinking much was held to be a virtue. For further discussion of the symposium, see Baruch

philosophical entertainments.[7] Philo attests the extent to which the institution needed to be protected from abuse (cf. *De Continentia* 57, 64). The Pauline and Lukan phrase, "after having supped," coordinates the supper with a well-ordered and comparatively sober philosophical symposium.

The generally Synoptic portrayal of the "last supper" implies a similar degree of sobriety, and the Lukan presentation expressly limits the consumption of wine that may take place in connection with any repetition of the meal. In Matthew and Mark, the action unfolds "while they were eating" (Matthew 26:26//Mark 14:22), and presumably drinking as well. The present form of the Lukan text manages to reduce the amount of drinking that may be imagined in connection with the meal by means of a more specific order of events: reference to the Passover (22:15, 16), sharing of wine with reference to the kingdom (vv. 17, 18), eating bread in remembrance (v. 19), and drinking again "after having supped" (μετὰ τὸ δειπνῆσαι) in view of the new covenant and the kingdom (v. 20).[8] Two cups, and two cups only, are associated with the meal in Luke. With varying degrees of rigor, Paul and the Synoptics mandate sobriety at the dominical symposium.

The Hellenistic innovations within the Petrine teaching which Paul handed on went further. First, the phrase "this is my blood of the covenant" became "This cup is the new covenant in my blood" (1 Corinthians 11:25, τοῦτο τὸ ποτήριον ἡ καίνη διαθήκη ἐστίν ἐν τῷ ἐμῷ αἵματι). The linguistic changes involve several substantive consequences. The fuller phrase, simply in terms of its structure, is more stately. The thought is more developed than the direct metaphor, "This (is) my blood;" the assertion is explicated so as to avoid

---

M. Bokser, *The Origins of the Seder. The Passover Rite and Early Rabbinic Judaism* (Berkeley: University of California Press, 1984) 50-66.

[7] Smith, p. 621, citing Plato, *Symposium* 176E; Athenaeus, *Deipnosophists* 5.186a. The former passage (immediately prior to the reference Smith has in mind) also attests the greater attention to the consumption of wine which should distinguish a philosophical symposium from others. Likewise, Athenaeus' observations may be gathered better, in their criticism of drinking too much, by reading from 5.179e until 5.190a.

[8] Smith, p. 628, argues that a "short version" of the Lukan eucharistic text (vv. 15-19a) better suits the Gospel's theology than the inclusion of the longer reading. What he fails to consider is (1) that his proposal results in reversing symposial order in relation to the meal, and (2) that the control of the consumption of wine was of concern within the Hellenistic world generally, and the early Church in particular.

misunderstanding Jesus' actual blood as a repeated offering. That misunderstanding, in turn, can only have arisen after the "supper" had ceased to be viewed as a natural and immediate surrogate of sacrifice. Instead, Jesus' blood was seen within Hellenistic Christianity as comparable to that of the heroic martyrs of 2 Maccabees and 4 Maccabees, as will be discussed further below. The notion of the necessary repetition of human bloodshed was therefore an inference to be avoided.

At the same time, the correctly taken cup is now made a covenant in the sense of a rite to be replicated correctly. Zechariah 9:11 provides a key to the grammatical structure and the sense of the Hellenistic version of Petrine tradition which Paul hands on in 1 Corinthians 11:25. Just as God in Zechariah had promised to rescue the captives of of Zion "by the blood of your covenant" (בְּדַם בְּרִיתֵךְ[9]) so the Petrine tradents portrayed eucharistic celebrations as a paradigmatic sacrifice of sharings in the manner of Moses on Sinai which promised salvation.[10] Finally—and most strikingly—the covenant here is "new." The usage of language from Jeremiah 31:31 is less important for its biblical pedigree than for its insistence, within the innovative grammatical form of the statement, that Jesus' act amounts to a covenantal requirement which is to be discharged "as often as you drink, in remembrance of me" (1 Corinthians 11:25). Unlike the Jacobean limitation to Passover, Paul's appropriation of the Petrine tradition envisages frequent celebration by all those who could eat together. As far as Paul was concerned, *pace* James, Peter, and Barnabas (as we have seen in the last chapter), that included all baptized persons.

The repetition which is enjoined in 1 Corinthians 11:25 is, then, by no means incidental for Paul. "As often as you drink" (ὁσάκις ἐὰν πίνητε) within the tradition of the Petrine circle is used as a bulwark against the limitations implicit within the association of eucharist with Passover, and especially the paschal chronology, of

---

[9] The sense of the phrase is, "my covenant with you," as in the Revised Standard Version. The Septuagint omits the pronoun altogether.

[10] The prominence of the book of Zechariah within the tradition of Jesus' passion would suggest that the Petrine model of eucharist had already been influenced by that book at the time Paul wrote; see F.F. Bruce, "The Book of Zechariah and the Passion Narrative," *Bulletin of the John Rylands Library* 43 (1960-61) 336-353; *The Temple of Jesus*, 135-136.

Jacobean tradition. The positive significance of the phrase for Paul becomes apparent in the next verse:

> For as often (ὀσάκις) as you eat this bread and drink the cup, you announce the Lord's death until he comes.

Paul repeats a key term within the Petrine tradition in his own voice, and draws his conclusion ("for," γάρ), which is that the significance of the eucharist is to be found in the death of Jesus. Drinking the cup is an act which declares that Jesus died and awaits his *parousia* at one and the same time.

Paul's assumption is that Jesus' last meal, the paradigm of the Lord's supper, was of covenantal significance, a sacrificial "memorial" which was associated with the death of Jesus in particular. The wording of that later version of Petrine tradition agrees most closely with Luke, the Synoptic Gospel which has the strongest associations with Antioch. It is likely that Paul's version of the Petrine tradition derived from his period in Antioch, his primary base by his own testimony (in Galatians 2) until his break with Barnabas.

"The cup" by the Antiochene phase of the Petrine tradition is doubly symbolic. It stands for the new covenant which Jesus mediates by his death, and it also takes the place (by metonymy) for the blood which seals Jesus' death. Neither transfer of meaning would have been possible, without the previous understandings that the wine within the cup was in some sense Jesus' blood, and that the blood was of covenantal significance. In both those aspects, 1 Corinthians 11:25 and Luke 22:20 give the appearance of being developed forms of Petrine tradition, the usage which developed in Antioch. Paul's symposial strategy is to apply the authority of eucharistic practice in Antioch, prior to the influence of James' circle, against the influence of the Jacobean identification with Passover and its attendant (in Paul's view, limited) insistence upon purity.

The Blood of the Ḥaṭaʾat

The perspective of Antioch, attested in the double symbolism of the cup in both Paul and Luke, involves a fresh conception of the place of "blood" in eucharist. The earlier form of the Petrine tradition (which was closely related to Jesus' practice) simply had it that the wine was blood, a surrogate of covenantal sacrifice. In the Hellenistic environment of Antioch, such a meaning could easily be confused with the notion of drinking a deity's blood in one of the Mysteries. The association of Jesus' last meal with his execution, which was already a feature of the Petrine tradition (see chapter 3) would have further encouraged the confusion. The Antiochene wording avoided any confusion of that kind, by making the cup the point of comparison with the new covenant, and describing the covenant as achieved "in" or "by" (ἐν) Jesus' blood.

Although the phrase "in my blood" (1 Corinthians 11:25; Luke 22:20) excludes a possible misunderstanding of the Petrine eucharist, it also conveys a positive appraisal of Jesus' own "blood," that is, his death. The offering commemorated in the bread and wine is not simply a covenantal sacrifice of sharings in the general sense established within the Petrine cycle, but the particular form of the sacrifice of sharings known as the sacrifice for sin, or ḥaṭaʾat (cf. Leviticus 4). When Paul conceives of Jesus' death sacrificially, he does so as such a sacrifice ("for sin," περὶ ἁμαρτίας, Romans 8:3). Indeed, by the time he came to compose Romans, he had been referring to Jesus' death in that way for some five years; in Galatians 1:4, Jesus is also described as having given himself for our sins.[11]

Of course, the phrase "for sin(s)" (περὶ ἁμαρτίας/ἁμαρτιῶν) by itself might be taken to be an odd way of referring to the sacrifice for sin (חטאת) of Leviticus, but that it precisely the equation made in the Septuagint (see especially Leviticus 16:3, 5, 6, 9, 11, 15). Paul cites the Hebrew scriptures in a Septuagintal version, so that the identity of phrasing might alone be taken to suggest that he presented Jesus' death as a species of ḥaṭaʾat. In addition, both Pauline passages proceed to conceive of Jesus' death in a manner congruent with the image of a sacrifice for sin. In Galatians 1:4, the purpose of his death is redemption from the present, evil age, while Romans 8:3 contrasts God's sending his son to the flesh of sacrifice. In all probability, Paul conceived of Jesus sacrificially as "having given himself for our sins" (Galatians 1:4, and see 2:20) in the years intervening between his writing a letter to the Galatians and a letter to the Romans, when he wrote several letters to the Corinthians. His conception was not original, but derived from the Antiochene practice of eucharist which he had taught during his catechesis at Corinth.

---

[11] Certain texts read ὑπέρ for περί, but the relationship between Sinaiticus and the first corrector thereof shows the likely direction of change.

The fundamental conception of the ḥaṭaʾat is that the sacrifice creates or recreates a sacred environment which was once polluted.[12] Once that perspective is appreciated, the sense of what has long been a *crux criticorum* becomes plain. In his most vivid application of the image of Jesus as a sacrifice for sin, Paul will refer to Jesus in Romans 3:25—shortly after his correspondence with Corinth (c. A.D. 57)—as a site of sacrificial appeasement, a ἱλαστήριον.[13] By way of analogy, we might recall Eleazar's prayer in 4 Maccabees 6:29, that God make his blood the purification of the people, and accept his life as their ransom (καθάρσιον αὐτῶν ποίησον τὸ ἐμὸν αἷμα καὶ ἀντίψυχον αὐτῶν λαβὲ τὴν ἐμὴν ψυχήν). In the case of both Romans and 4 Maccabees, a document of Hellenistic Judaism[14] presents a martyr's blood as the means of a purifying sacrifice for sin, and his death as a sacrificial appeasement. In his usage of such a motif in respect of Jesus, Paul availed himself of an ambient understanding of Jesus' death which was mediated to him by the development of Petrine tradition in Antioch. He resisted the Jacobean program of purity, and the association of eucharist with Passover, by appealing to the Hellenistic motif of Jesus himself as heroic ḥaṭaʾat.

The Synoptic Symposia

The Synoptic Gospels reflect the conception of Jesus as the heroic ḥaṭaʾat which characterized the Hellenistic catechesis invoked by Paul. The blood of the covenant is here "poured out" for a specific, purifying purpose, in the manner of the blood of the sacrifice for sin (Matthew 26:28//Mark 14:24//Luke 22:20). That purposive oblation of blood, which is characteristic of the ḥaṭaʾat (see Leviticus 4:5-7, 16-18, 25, 30, 34), is a feature of the commonly Synoptic presentation of Jesus' statement concerning the wine.

Although the Synoptic presentations are comparable, the motif is

---

[12] See David P. Wright, *The Disposal of Impurity*; Chilton, *The Temple of Jesus*, "Sacrifice in 'Classic' Israel," 45-67, 58-60.

[13] See Appendix 5, "The Pauline ἱλαστήριον and the Offering of the Nations."

[14] See Hugh Anderson, "4 Maccabees," *The Old Testament Pseudepigrapha* 2 (ed. J.H. Charlesworth; Garden City: Doubleday, 1985) 531-564, 533-537. His treatment of the dating of 4 Maccabees is representative, although a date after the destruction of the Temple may not be excluded; cf. Douglas A. Campbell, "Appendix 3. The Date of *4 Maccabees*," *The Rhetoric of Righteousness in Romans 3.21-26*: Journal for the Study of the New Testament Supplements 65 (Sheffield: Sheffield Academic Press, 1992) 219-228.

spelled out differently in each Gospel. In Matthew 26:28, the blood is "poured out for many for the forgiveness of sins" (τὸ περὶ πολλῶν ἐκχυννόμενον εἰς ἄφεσιν ἁμαριῶν); the wording fastens upon the issue of forgiveness, which is developed particularly within Matthew by means of uniquely Matthean material (see 5:23, 24; 16:19; 18:15-18, 23-35). The diction chosen to refer Jesus' "blood" to such forgiveness ("for...sins," περὶ...ἁμαρτιῶν) echoes the Septuagintal and Pauline reference to the ḥaṭaʾat as described in the last section of the present chapter.[15] The wine of eucharist is here understood to effect a purifying forgiveness in terms more immediately evocative of cultic worship in the Temple than any others in the New Testament.

In Mark 14:24, the blood is "poured out on behalf of many" (τὸ ἐκχυννόμενον ὑπὲρ πολλῶν). It has been suggested[16] that "on behalf of" (ὑπέρ) is an echo of what the servant does in Isaiah 53:12, and it is notable that the servant's offering of his life is associated in the Septuagint, but not in the Masoretic Text, with the sacrifice for sin (see 53:10, περὶ ἁμαρτίας).[17] Conceptually, the famous passage from Isaiah in its Septuagintal form, with its express reference to the sacrifice for sin in v. 10, may be taken to support the development of the motif of the heroic ḥaṭaʾat within the milieu of Hellenistic Judaism and Christianity. But it is precisely the express reference to sin which is absent from Mark (and from Luke), and the usage of "many" and "on behalf of" (the latter of which does not even appear in Isaiah 53:12 in the Septuagint) establishes no explicit connection with the Isaian servant. The more obvious connection in Mark is with the son of man in 10:45, who is said to give his life as a ransom "for the sake of many" (ἀντὶ πολλῶν).[18] The echo between the unqualified usage of "many" in 10:45 and in 14:24 is a

---

15 See also Alan Hugh McNeile, *The Gospel According to St. Matthew* (London: Macmillan, 1957 [from 1915]) 382, 383.

16 See, for example, Vincent Taylor, *The Gospel according to St. Mark* (London: Macmillan, 1966) 546.

17 In the Masoretic Text, the sacrifice is an ʾasham, a sacrifice for guilt. Treated of in Leviticus 5, the sacrifice for guilt had a strong affinity with the sacrifice for sin (see *The Temple of Jesus*, 60, 61).

18 So Xavier Léon-Dufour, *Le partage du pain eucharistique selon le Nouveau Testament* (Paris: Editions du Seuil, 1982) 201. He is insistent that the meaning of ὑπέρ originally was not sacrificial, but salvific (pp. 143-147). Although he is correct that the term in itself is not sacrificial, any more than it is an obvious reference to Isaiah 53:12, the Markan context is sacrificial (and, indeed, paschal).

unique feature of Mark,[19] and clearly links Jesus' intention to die with the sacrificial wine of eucharist. Both sayings may or may not be inspired by the image of the Isaian servant; that they are related to one another within the Markan presentation, however, is a straightforward inference.

In Luke 22:20, the blood is "poured out on your behalf" (τὸ ὑπὲρ ὑμῶν ἐκχυννόμενον); the result is to coordinate Jesus' statement with what he says in Luke regarding his body, which is "given on your behalf" (22:19, τὸ ὑπὲρ ὑμῶν διδόμενον). "On your behalf" is also how Jesus' body is qualified in 1 Corinthians 11:24,[20] a fact which confirms the affinity already noted between Paul and Luke. Luke's contextual development is much richer than Paul's, of course, just as the Lukan phrasing is fuller. "On your behalf" puts the promise in precisely the same key as the address to the "you" who have endured with Jesus in Luke 22:24-30 (especially vv. 28-30), a discourse uniquely presented in its current context in the third Gospel, just after Jesus' identification of the bread and the cup (vv. 17-20) and his designation of his betrayer (vv. 21-23). Rhetorically and contextually, then, "you" are those who are in eucharistic fellowship with Jesus (vv. 17-20), who remain loyal to Jesus (vv. 21-23), avoid hierarchy (vv. 24-27), and whose faithful endurance promises a place in the eschatological feast and in the final judgment (vv. 28-30). No Gospel as clearly relates the eucharist, those whom it benefits, and the ethical grounds of that benefit, as does Luke's.

Jesus is the heroic ḥaṭaʾat in Matthew, Mark, and Luke, then, but that identification is achieved by unique means of narrative, diction, discourse, and/or context in each. The forgiveness of Matthew 26:28 relates to a particular emphasis upon forgiveness developed in uniquely Matthean material, and the language of the statement concerning Jesus' "blood" is evocative of the cultic sacrifice for sin. The "many" of Mark 14:24 manifests a uniquely Markan symmetry with the motif of Jesus' vocation to die in the service of a ransoming death. Luke 22:20 is developed from an insistence upon the efficacy of eucharist for participants ("on your behalf") in the Hellenistic version of the Petrine tradition which Luke shares with

---

[19] Matthew also relates the saying in which the son of man is a ransom for the sake of many (20:28); the uniquely Markan feature is the symmetry with what Jesus says about the wine of eucharist by means of an unqualified usage of "many."

[20] Paul, however, cites an abbreviated formula, without "given."

Paul; the ethical requirements of their participation are spelled out contextually and by means of rhetoric in a uniquely Lukan manner.

In the substance of their presentation of Jesus' last meal, the Synoptic Gospels relate more closely to one another than to Paul, and yet they are not simple copies, one from another. At the Synoptic stage, as earlier, the tradition was protean, subject to local variation, shifts of perspectives, and structural evolution, as well as actual changes of wording. Nonetheless, the agreement in the substance and method of presentation suggests that the transformation of Jesus' eucharist into a heroic ḥaṭaʾat at the stage of the Synoptics was definitive for each of them, and that the distinctions of each Gospel from the others are a function of distinctive construals of that common transformation.[21]

The most basic instrument of the Synoptics' transformation of Jesus into a heroic ḥaṭaʾat is narrative contextualization. From the moment Jesus is portrayed as heading toward Jerusalem, a heroic motif comes into play, and it is striking that the Synoptics have him make the decision to do so as "the son of man." By using that phrase, borrowed from Daniel 7, they make Jesus' heroism more than noble: it is the historical antecedent of the apocalyptic drama which began with his death and which is to climax in his *parousia*.[22]

There is a particular focus on Jesus' heroism within the complex in which the "last supper" is a dramatic moment. The anointing in Bethany is a good point from which to describe the heroic Jesus of the Synoptic transformation (Matthew 26:6-13//Mark 14:3-9). The pericope interrupts the linear movement of the narrative from the notice of the authorities' resolution concerning Jesus (Matthew 26:1-5//Mark 14:1, 2) to the notice of Judas' act (Matthew 26:14-16//Mark 14:10, 11).[23] The scene focuses on Jesus' "body" as prepared for burial (Matthew 26:12//Mark 14:8), and rewards the woman who anoints him—on the authority of a dominical saying—

---

[21] For the background of the terminology here applied, see *Profiles of a Rabbi*, pp. 139-189.

[22] Cf. Douglas R.A. Hare, *The Son of Man Tradition* (Minneapolis: Fortress, 1990) 213-256.

[23] Lane, p. 491, rightly sees that the story is in the nature of an expansion, although he attributes its position directly to Mark the Evangelist. Within the present study, specifically literary activity is only postulated when the text in question appears to be the product of a choice among options which included a prior, fixed order of narration or diction from which an author self-consciously departs (for specifiable reasons).

with inclusion in the preaching of the gospel (Matthew 26:13//
Mark 14:9). She alone, in the face of resistance from the disciples
(Matthew 26:8-10//Mark 14:4-6), confirms Jesus' intention to die.

The body anointed is implicitly presented as the counterpart of
the body given as bread, and the parallelism itself is made a part of
the gospel: whenever Jesus' statement, which makes bread his body,
is remembered, what the woman did for his body will be recalled.
The significance of the woman's act is not only that it is included in
a narrative which can be called a gospel (or passion narrative, as
contemporary scholarship would have it). What she did is to be
spoken of "in memory of her" (εἰς μνημόσυνον αὐτῆς, Matthew
26:13//Mark 14:9), because she warrants the unfolding action which
is to be recalled every time Jesus' "body" and "blood" are given
and received (Matthew 26:26-28//Mark 14:22-24). In her the Hellenistic constituency of the Synoptics is embodied within Jesus'
movement.

Luke's location of a scene of anointing earlier in the ministry of
Jesus (7:36-50) reflects an awareness that it is anachronistic within
the narrative of his passion. Anointing can be "beforehand for my
burial" only in the Hellenistic world in which Judaic practice is
transmuted into the realm of symbolism. As we shall see repeatedly,
the Lukan concern to tell the catechetical story "in order" (1:3)
causes the Evangelist to change the order of the commonly Synoptic
transformation when he suspects it of anachronism. In any case,
Luke in his account combines the reference to the authorities' resolution directly with a notice of Judas' "betrayal" (Luke 22:1-6),[24]
in an attempt to approximate to the earlier, probably Petrine cycle
of tradition.

Judas has a straightforward place here (Matthew 26:14-16//Mark
14:10, 11), but his specification as one of the twelve betrays the constituency of the Synoptics: despite his position, he belongs to the opposition as unequivocally as the anonymous woman of Bethany belongs to the gospel. Luke, absent the pericope of anointing in its
Matthean and Markan position, uses other means to convey the
contrast between Judas and faithful discipleship; instead, Satan

---

[24] But Luke appears to be aware of the version of Matthew and Mark, in that
the Pharisee of Luke 7:36-50 turns out to be named Simon (vv. 40, 43, 44, cf.
Matthew 26:6//Mark 14:3). Moreover, we shall see shortly that Luke knowingly
manipulates the order in which his next pericope concerning Judas is presented.

enters Judas, who is still described as from the number of the twelve
(22:3-6, v. 3, cf. John 13:2). The notice of Satan would appear to
compensate for the absence of a contrast with the woman in the
pericope of anointing at this point in the narrative. That is one of
the features which betrays that Luke's activity is literary, a conscious (although far from arbitrary) departure from the generically
Synoptic presentation.

Next comes the Jacobean passage concerning the preparation of
Passover (Matthew 26:17-20//Mark 14:12-17//Luke 22:7-14), but
the immediate return to the matter of Judas (Matthew 26:21-25//
Mark 14:18-21) demonstrates the focus of the Synoptic transformation. The diction of "betraying" Jesus contributes to two portrayals
of his stature. At one level, Judas is used to highlight Jesus' isolation
as the hero. But at another level, Judas will hand over Jesus even
as Jesus gives himself: the use of παραδίδωμι establishes the action
as part of the apocalyptic drama, whatever Judas' motivation.[25]
That verb is also the link to the gnomic statement regarding the man
by whom the son of man is betrayed (Matthew 26:24; Mark 14:21
cf. Luke 22:21, 22). In origin, that is a saying regarding one person
who betrays another, a "son of man" in the sense of an instance of
humanity; but the human reference of the Aramaic idiom has been
harnessed in the service of the Synoptic transformation of Jesus
alone into that Danielic son of man whose death is the necessary
prelude to his definitive vindication.[26]

Luke (22:21-23) has delayed his next reference to Judas: a betrayer is designated *after* the consumption of wine, bread and wine again
(vv. 15-20), rather than before the consumption of bread and wine
(as in Matthew 26:21-25//Mark 14:18-21). The use of additional
material in vv. 15-18, derived (as we have suggested previously)
both from "Q" (vv. 15-17) and the commonly Synoptic source
(v. 18), compensates the delay with a self-conscious reference by
Jesus to his own suffering (which will obviously be occasioned by
Judas, within the understanding of the present, narrative context).

---

[25] Cf. Norman Perrin, "The Use of παραδιδόναι in Connection with the Passion of Jesus in the New Testament," *Der Ruf Jesu und die Antwort der Gemeinde* (eds
E. Lohse, C. Burchard, B. Schaller; Göttingen: Vandenhoeck und Ruprecht,
1970) 204-212.

[26] Cf. Barnabas Lindars, *Jesus Son of Man. A Fresh Examination of the Son of Man
Sayings in the Gospels in the Light of Recent Research* (Grand Rapids: Eerdmans, 1983)
60-84.

The later placement of the pericope concerning the betrayer enables Luke to use the negative example of Judas to introduce a set of sayings—framed as a discourse addressed (as we have seen) to "you"—which calls upon Jesus' followers to forgo honor, serve one another, remain constant in temptation, and so reign with Jesus (22:24-30).[27]

The Lukan discourse provides a compelling preamble to the story of Peter's denial, which is already a stark caution within the commonly Synoptic presentation: even the font of the tradition may be challenged when he assumes his own power will enable him to withstand the duress of testimony (Matthew 26:30-35//Mark 14:26-31// Luke 22:31-34). The Lukan context even associates such failure with Judas' betrayal, by delaying Jesus' reference to "the betrayer" until after the meal (vv. 21-23). The numerical device in Jesus' response to Peter, in a formulation which is not entirely stable (see Matthew 26:34; Mark 14:30; Luke 22:34), is—as shall appear below—a signature of the commonly Synoptic imagination. In the present case, the device underscores Peter's unreliability, no matter which numbers are accepted: Peter is told he will squawk more prematurely than a cock, and so he does (Matthew 26:57-75//Mark 14:53-72//Luke 22:54-71).

Jesus, however, remains constant in all the Synoptics, to the extent that his statement about drinking wine is now taken as a vow of abstinence, against its original sense (as discussed previously). Distance from the origins of the tradition permits an emphatic promise of the kingdom's coming and its association with Jesus' meals to be taken as a refusal to drink wine which is inconsistent with the imagery of feasting in the kingdom which was a hallmark of Jesus' preaching. The narrative problem posed by the myrrhed wine of Matthew 27:34//Mark 15:23 is resolved by passing over the incident in silence in Luke 23:33. But the strength of the Synoptic tradition in the reference to vinegar (Matthew 27:48//Mark 15:38// Luke 23:36) was such that it was not repressed within any of the Synoptic Gospels, despite its evident contradiction of the idea that Jesus actually vowed abstinence. The portrayal of Jesus as a heroic martyr within the Synoptics reflects the Hellenistic phase of the develop-

---

[27] The Matthean and Markan analogs of vv. 24-30 are presented earlier, at Matthew 20:24-28; 19:28//Mark 10:41-45.

ment of their tradition, and manifests occasional tension with earlier portrayals.

The portrayal of Jesus as heroic martyr has recently been linked to the motif represented in Maccabean literature that the suffering martyr functions as a kind of sacrifice, and more specifically that the martyr's death might make atonement for his people.[28] Care must be taken not to homogenize what in the Maccabean literature is a motif which emerges gradually, and with variegation. The notion of the sacrificial efficacy of the martyr in his death appears to have been articulated only with 4 Maccabees. Prior to that document, the portrait of the martyr might more appropriately be characterized as that of a heroic victim of faith: loyalty brings an exemplary death, not cultic atonement in the first instance (see 1 Maccabees 2:37; 6:43-46; 2 Maccabees 6:18-31; *Testament of Moses* 9:4-7).[29]

4 Maccabees was probably composed near the time that the Synoptic Gospels developed. Hugh Anderson dates it earlier than the Gospels, largely on the grounds of Elias Bickerman's observation that the reference in 4:2 to Syria, Phoenicia, and Silicia as the ambit of Apollonius' power corresponds well to Roman administrative arrangements between A.D. 19 and A.D. 54.[30] But Douglas Campbell argues convincingly that the reference in 4 Maccabees 4:2 is regional, rather than administrative, and that in any case the author does not exhibit care in regard to political arrangements.[31]

Campbell attempts by means of two arguments to place the composition after A.D. 135. First, he claims that the term τροχαν-τήρ, in reference to an instrument of torture, "is only attested in Galen."[32] But in that the term properly means "runner," it might have been applied to such an instrument, designed to run along

---

[28] Cf. David Seeley, *The Noble Death: Graeco-Roman Martyrology and Paul's Concept of Salvation*: Journal for the Study of the New Testament Supplement 28 (Sheffield: Sheffield Academic Press, 1990); James Tabor, "Martyr, Martyrdom," *The Anchor Bible Dictionary* 4 (ed. D.N. Freeman *et al.*; New York: Doubleday, 1992) 574-579.

[29] So Tabor, p. 575-577, citing further examples.

[30] Cf. H. Anderson, "4 Maccabees," *The Old Testament Pseudepigrapha* 2 (ed. J.H. Charlesworth; Garden City: Doubleday, 1985) 531-564, 534. Anderson wisely rejects the argument *ex silencio* that the absence of an allusion to Caligula suggests a date prior to A.D. 38.

[31] Campbell, "Appendix 3: The Date of *4 Maccabees*," *The Rhetoric of Righteousness*, pp. 219-228.

[32] Campbell, p. 226.

the victim's flesh, in any period; in fact, several manuscripts of
4 Maccabees 8:13 read τροχαντήριον, a form (cf. ἱλαστήριον!) even
more suggestive of the fresh application of a word in a transferred
sense.[33] In any case, Galen uses the term with a distinct meaning,
of "the processes at the end of the thigh bone,"[34] which would suggest (as may seem obvious) that he is traveling in quite a different
circle from that of 4 Maccabees. Next, Campbell argues that, because the threat envisaged in 4 Maccabees is against the practice of
the law, rather than the Temple, the context implicitly corresponds
"to the Hadrianic persecution, rather than the first revolt."[35] But
such an emphasis upon the law is simply characteristic of the Maccabean literature,[36] and should not be used as a criterion of dating.

The best argument for dating 4 Maccabees after A.D. 70 is that
sacrificial efficacy is attributed to martyrs, apparently in compensa-
tion for what had been lost on Mount Zion. But the destruction of
the Temple is not taken to be definitive. The author maintains a distinction between God's pleasure in sacrifice, and the means of that
sacrifice. In 6:28, 29, God is asked to be pleased with his people
(ἵλεως γενοῦ τῷ ἔθνει) by Eleazar, and to make his blood their purification (καθάρσιον) and his life their ransom (ἀντίψυχον). The plea
is that heroic martyrdom be accepted in an unusual way in the light
of a radical challenge to the usual means of sacrifice. Then, in chapter seventeen, it is said of the seven brothers that, in the manner of
Eleazar, they purified the homeland in that they became a ransom
of the sin of the nation (17:21, τὴν πατρίδα καθαρισθῆναι ὥσπερ
ἀντίψυχον γεγονότας τῆς τοῦ ἔθνους ἁμαρτίας). The language of
purification and ransom is consistently used, in chapters six and
seventeen, to refer to the deaths of martyrs in cultic terms, but on
the understanding that such terms need carefully to be spelled out.
4 Maccabees does not envisage the permanent replacement of cultic
sacrifice, but its re-establishment in the Temple as a result of the sort
of heroic sacrifice that is praised.

One might expect a document composed shortly after the Temple
had been destroyed to attribute cultic efficacy to a martyr's faithful-

---

[33] As Anderson, pp. 532, 533, points out, the author was fond of rare forms
and neologisms.
[34] Cf. Henry George Liddell and Robert Scott, *A Greek-English Lexicon* (Oxford:
Clarendon, 1901) 1584.
[35] Campbell, p. 226.
[36] Cf. Tabor, pp. 576, 577.

ness, and at the same time to look forward to the restoration of the cult. The probability that 4 Maccabees was composed in Asia Minor[37] strengthens the impression that when Jesus as the son of man is said in the Synoptic tradition to have come to give his life as a ransom for many (δοῦναι τὴν ψυχὴν αὐτοῦ λύτρον ἀντὶ πολλῶν, Matthew 20:28; Mark 10:45), the operative theology is in the Hellenistic key of the Maccabean discourse concerning sacrificial martyrdom. The meanings which went before, of eucharist as an anticipation of the kingdom, as a surrogate for sacrifice, as sacrifice of sharings, as Passover, and as sacrifice for sin, could all be subsumed within the narrative claim that those meanings were derived from the hero's nobility.

Participation in the Synoptic Symposia

The heroic *ḥaṭa'at* of the Synoptics is not simply a representation of Jesus, but a paradigm of communal practice. The differences among the first three Gospels have to do, not only with the significance attached to the meal, but with what is to be done at the meal.

Matthew (26:26 see 26:21) and Mark (14:22 see 14:18) agree that Jesus took, blessed, broke and gave bread as his body "while they were eating;" the community's fellowship at an actual meal is of the nature of what occurs. In contrast, Luke (22:15-19) has Jesus take bread, give thanks over it, break and give it as his body within a sequence which (as we have seen) restricts the amount of consumption which is possible and frames the entire meal which is completed before the second cup (22:20) within the terms of reference of Jesus' commandments. Such differences are as significant in practical terms as the distinctive pattern of two cups, one before and one after the giving of bread, which Luke (22:17-20) establishes.

In each of the Synoptic Gospels, by characteristic and distinctive means, the participation of all present in Jesus' meal is insisted upon. Luke has Jesus say over the first cup that the participants are to take it and divide it among themselves (22:17), while in Matthew they are all commanded to drink from it (26:27) and in Mark (14:23) it is said that they all actually did so. But if the last meal of Jesus with his disciples is taken as a paradigm of eucharist, then—against the

---

[37] Cf. Anderson, pp. 534-537, and Campbell, p. 222 n. 3.

program of the Jacobean circle (see chapter 4)—Jews and non-Jews are fully to participate.

By means of its narrative of what is at one and the same time an ideal meal of Jesus' and a paradigm of continuing fellowship, ideological claims of inclusion are articulated in the Synoptic tradition. The limitation of Passover is transcended, because paschal motifs are transformed from *halakhoth* into themes. The Seder is no longer the norm of how eucharist is to be observed, but the symbol of what is celebrated by all participants. The Synoptic tradition succeeded in taming the Jacobean program where Paul did not. Paul had attempted to grant that Jesus was a kind of Passover (1 Corinthians 5:7), without granting there was a direct connection between Christ as Passover and the significance or chronology of the dominical supper (1 Corinthians 11:23-26).[38] The Synoptics include the paschal dimension of eucharist within the tradition of the supper itself, and then symbolize that dimension so thoroughly that Gentiles are not thereby excluded from full participation.

Jesus' "last supper" in the Synoptic Gospels is redolent of so many meanings that it can be restricted to none of them. Particularly, participation may be limited to adherents of the twelve as little as Judas is loyal and Peter is constant. The anonymous woman is the seal that, in the Synoptic catechesis, the Hellenistic community took ownership of the eucharist.

The symbolic imagination of that community is instanced in the two signs of feeding, of the 5,000 and the 4,000. In the first story (Matthew 14:13-21//Mark 6:32-44//Luke 9:10b-17), the eucharistic associations are plain:[39] Jesus blesses and breaks the bread prior to distribution (Matthew 14:19//Mark 6:41//Luke 9:16). That emphasis so consumes the story, the fish—characteristic among Christian eucharistic symbols[40]—are of subsidiary significance by the end of

---

[38] As Conzelmann recognized, p. 197.

[39] See Alan Hugh McNeile, *The Gospel According to St. Matthew* (London: Macmillan, 1957) 216 and C.E.B. Cranfield, *The Gospel according to St Mark*: The Cambridge Greek Testament Commentary (Cambridge: Cambridge University Press, 1963) 222, 223. Cranfield also notes the associations between the feeding stories, eucharistic celebration, and the motif of the *manna* in the wilderness. Moreover, he picks up the sense of συμπόσια συμπόσια in Mark 10:39 (p. 218). See also W.D. Davies and Dale C. Allison, *A Critical and Exegetical Commentary on the Gospel according to Saint Matthew* II: The International Critical Commentary (Edinburgh: Clark, 1991) 481, 493, 494.

[40] Cf. C.H. Dodd, *Historical Tradition in the Fourth Gospel* (Cambridge: Cam-

the story (compare Mark 6:43 with Matthew 14:20 and Luke 9:17). Whatever the pericope represented originally, it becomes a eucharistic narrative in the Synoptic transformation of meaning. Jesus gathers people in orderly way (see Matthew 14:18//Mark 6:39, 40// Luke 9:14, 15), by "symposia" as Mark literally has it (6:39); without that order, they might be described as sheep without a shepherd (Mark 6:34).

The *Didache* 9:4 relates the prayer that, just as bread is scattered on the mountains (in the form of wheat)[41] and yet gathered into one, so the Church might be gathered into the Father's kingdom. The 5,000 congregate in such a manner, their very number a multiple of the prophetic gathering in 2 Kings 4:42-44,[42] and Luke 9:11 has Jesus speaking to them concerning the kingdom.

The authority of the twelve is a marked concern within the story. Their return in Matthew 14:12b, 13//Mark 6:30, 31//Luke 9:10a after their commission (see Matthew 10:1-42//Mark 6:7-13//Luke 9:1-6) is what occasions the feeding, and their function in the proceedings is definite: Jesus gives them the bread, to give it to others (Matthew 14:19//Mark 6:41//Luke 9:16). Their place here is cognate with their position within another pericope (from the Jacobean cycle) which features the twelve, the parable of the sower, its interpretation, and the assertion that only the twelve possess the mystery of the kingdom (Matthew 13:1-17//Mark 4:1-12//Luke 8:4-10).[43] Such a mystery is also conveyed here, in the assertion that twelve baskets of fragments were gathered after the 5,000 ate. The lesson is evident: the twelve will always have enough to feed the Church.

---

bridge University Press, 1965) 200, 201. W.D. Davies and Dale C. Allison, p. 481, refer to 2 Baruch 29:3-8 and 4 Ezra 6:52 to support their suggestion that "both bread (or manna) and fish (or Leviathan) are associated with the messianic feast in many Jewish texts."

[41] Charles Taylor cited Psalm 72:16 in order to instance the imagery of grain growing on mountains, *The Teaching of the Twelve Apostles* (Cambridge: Deighton Bell, 1886) 129, 130.

[42] V. 43 specifies 100 men, which in the Synoptic transformation is multiplied by 10 and by 5. The number "10" is of symbolic significance within the biblical tradition (cf. Jöram Friberg, "Numbers and Counting," *Anchor Bible Dictionary* 4 [ed. D.N. Freedman; New York: Doubleday, 1992] 1139-1146, 1145). The number "5," however, is better taken of the Pythagorean number of man, the pentagram; cf. Annemarie Schimmel, "Numbers. An Overview," *The Encyclopedia of Religion* (ed. M. Eliade; New York: Macmillan, 1987) 13-19.

[43] Cf. *A Galilean Rabbi*, pp. 95, 96.

The story of the feeding of the 4,000 (Matthew 15:32-39//Mark 8:1-10) follows so exactly that of the 5,000, its omission by Luke—perhaps as a redundant doublet—may seem understandable. The 4,000 are a multiple of the four points of the compass, the story follows that of the Canaanite or Syrophoenician woman (Matthew 15:21-28//Mark 7:24-30), and concerns a throng from a number of different areas and backgrounds (see Matthew 15:21, 29//Mark 7:24, 31). Likewise, the number 7, the number of bushels of fragments here collected, corresponds to the deacons of the Hellenists in the Church of Jerusalem (cf. Acts 6:1-6), and is related to the traditional number of the seventy nations within Judaism.[44] Moreover, the reference to Jesus as giving thanks (εὐχαριστήσας) over the bread in Matthew 15:36//Mark 8:6 better corresponds to the Hellenistic version of the Petrine eucharist in Luke 22:17, 19; 1 Corinthians 11:24 than does εὐλόγησεν in Matthew 14:19//Mark 6:39, which better corresponds to the earlier Petrine formula in Matthew 26:26//Mark 14:22.[45]

The Lukan omission of such stories, in fact of the whole of what corresponds to Mark 6:45-8:26 (conventionally designated as "the great omission" of Mark by Luke) seems natural, once their meaning is appreciated: they concern the sense of Jesus in an environment characterized by a mixture of Jews and Gentiles.[46] Luke takes up that theme in Acts, and regards its reversion into the ministry of Jesus as anachronism.

After the second feeding, Jesus rebukes his disciples for a failure to understand when he warns them about the leaven of the Pharisees and Sadducees, and asks whether they truly grasp the relationship between the number 12 and the 5,000 and the number 7 and the 4,000 (Matthew 16:5-12//Mark 8:14-21). In the mind of the Hellenistic catechesis, the meaning is clear, and its implications for eucharistic discipline are evident.[47] Celebration is neither to be

---

[44] Cf. Friberg, p. 1145.

[45] See Davies and Allison, pp. 562-565, for a discussion of the features here adduced. Their conclusion that the story does not concern only Gentiles, but (in the Matthean formulation) "the lost sheep of the house of Israel" (p. 564), seems justified. Nonetheless, the geographical references which precede the second feeding make it apparent that the 4,000 were not simply Jews in a conventionally recognizable sense.

[46] That the feeding of the 4,000 relates particularly to Gentiles is argued, for example, in John W. Bowman, *The Gospel of Mark. The New Christian Passover Haggadah*: Studia Post-Biblica (Leiden: Brill, 1965) 176-178.

[47] See Paul J. Achtemeier, *Mark*: Proclamation Commentaries (Philadelphia:

limited to Jews at Passover, as the Jacobean program would have it, nor forced upon communities in a way which would require Jews to accept reduced standards of purify, as the Pauline program would have it. There is for the Hellenistic catechesis of which the Synoptic transformation is a monument, an on-going apostolate for Jews and for Gentiles, prepared to feed as many of the Church that gather.

Fortress, 1986) 29, who rightly observes that the statement attributed to Jesus "presupposes not only the present order of events in Mark, but also the present form of the Greek prose." His conclusion of particularly Markan authorship, however, is not warranted.

CHAPTER SIX

THE MIRACULOUS FOOD OF PAUL AND JOHN

Manna *and Flesh*

Paul needed to acknowledge, in the face of its overwhelming acceptance, the aspect of the Jacobean claim which portrayed eucharistic gatherings as a kind of Passover. The Synoptic tradition, a form of catechesis within the Hellenistic Church which became dominant, accepted the Jacobean chronology, but did not accept the limitation of eucharistic fellowship to Jews alone (see chapter 5). Paul's means of coming to terms with James' influence, without relenting in his adherence to a Petrine construction of the meals themselves, was to portray *Christ* as the Passover who was sacrificed (1 Corinthians 5:7b). A direct comparison of the eucharist with the Seder is therefore avoided.[1]

Paul makes his assertion succinctly, in the context of applying the image of leaven in order to warn against fornication (5:1-13), and he maintains a clear distinction between paschal theology and eucharistic theology. There is nothing in the allusion to Passover here to warrant the conclusion that it is a Pauline innovation. What is coming to expression in Paul's reference to Christ as Passover is rather a common understanding of Hellenistic Christianity comparable to that of the Synoptic Gospels, that the paschal truth of Jesus' last supper was the efficacy of his death as a heroic martyr, not the limitation of the meal to Jews in a state of purity.

Paul's conception of Christ himself as the typological meaning of Passover is further applied to the *manna* provided in the wilderness in 1 Corinthians 10. In fact, the complex of the exodus, including crossing the sea and eating miraculous food (Exodus 13-17), is presented as type in 1 Corinthians 10:6. The cloud which led Israel, and the sea they crossed, correspond to baptism (vv. 1, 2), while the

---

[1] The phrase "on our behalf" (ὑπὲρ ἡμῶν) in some manuscripts is a later addition which establishes a resonance with the words of institution in their Hellenistic phase (see 1 Corinthians 11:24 with Luke 22:19, 20; Mark 14:24, and the discussion in chapter 5).

food they ate and the water provided from the rock correspond to eucharist (vv. 3-4).[2] The notion of typology will enable Paul to make the connection between the idolatry in the wilderness and the fornication in Corinth which is one of his preoccupations (vv. 6-14), but the initial correspondence, between exodus and both baptism and eucharist, is essential to his argument, and he labors the point with the introduction, "I would not have you ignorant, brethren ..." (v. 1). Yet Paul does not make one obvious connection between the exodus and the practice of Christianity: a typology between Seder (Exodus 12) and eucharist is no part of his argument. His recent defeat at the hands of James' circle (reflected in Galatians 2, as discussed in chapter 5) does not admit of that logical development.

Within the order of exposition Paul follows, the imagery begins with the cloud and the sea, proceeds through the food in the wilderness, and ends with the water from the rock; the correspondence is to the water (and spirit) of baptism, the bread of eucharist, and the wine of eucharist respectively (1 Corinthians 10:1-4). Nonetheless, the typological key to the sequence is provided by the Pauline exposition of the rock from which drink flowed: "and the rock was Christ" (10:4).[3] As ever in the development of the eucharistic teaching we have surveyed, the wine proves to be key to the ideology involved, and Paul may here betray an awareness that it was the foundational element (see chapter 2). In any case, he demonstrates how, in the setting of Hellenistic Christianity, a paschal reading of the eucharist was side-tracked within a typology of Jesus himself as Passover. That development would have profound consequences for the explication of the feeding of the five thousand, a story which was central to the Synoptic transformation of the Jacobean program (see chapter 5).

The Gospel according to John (6:1-15) signally develops the eucharistic and paschal aspects of the feeding of the five thousand within the Hellenistic catechesis. Together with the discourse concerning the bread of life in John 6:22-59, the entire complex (which includes the feeding and the crossing of the sea of Tiberias in vv. 16-

---

[2] For a useful exposition, see Gordon D. Fee, *The First Epistle to the Corinthians*: The New International Commentary (Grand Rapids: Eerdmans, 1987) 443-450.

[3] See Oscar Cullmann, "πέτρα," *Theological Dictionary of the New Testament* VI (ed. G. Friedrich, tr. G.W. Bromiley; Grand Rapids, 1979) 95-99, 97.

21) amounts to coherent guidance for the Johannine community regarding the nature of eucharist.

The paschal setting of the scene (6:4) appears in a belated, self-conscious reference to "Passover, the feast of the Jews." The actual beginning is marked simply with the phrase "after this" (μετὰ ταῦτα in v. 1), linking what follows to Jesus' reference at the close of chapter 5 to Moses.[4] That reference, in 5:45-47, is designed to take up and bring to a climax the theme that the scriptures, associated with the word of God (5:38), attest to Jesus' identity (vv. 39-44) in a manner consistent with the witness of John the baptist (vv. 33-35) and Jesus' own acts (v. 36). The notion that the movement from Moses to Jesus is a movement from grace to ever more grace is paradigmatically Johannine (see 1:16, 17, immediately preceded by reference to John's witness in v. 15). The connection between Moses and Jesus (5:45-6:1) is more basic to an understanding of the feeding of the five thousand in John than the reference to the Passover (6:4) which serves in the interest of that connection.

The intrinsic relationship between Moses and Jesus is articulated in their mutual expression of the divine *logos*, as may be seen in 1:16, 17. The connection is all the more obvious, when v. 16 is read in the context of the status of the creative *logos* in its primordial role:

> For from his (αὐτοῦ) fullness we have all received, even grace upon grace.

Αὐτοῦ, whether taken of the *logos* or of Jesus, is a masculine pronoun, but the statement seems a resumption of what has been said in vv. 1-5, 14: we live from devolutions of the *logos*, the dynamic structure of word, light and life in which all things have their beginning.

The understanding that God's primordial "word" is still the essential issue in play within v. 16 makes the transition to the next topic straightforward (v. 17):

> For the law was given through Moses, grace and truth came through Jesus Christ.

---

[4] See Anthony Tyrrell Hanson, *The Prophetic Gospel. A Study of John and the Old Testament* (Edinburgh: Clark, 1991) 69-95; Raymond E. Brown, *The Gospel according to John (i-xii)*: The Anchor Bible (Garden City: Doubleday, 1966) 235, 236. Brown correctly observes that to reverse the order of chapter 5 and chapter 6 is to give "undue emphasis" to issues of geography and chronology.

The connection of *logos* to the revelation through Moses is evident (and is made again in 5:38). Moreover, the syntax and logic of v. 17 coheres with that of v. 16; the coordination of God's activity in creation with his donation of the law through Moses and the grace given through Jesus Christ is a thematic concern of the prologue. The link between the verses is literal, as well. The "grace" (ἡ χάρις) which came through Jesus Christ (v. 17) is akin to the "grace upon grace" (χάριν ἀντὶ χάριτος) we have all received (v. 16).[5]

There is a constant and consistent activity of God's *logos* from the creation and through the revelations through Moses and through Jesus. The *logos* in John is simply a development of conventional notions of the *memra*, God's word of command, within early Judaism.[6] At no point and in no way does the prologue present the revelation through Jesus as disjunctive with the revelation through Moses: any such disjunction is an artifact of imposing an anachronistic christology upon the text.

On the basis of a paradigmatic linkage within John, the story of the feeding of the 5,000 naturally triggered a reminiscence of the *manna* provided in the wilderness in Exodus 17, just the image taken up in the uniquely Johannine discourse concerning the bread of life (6:31-51). The connections between Jesus and Moses, and between eucharist and the miraculous provision after Passover, are developed in a way which makes them primary criteria of the meaning of the passage in John. The typology of Jesus' crossing the sea[7] and providing bread is completed by the specification that Passover, "the feast of the Jews," was near (6:4). The paschal interest is so marked as to be unmistakable.

The paschal aspect of the feeding of the five thousand in John is manifest, and its relevance for eucharistic practice within Hellenistic Christianity is equally plain. In 6:1, the sea Jesus is said to go to the other side of, in a departure from the Synoptic terminology, is

---

[5] See Brown, pp. 16, 35, 36.

[6] See my article, "Typologies of *memra* and the fourth Gospel," *Targum Studies* 1 (1992) 89-100.

[7] It is perhaps necessary to recollect that the Johannine story does not specify that Jesus "walked on" water, in that the meaning of v. 19 is somewhat obscure (see Brown, 251, 252). The issue of concern is marked in 6:25 as "when" Jesus arrived on the other side of the sea. The confused explanation of 6:16-24 leaves it unclear just what is supposed to have happened. The operative issue within John is that Jesus returned to the other side of the sea of Galilee by unknown means. Brown, p. 255, discusses the possibility of paschal symbolism.

doubly qualified as both "of Galilee" and "of Tiberias" (τῆς Γαλι-
λαίας τῆς Τιβεριάδος): "Tiberias" is a connective locus all the way
through the complex, in that other boats (beside the disciples') are
said after Jesus (re)crosses the sea to arrive from Tiberias (6:22, 23),
and the crowd on board commences the questioning (vv. 24, 25)
which leads into the discourse concerning the bread of life (vv. 26-
59). Indeed, "Tiberias" as the qualification of the sea of Galilee has
an even more resonant place in the Gospel, as the place where the
risen Jesus manifested himself in the context of a meal (21:1-14).[8]

The particular disciples mentioned during the course of the action, as reporting on the need for bread and the amount present, are
Philip and Andrew (6:7-9). The same two disciples are named later
in the narrative, as mediating the request of certain "Greeks,"
present for the feast in Jerusalem, that they might "see Jesus"
(12:20-22). Philip, of course, fulfills an independent role in the
Gospel (cf. 1:43-46; 14:8, 9a), but the pairing with Andrew brings
to expression the influence upon the present form of the text of
tradents within the Hellenistic environment of early Christianity.[9]
Within their transmission, as related in John, what accompanies the
five barley loaves[10] are not just two fish (cf. δύο ἰχθύες, Matthew
14:17, 19//Mark 6:38, 41//Luke 9:13, 16), but two ὀψάρια, that is,
prepared fish (6:9, 11). That is also precisely what the risen Jesus
offers his disciples, with bread, by the sea of Tiberias (21:1-14,
vv. 9, 10, 13).[11]

It is, then, no surprise that in the Johannine story of the feeding
of the 5,000, Jesus does not merely bless the bread and fish (so
Matthew 14:19//Mark 6:41//Luke 9:16), but offers thanks (εὐχαριστήσας) over the bread, and deals "similarly" (ὁμοίως) with the
prepared fish (John 6:11). The verb is associated with the bread in
the feeding of the four thousand in Matthew (15:36) and Mark (8:6),

---

[8] A connection between 6:1 and 21:1 is argued by Rudolf Schnackenburg (tr.
D. Smith and G.A. Kon), *The Gospel according to St John* 3: Herder's Theological
Commentary (London: Burns & Oates, 1982) 351.

[9] See Brown, p. 246. Aside from 6:8 and 12:22, Andrew is only mentioned—
and then incidentally—at 1:40, 44.

[10] The specification of the loaves as of barley in John 6:9, 13 is an evident reference back to 2 Kings 4:42-44, which is a likely paradigm of the feeding as a prophetic "sign" (John 6:14).

[11] Obviously, the picture of the disciples providing *prepared* fish from what they
have just caught (however miraculously) is strained; see Ernst Haenchen (tr.
Robert W. Funk), *John* 2: Hermeneia (Philadelphia: Fortress, 1984) 224.

as well as in the Hellenistic formula represented by Luke 22:19, and 1 Corinthians 11:24.[12] The term "likewise" (ὡσαύτως)—a virtual synonym of "similarly" (ὁμοίως)—is connected with the cup in Luke 22:20 and 1 Corinthians 11:25, and "similarly" (ὁμοίως) itself is used to pair the bread and the fish in 21:13. Later, in order to refer back to the scene, reference will be made to the place "where they ate the bread, the Lord having given thanks" (6:23). The bread is clearly at the center of concern even more emphatically than in the Synoptics, and explicitly eucharistic vocabulary is making itself felt.[13]

We have seen in chapter 5 that the cycle of feedings (and crossing the sea) ended with the riddle concerning the numbers involved (that is, 5,000 and 12 in one case, 4,000 and 7 in the other case; Matthew 16:5-12//Mark 8:14-21). The riddle, and the feeding of the 4,000 with which it is especially associated in Matthew and Mark, makes its appearance no more in John than in Luke. But John has a discourse in which Jesus provides the meaning of the bread which he gave (6:26-59).[14] The discourse provides the fundamental sense of eucharist according to John. The analogy with the literary order of the Synoptics is rather precise: the issue which introduces the discourse is said to be "signs" (6:14, 26), just as a saying of Jesus refers to a seeking for "signs" just before his riddle concerning the numbers involved in the feedings (Matthew 16:1-4//Mark 8:11-13). To be sure, the sense of the term varies qualitatively as one moves from the Synoptics to John, but that is consistent with the Hellenistic revision of several different traditions which appears to be the Johannine program.[15]

Capernaum is specified as the site of the discourse, where a crowd is depicted as having traveled from Tiberias in boats to find Jesus (6:22-25). Jesus immediately challenges them with the assertion that they do not seek him because they saw signs, but because they ate

---

[12] For the usage of the verb in connection with the cup, see Matthew 26:27; Mark 14:23; Luke 22:17.

[13] The usage in *Didache* 9 is even more emphatic, in that the noun, "eucharist," also appears (with the verbal equivalent, here and in chapter 10). Brown pursues the analysis of eucharistic similarities between John and the *Didache*, pp. 246-249.

[14] See Robert Tomson Fortna, *The Fourth Gospel and Its Predecessor. From Narrative Source to Present Gospel* (Philadelphia: Fortress, 1988) 79-93.

[15] See Ernst Haenchen (tr. Robert W. Funk), *John* 1: Hermeneia (Philadelphia: Fortress, 1984) 274.

their fill of bread (6:26). That becomes the occasion of a challenge to seek ''bread which endures for ever'' (v. 27), and the crowd replies with a challenge to perform a sign comparable to that of the *manna* in the wilderness (vv. 30, 31).[16] Jesus then asserts (vv. 32-40), in the thematic claim of the discourse (v. 35), that he is himself the bread of life which is given by God, the surety of eternal life and of resurrection on the last day (v. 40).

Conceptually, a daring advance beyond the Hellenistic catechesis represented in the Synoptics has already been achieved. Jesus no longer merely offers solidarity in martyrdom by means of his symbolic body and blood. Jesus now claims that he is what is consumed, the true bread of heaven. The fact that the new identification is developed within the complex of the feeding, rather than within a narrative of the ''last supper,'' may be an indication of the self-consciousness of creativity at this point. As Barrett observes, John is ''more, rather than less, interested in the eucharist'' than the Synoptic Gospels; the Johannine program is to identify Jesus himself with the bread ''to root the sacrament as observed by the church in the total sacramental fact of the incarnation.''[17]

For just that reason, the last meal of Jesus with his disciples in chapter 13 is a symposial gathering, in which heroic service is exemplified,[18] rather than the institution of what for John is an eternal reality. In that John appears to have been composed on the basis of familiarity with the Hellenistic catechesis which crystallized in the Synoptic Gospels,[19] the form of chapter 13 may be taken to confirm the reading of the Synoptic last supper as a heroic symposium (see chapter 5).

The name ''Capernaum'' also bears associations of the meaning of earlier ''signs'' in John. After the sign at the wedding, Jesus is said to depart from Cana to dwell in Capernaum with his family and his disciples (2:12). Later, while he is again in Cana, a royal official sends from Capernaum concerning his son's illness; the cure which follows is styled ''the second sign which Jesus did, while coming

---

[16] At this point, an analogy of the Johannine discourse with the signs of Matthew 16:1-4//Mark 8:11-13 becomes apparent.

[17] C.K. Barrett, *The Gospel according to St John* (London: SPCK, 1960) 42. See also Brown, pp. 272-275.

[18] Cf. Dodd, pp. 401-403; William Temple, *Readings in St. John's Gospel* (New York: Macmillan, 1939) 78-82.

[19] See Barrett, pp. 363-364.

from Judaea into Galilee'' (4:46-54).[20] Capernaum, then, is in John a place for the memory and interpretation of signs, as in the case of the discourse concerning the bread of life. In the discourse, however, Jesus interprets himself as the true bread given by God, bread which endures forever in the sense that to see the son and believe in him is to have eternal life and to be raised on the last day (6:35-40).

The scandal implicit in Jesus' assertion is fully articulated from 6:41, 42. The objection of ''the Jews'' that Jesus is knowable by his kin (and therefore not descended from heaven)[21] is simply rejected (v. 43), as Jesus goes on to assert his identity all the more emphatically. As the bread of life (v. 48), he offers what the *manna* could not: eternal life (vv. 49-51).

The final assertion of Jesus' answer to the Jews is the most scandalous. The claim that Jesus is in some sense the bread of life is already problematic, especially when his efficacy is compared positively to Moses'. The assertion of v. 51b, c, however, must be seen as deliberate provocation:

> If someone eats of this bread, he will live forever; and the bread which I will give is my flesh on behalf of the life of the world.

The full scandal of the identification of heavenly bread with a particular person is emphatic: Jesus' flesh is superior to the *manna* given by Moses, and must be eaten to be effective.

In v. 41, the response of ''the Jews'' is characterized with the verb γογγύζω: they grumble. But the climactic assertion in v. 51 effects a transition to the assertion in v. 52 that they quarrel with one another (μάχομαι). Jesus' donation of his flesh, his actual body (whether under the aspect of bread or *manna*), is held to constitute the crux of Jewish objections. Within the experience of the Johannine community in Ephesus, the ''flesh'' of Jesus constitutes the line of demarcation with Judaism, both as the body which is given in eucharist and as the body which died on the cross. The discourse concerning the bread of life identifies Jesus' flesh in precisely those two senses, and in that order.

The question of ''the Jews'' is, How is he able to give us his flesh

---

[20] The complex has an obvious associations with the Synoptic story of the healing of the centurion's servant, which is also set in Capernaum (Matthew 8:5-13// Luke 7:1-10), and with a story concerning Ḥanina ben Dosa in Berakhoth 34a (cf. *A Galilean Rabbi and His Bible*, 31, 32).

[21] A similarity with Matthew 13:53-8//Mark 6:1-6a may be noted.

to eat (6:52b)? Jesus' response is to exacerbate the potential for scandal: one must eat the flesh of the son of man, and drink his blood, to have life in oneself (v. 53). The eucharistic context of the assertion becomes all the more plain with the mention of ''blood,'' but an additional saying calls for one to ''chomp'' (τρώγω) the flesh and drink the blood (v. 54). The literalism of ''the Jews,'' as established in the scene between Jesus and Nicodemus (3:1-21, see especially v. 4) can only make such statements appear irredeemably scandalous, although within the community of the Gospel the eucharistic application will have been apparent.

The repetition of the assertion (vv. 55-57), and the favorable comparison of Jesus as the bread of life with the *manna* (v. 58), puts the discourse on a collision course with any ordinary understanding of Judaism before or after the destruction of the Temple. The Mishnah, in an effort to conceive of a heinous defect on the part of a priest involved in slaughtering the red heifer, pictures him as intending to eat the flesh or drink the blood (Parah 4:3). Because people had no share of such flesh or of blood, which belonged only to God, even the thought of consuming it was blasphemous. To imagine drinking human blood, consumed with human flesh, could only make the blasphemy worse. So if Jesus' words are taken with their Johannine, autobiographical meaning, his eucharist can only be understood as a deliberate break from Judaism. The location of the discourse within a synagogue in Capernaum (v. 59) makes the break explicit.

The reaction of Jesus' own disciples constitutes a final coda after the discourse. ''Many'' of them complain that Jesus' claim is ''hard'' (σκληρός), and impossible to sustain (v. 60). His response is that the ascent of the son of man to where he formerly was is the substantiation of his claim (vv. 61, 62): the flesh he gives is of the nature of his origin, which is why eating his flesh enables one to partake of the life with which the father endows him (v. 56, 57).

Notably, the grumbling of many of Jesus' disciples is described by means of the same verb (γογγύζω; 6:61) which had been used earlier to characterize the response of ''the Jews'' to Jesus' assertion that he is the bread of life (v. 41). The identification of ''the Jews''' perplexity and that of the disciples is obviously a moment of drama, and is skillfully exploited within the Gospel in what follows. Some disciples are perceived by Jesus so to disbelieve him as to be associated with Judas's betrayal, which he also foresees (6:64-65), and the events which follow fully justify his perception (vv. 66-71). The close of that complex includes Jesus' assertion that one of the twelve is "the devil," and the identification of that person as Judas (vv. 70-71). Immediately thereafter, reference of the plot of "the Jews" in Judaea to kill Jesus is made (7:1): the association of disbelieving, betraying disciples with overtly conspiratorial "Jews" is evident.

That association has occurred because neither group has understood that Jesus' flesh, as the bread of life, must be eaten. The specificity of the Johannine conception becomes plain in 6:63:

> The spirit is that which gives life, the flesh avails nothing; the sayings which I have spoken to you are spirit and life.

The usage of "flesh" here involves the typical contrast with spirit: the disciples who fail to grasp Jesus' meaning are aligned with Nicodemus (3:6). By implication, therefore, the flesh which Jesus gives for the life of the world in v. 51 must differ from flesh as ordinarily understood. The bread of life seems to be identified with Jesus in his death, although earlier it was said that the bread which comes down from heaven gives life to the world (v. 33). The potential dilemma, generated by the seemingly paradoxical relationship between the man Jesus and God's life-giving *manna* which animates the entire chapter, is resolved in v. 63. Jesus enunciates life-giving spirit, so that the flesh which he gives, an embodiment of that enunciation, is not of the same nature as ordinary flesh.

The Johannine claim is only possible on the basis of the prior identification, within the developments discussed in the previous two chapters, between the feeding of the 5,000 and a paschal understanding of eucharist. The Gospel, indeed, emphasizes that identification, in order to develop its own analogy between the *manna* and Jesus' "flesh," bread as the sign of his life-giving sayings and death. And having managed that analogy as a prerequisite of understanding Jesus, without which one is classed with conspiring "Jews" and treacherous disciples, the request, "Lord, give us this bread always" (6:34) is utterly natural. The Quartodeciman limitation of eucharist to Passover is overcome, but by means unlike those used by Paul. There is no appeal to a Petrine interpretation distinct from the Jacobean; rather the paschal identification of James is accepted, only to be transcended by the analogy between *manna* and Jesus' "flesh." In its eucharistic teaching, John's Gospel represents the attempt to revise the Jacobean program without contending its influence.

The extent of the Johannine revision in the direction of Hellenistic Christianity is most apparent in the commandment that Jesus' followers eat his flesh and drink his blood. The difficulty of such a notion within Judaism, and within the company of Jesus' Jewish followers, is explicitly recognized in the discourse concerning the bread of life, as we have seen. Nonetheless, consuming Jesus' life-giving flesh and blood is a requirement of Johannine fellowship, apart from which one is an enemy or a traitor, and, in either case, dead in respect of God.

At least as early as the Synoptic presentation of the last supper as a heroic *ḥaṭaʾat*, the bread and the wine were related to Jesus' body and blood in a personal sense. The flesh and blood of sacrifice had been transformed, in ways we have traced through chapters 1-5, into means of solidarity with a noble martyr. That transformation was not merely a function of the linguistic decision to render "flesh" (בִּסְרָא) in Aramaic with "body" (σῶμα) in Greek, but that decision fed a cultural process of transformation. There was no possibility of preventing at least some Christians who followed the eucharistic practice of Paul and the Synoptics from conceiving of Jesus himself as consumed in the bread and wine.

Jesus' last supper was naturally compared to initiation into Mystery within Hellenistic Christianity. He was a new Dionysos, historical rather than mythical, who gave himself, flesh and blood, in the meals which were held in his name. After all, he had said "This is my body," and "This is my blood." For many Hellenistic Christians, that could only mean that Jesus referred to himself: bread and wine were tokens of Jesus, which became his body and blood when believers consumed them.[22]

The Johannine discourse concerning the bread of life, following upon a paschal reading of the feeding of the 5,000, addressed the challenges of a Hellenistic reading of eucharist as Mystery. By means of a nuanced tension between "flesh" in its ordinary sense (6:63), as alien from God, and Jesus' "flesh" as the medium through which the son of man was sent by God to offer life (6:53-59), the Johannine discourse avoided any crude reduction of eucharist to

---

[22] See Samuel Angus, *The Mystery-Religions and Christianity. A Study in the Religious Background of Early Christianity* (London: Murray, 1925) 127-133; Kurt Rudolf (tr. M.J. O'Connell), "Mystery Religions," *The Encyclopedia of Religion* 10 (ed. M. Eliade; New York: Macmillan 1987) 230-239.

the consumption of a god. Jesus' flesh is that bread which he gives (6:51), the true *manna*, a miracle which animates the world (6:32, 33), because he is himself the bread of life (6:35, 48, 51). The essential nuance, apart from which the discourse is not understandable, is that Jesus' "flesh" as consumed in eucharist is not flesh in the usual understanding, but the means by which he offers spirit and life (6:63). Yet however sophisticated the discourse may be, it implicitly accepts that the language of Mystery is appropriate, suitably refined, for the description of eucharist. For that reason, the fourth Gospel marks the point at which the Christian practice of eucharist self-consciously and definitively parted from Judaism, even as paschal imagery was embraced and developed.

The Lamb which was slain

Paschal imagery permeates the fourth Gospel with eucharistic meaning. The moment of Jesus' death in John corresponds to the time at which paschal lambs were normally slain: that Jesus was crucified during the afternoon of the day of preparation, just prior to Passover, is emphasized (19:14, 31). Moreover, John 19:36 cites a regulation concerning the paschal lamb, that no bone shall be broken (Exodus 12:46), in respect of Jesus' body on the cross. The sponge of vinegar raised on hyssop (specified only in John 19:29) may recollect the hyssop which was used to apply the paschal blood in Exodus (12:22).[23]

The timing of the crucifixion in John formally excludes a strictly Quartodeciman construction of eucharist as Passover, since the Seder would not have been observed until the day after the crucifixion. Much as Paul beforehand (in 1 Corinthians 5:7), but now in narrative rather than theological terms, John's Gospel affirms the Hellenistic creed that Jesus is himself the true Passover which benefits all who are baptized, not Jews alone.

When John the baptist identifies Jesus as "the lamb of God which takes away the sin of the world" (1:29, cf. v. 36), an association with Passover is evident. It has been objected that the image of the lamb here is not necessarily paschal, and that the removal of sin might more readily be associated with the daily offering (the *tamid*) than

---

[23] See Barrett, pp. 146-147; Brown 61-63.

with the paschal lamb. When the image is taken in isolation, that observation is apposite. But the connection between the death of Jesus
(and therefore eucharist) and the sacrifice for sin had already been
made within the Hellenistic catechesis of the Synoptic Gospels by the
time John was produced (see chapter 5), and the Gospel itself
betrays an awareness of that traditional theme in its conviction that
Jesus is a lamb which takes away sin. The Johannine contribution
is to make that conviction more specific: Jesus he is the paschal
lamb, just as he is the true *manna*.[24]

The Revelation takes up the paschal imagery of the Gospel within
its own version of the Johannine portrayal of eucharist. The document itself is written in a Semitized Greek, with self-consciously bad
grammar: some errors of case and tense, for example, are below a
rudimentary level.[25] Such attempts at archaism can scarcely con-
vince, when Jewish congregations are dismissed as instances of a
"synagogue of Satan" (2:9; 3:9).

Separation from Judaism is also flagged in the Revelation by a
theological development: Jesus as the divine lamb is now explicitly
an object of worship. The ἀμνός of John 1:29, 36[26] has become a
surreal "lamb standing as slain" (ἀρνίον ἑστηκὸς ὡς ἐσφραγμένον;
Revelation 5:6). The attribution to the ἀρνίον of divine status is obvious both in its placement, in the midst of the throne and the living
creatures, among the elders, and in its possession of seven eyes
"which are the spirits of God sent out into all the earth." Although
the term ἀρνίον in Koine appears unequivocally to connote the help-
lessness of a lamb,[27] so that the fact of its slaughter is emphasized,

---

[24] See Haenchen, *John* 1, 155, 156.

[25] See R.H. Charles, *A Critical and Exegetical Commentary on the Revelation of St.
John* 1: The International Critical Commentary (New York: Scribner's, 1920)
cxvii-clix. The unique character of the Revelation's Greek style is well described
on pp. cxliii, cxliv, but I cannot agree that the best explanation is that *"while he* (sc.
the author) *writes in Greek, he thinks in Hebrew."* A more likely explanation is that
"the author uses early Christian prophetic-apocalyptic traditions and understands
the words of the book as prophetic *Geistrede* (speech of the Spirit)," see Elisabeth
Schüssler Fiorenza, "The Quest for the Johannine School: The Book of Revelation
and the Fourth Gospel," *The Book of Revelation, Justice and Judgment* (Philadelphia:
Fortress, 1989) 85-113, 106.

[26] See Acts 8:32; 1 Peter 1:19; Philip Edgcumbe Hughes, *The Book of the Revelation. A Commentary* (Grand Rapids: Eerdmans, 1990) 79, 80.

[27] Cf. Joachim Jeremias, "ἀμνός, ἀρήν, ἀρνίον," *Theological Dictionary of the
New Testament* I (ed. G. Kittel, tr. G.W. Bromiley; Eerdmans: Grand Rapids,
1978) 338-241.

the focus of the Revelation is the power which proceeds from the lamb as a consequence of its slaughter. The lamb is worthy of heavenly and human worship (5:8, 13; 7:9-10) precisely as slain (5:12). That is the source of its authority to open the seals (5:1-5, 7; 6:1f.) and exercise judgment with God (6:15-16; cf. 14:9, 10; 17:12-14).

The essential focus of the Synoptic catechesis regarding eucharist, the solidarity of believers in the witness of a faithful martyr, is assumed in the Revelation. Indeed, that solidarity is combined with the imagery of Jesus as a sacrifice for sin in the portrayal of Christian martyrs as those who have whitened their robes in the blood of the lamb (7:14). They enjoy the presence of the lamb in their midst, now portrayed as shepherding them (7:17). It is telling that the image appears after reference to the sealing of the 144,000 of Israel (7:4-8) and to the worshiping throng "from every country, tribe, people and tongue" (7:9-12, 9). The union of Jewish and non-Jewish followers of Jesus within the heroic *ḥaṭaʾat*, implicit within the Synoptics, is unmistakable within the Revelation. The notion of whitening in blood is no paradox, once it is understood that the underlying issue is the purification which Christ as *ḥaṭaʾat* effects.[28] And the imagery of the lamb's blood is explicitly linked with the theme of Christian witnessing in 12:11: the heroism of this *ḥaṭaʾat* extends to those who worship, as well as to what they worship.

There is genuine creativity in conceiving of the lamb as slain from the foundation of the world (13:8). That conviction is expressed in the same verse which regards the book of life as belonging to the lamb; indeed, the phrase "from the foundation of the world" might be read as qualifying the lamb or as qualifying the book of life.[29] The ambivalence is deliberate: both the lamb and its book in the Revelation are as primordial as the *logos*, a conception shared with the fourth Gospel which is developed visually and radically in the Revelation (19:13).[30] Jesus' death is now viewed as an eternal sacrifice which both gives him access to the divine throne and offers his followers solidarity with his triumphant purity. For that reason, those followers—or at least 144,000 of them, marked especially for purity—are to appear with the lamb on Mount Zion and offer wor-

---

[28] See Charles, *Revelation* 1, 213, 214.
[29] See Charles, *Revelation* 1, 353-355; Hughes, 149.
[30] See Charles, *Revelation* 2, 134, Fiorenza, 97-99.

ship in the presence of the throne, the four beasts, and the elders (14:1-5). Ultimately, however, all those who conquer the beast and its image are to join in the song of Moses and of the lamb (15:2-4; cf. 21:22-27).

The festal quality of the solidarity of faithful followers with the lamb leads to the unlikely imagery of the marriage of the lamb with his bride, a symbol of the Jerusalem which is to come (21:1-14). The earlier blessing pronounced on those who are called to ''the wedding supper of the lamb'' (19:9, see v. 7 also, and the context from v. 1) is here developed in the idiom of the seer's vision. A likely source of the motif,[31] reference in the Synoptics to invitation to a wedding feast (see Matthew 22:1-14; Luke 14:7-14), has joined with the Synoptic conception of the eucharist in which solidarity with Christ is effected by participation. It is a solidarity which makes the seer, and any faithful Christian, a fellow servant with the angelic host (see 19:9-10), a citizen of the new Jerusalem whose purpose is the worship of God and the lamb (22:1-5).

---

[31] For the usage of Synoptic traditions in the Revelation, see Charles, lxxxiii-lxxxvi; Fiorenza, 101-106.

CHAPTER SEVEN

CONCLUSION:
THE GENERATIVE EXEGESIS OF EUCHARISTIC TEXTS

Typologies of Meaning

Generative exegesis is concerned with the meanings and linguistic complexions of texts, their likely social settings and histories of formation, as well as with the literary motifs, contexts, and patterns with which they frame their meanings. The chapters which precede have involved themselves with those issues in respect of the eucharistic texts of the New Testament, in as much detail as seemed necessary to address critical questions which have long concerned exegetes. Generative exegesis is simply one form of critical reading, and—in the case of documents from the past—historical reading.

A generative exegesis maintains a particular focus in the midst of the many critical questions which might arise in the course of reading. The issue of generation is: in association with what practice and in which community did a text arise, so as to attest that practice and the meaning attributed to it? In the case of the eucharistic texts of the New Testament, the obvious diversity of extant witnesses alerted us (in the Introduction) to the possibility that a variety of practices and communities might be reflected. In the event, our six chapters of analysis are designed to show that six types of practice interacted sequentially to produce the texts we can read today. The types of practice may be briefly reviewed now, on the understanding that they have been developed in exegetical terms during the previous chapters.

Jesus joined with his followers in Galilee and Judaea, both disciples and sympathizers, in meals which were designed to anticipate the coming of God's kingdom. The meals were characterized by a readiness to accept the hospitality and the produce of Israel at large. A willingness to provide for the meals, to join in the fellowship, to forgive and to be forgiven, was seen by Jesus as a sufficient condition for eating in his company and for entry into the kingdom.

Jesus' view of purity was distinctive, and—no doubt—lax in the estimation of many contemporary rabbis. In one regard, however,

he typifies the Judaism of his period: there was an evident fit between his practice of fellowship at meals and his theory of what was
clean. Meals appear to have been a primary marker of social group-
ing within the first century in Palestine. Commensal institutions,
formal or not, were plentiful. They included the hierarchical banquets of Qumran, but also occasions of local or national festivity
throughout the country. Any patron who mounted a banquet would
appropriately expect the meal to reflect his or her views of purity,
and guests would not be in a good position to militate in favor of
other views. But meals need not be on a grand scale to be seen as
important, and much more modest events might be subject to custom: a household might welcome a feast or sabbath with a cup of
sanctification (the *kiddush*), and bless bread as a prelude to a significant family affair (the *berakhah*). In addition, collegial meals shared
within fellowships (*haburoth*) at which like-minded fellows (*haberim*)
would share the foods and the company they considered pure would
define distinct social groups.

Jesus' practice coincided to some extent with that of a *haburah*, but
his construal of purity was unusual. Given the prominence accorded
wine in his meals, we might describe the first type of his meals—the
practice of purity in anticipation of the kingdom—as a *kiddush* of the
kingdom. But his meals were not limited to households. Any analogy with the meals of Qumran would seem to be strained, unless
the feedings of the 5,000 and the 4,000 are held originally to have
been staged as massive banquets designed to instance Jesus' theory
of purity and his expectation of the kingdom.

Indeed, there is practically no meal of Judaism with which Jesus'
meals do not offer some sort of analogy, because the meal was a seal
and an occasion of purity, and Jesus was concerned with what was
pure. But both the nature of his concern and the character of his
meals were distinctive in their inclusiveness: Israel as forgiven and
willing to provide of its own produce was for him the occasion of
the kingdom. That was the first type in the development of the
eucharist.

Jesus brought about the final crisis of his career. His teaching in
regard to the kingdom and its purity, including his communal meals
as enacted parables, might have been continued indefinitely (for all
the controversy involved) outside of Jerusalem. But he sought to
influence practice in the Temple, where the purity of Israel was
supremely instanced and where the feast of all nations promised by

the prophets was to occur. A dispute over the location of vendors of animals for sacrifice was the catalyst in a raging dispute over purity between Jesus (with his followers) and the authorities in the Temple.

The riot in the Temple which Jesus provoked may have been sufficient by itself to bring about his execution, given the importance of the Temple within both Judaism and the settlement with Rome. But he compounded his confrontation with the authorities by putting a new interpretation upon the meals people took with him in their expectation of the kingdom. As he shared wine, he referred to it as the equivalent of the blood of an animal, shed in sacrifice; when he shared bread, he claimed its value was as that of sacrificial flesh. Such offerings were purer, more readily accepted by God, than what was sacrificed in a Temple which had become corrupt. Here was a sacrifice of sharings which the authorities could not control, and which the nature of Jesus' movement made it impossible for them to ignore. Jesus' meals after his failed occupation of the Temple became a surrogate of sacrifice, the second type of eucharist.

The third type is that of Petrine Christianity, when the blessing or breaking of bread at home, the *berakhah* of Judaism, became a principal model of eucharist. A practical result of that development was that bread came to have precedence over wine. More profoundly, the circle of Peter conceived of Jesus as a new Moses, who gave commands concerning purity as Moses did on Sinai, and who also expected his followers to worship on Mount Zion. As compared to Jesus' practice (in its first and second stages), Petrine practice represents a double domestication. First, adherents of the movement congregated in the homes of their colleagues, rather than seeking the hospitality of others. Second, the validity of sacrifice in the Temple was acknowledged. Both forms of domestication grew out of the new circumstances of the movement in Jerusalem and fresh opportunities for worship in the Temple; they changed the nature of the meal and the memory of what Jesus had said at the "last supper."

The fourth type of eucharist, the contribution of the Jacobean circle, pursued the tendency of domestication further. The eucharist was seen as a Seder, in terms of both its meaning and its chronology. So understood, only Jews in a state of purity could participate in eucharist, which could be truly recollected only once a year, at Passover in Jerusalem. The Quartodeciman controversy (concerning the timing of Easter) of a later period, fierce though it appears, was but a shadow cast by much a more serious contention concerning the nature of Christianity. The Jacobean program was to integrate Jesus' movement fully within the liturgical institutions of Judaism, to insist upon the Judaic identity of the movement and upon Jerusalem as its governing center.

Paul and the Synoptic Gospels represent the fifth type of eucharist. Paul more vehemently resists Jacobean claims, by insisting Jesus' last meal occurred on the night in which he was betrayed, not on Passover. He emphasizes the link between Jesus' death and the eucharist, and he accepts the Hellenistic refinement of the Petrine type which presented the eucharist as a sacrifice for sin. That type is also embraced in the Synoptic Gospels, where the heroism of Jesus is such that the meal is an occasion to join in the solidarity of martyrdom. The Synoptic strategy is not to oppose the Jacobean program directly; in fact, its chronology is accepted (although not without internal contradiction). Instead, the Synoptics insist by various wordings that Jesus' blood is shed in the interests of the communities for which those Gospels were composed, for the ''many'' in Damascus (Matthew) and Rome (Mark), on behalf of ''you'' in Antioch (Luke). The Synoptic tradition also provided two stories of miraculous feeding which symbolized the inclusion of Jews and non-Jews within eucharist, understood as in the nature of a philosophical symposium.

The feeding of the 5,000—understood as occurring at Passover—is taken up in John in a fully paschal sense. Jesus himself is identified as the *manna*, miraculous food bestowed by God upon his people. The motif was already articulated by Paul, but John develops it to construe the eucharist as a Mystery, in which Jesus offers his own flesh and blood (carefully defined to avoid a crude misunderstanding). That autobiographical reading of Jesus' words—as giving his personal body and blood in eucharist—had already occurred to Hellenistic Christians who followed Synoptic practice. The Johannine practice made that meaning as explicit as the break with Judaism is in the fourth Gospel. Both that departure and the identification of Jesus himself (rather than his supper) as the paschal lamb are pursued in the Revelation. The sixth type of eucharist can only be understood as a consciously non-Judaic and Hellenistic development.

Sources of Meaning

As the analysis has progressed, meanings and the circles within which they emerged have been identified. A generative exegesis properly focuses on the issue of meanings itself, but the corollary matter of cultural milieu cannot be avoided. Consequently, circles of meaning have been characterized: dominical, Petrine, Jacobean, Synoptic, Pauline, Johannine. By means of inference, it is possible to speculate on the periods in which their traditions emerged, how they interacted, and (in some cases) who the likely tradents were.

For most of his career, Jesus' meals with his disciples represent the practice of purity in anticipation of the kingdom. The principal witness of his practice is Matthew 26:29//Mark 14:25//Luke 22:18. The foundational saying plainly speaks the language of anticipation, and warrants that each meal is a pledge that the kingdom is to come: "I shall not again drink of the fruit of the vine until I drink it new in the kingdom of God." The intention of the saying within its originating context was to assure Jesus' followers that each meal taken in fellowship was a warrant of the festal kingdom which was shortly to come, and Jesus himself undertook to consume wine in no other way (see chapter 1). The wide attestation of the saying, despite its asymmetry with later understandings of eucharist, would suggest that it was widely understood by Jesus' first followers to be his ideology of fellowship at meals.

After Jesus' occupation of the Temple, and his failure to reform cultic worship, he presented his "blood" and "body" as the replacement of conventional sacrifice. Matthew 26:26-28//Mark 14:22-24//Luke 22:19, 20 (with v. 17 in respect of the correct order)//1 Corinthians 11:24, 25 reflect that development clearly, although in an indirect and elaborated form. At the level of dominical practice, however, the sense of the gesture is plain: pure wine and bread, shared in a community created by mutual forgiveness, is a better sacrifice than the priesthood of the Temple is willing to permit (see chapter 2). The sense of the gesture is confrontative, but does not involve the formal blasphemy which a later, autobiographical interpretation of the saying would require. Again, wide attestation suggests that the saying was a matter of a consensual tradition.

The eucharistic teachings of Jesus did not, of course, exert a direct influence upon the text of the Gospels. They were already incorporated, and given a new meaning, within a cycle of narrative catechesis associated with Peter and his fellow "pillars." The Petrine cycle must have been available in Aramaic by c. A.D. 35, in time for Paul to be informed of it at the time of his visit to Jerusalem. But the very name "Peter" attests early translation into Greek, in association with the wider field of preaching for which that apostle accepted responsibility. The Petrine cycle substantially included the initial call of the first disciples, the healing of Jairus' daughter, the confession at Caesarea Philippi, the transfiguration, the eucharist, and the struggle in Gethsemane. By design and in fact, the Petrine usage of narrative for the purpose of catechesis established a paradigm in the primitive Church; the Synoptic Gospels are a monument to that narrative strategy.

The purpose of the Petrine teaching of the eucharist is indicated by the sense of "covenant" (διαθήκη) in Matthew 26:28; Mark 14:24. "New covenant" in Luke 22:20; 1 Corinthians 11:25 represents a Hellenistic phase of the Petrine cycle. The reference to the covenant represents the meal as under the type of Moses' covenantal sacrifice of sharings (Exodus 24), so that Jesus is accorded foundational importance, but any perception of competition with the Temple is avoided. Towards the same end, the "memorial" (ἀνάμνησις) in Luke 22:19; 1 Corinthians 11:24, 25 links Jesus action to what is immolated on the altar for the purpose of a sacrifice such as Moses offered. Because the meal of Jesus with his disciples is presented as a covenantal sacrifice, a type of sacrifice of sharings, the continuing validity of worship in the Temple is presupposed, while the Mosaic stature of Jesus is also conveyed (see chapter 3).

Passover became the principal association with eucharist in the circle of James. However emphatic the association (Matthew 26:17-20; Mark 14:12-17; Luke 22:7-14), it is also artificial (see Matthew 26:1-5; Mark 14:1, 2; Luke 22:1, 2, 15, 16), an example of interpretation by addendum. The paschal connection of the meal was a most effective means of incorporating Jesus' movement fully within the cultic worship of conventional Judaism, which was the program of James. In a stroke, the meal was more tightly linked to the liturgical year than it ever had been before, and its only possible occasion was in Jerusalem. The dominical and Petrine meals were repeatable anywhere and frequently. The Jacobean transformation of what is now a last Passover could only truly be enacted "between the evenings" of 14 and 15 Nisan, and in the vicinity of the Temple, where the paschal lambs were slain (see chapter 4).

What was produced within James' circle was not an independent cycle, but substantial recastings (summarized below) of the Petrine cycle and the source of sayings known as "Q." Both the Petrine cycle and the Jacobean revision of that cycle were known in Antioch prior to the council in Jerusalem which took place c. A.D. 49 (see Galatians 2). The Jacobean revision itself may be dated c. A.D. 40, since it went through some development before Paul became acquainted with it in Antioch, although he was not apprised of it at the time of his visit with Peter c. A.D. 35.

The source of Jesus' sayings known as "Q" has contributed little to the texts as they may be read today. But Jesus' wistful statement that he had greatly desired to eat the Passover (but could not), attested only in Luke 22:15-17, manifests no incorporation within the Jacobean program. In its earliest phase, "Q" was a collection of sayings in the nature of a mishnah which a rabbi's disciples might learn, virtually contemporaneous with the Petrine cycle. In the present case, the mishnaic source confirms that, prior to the Petrine cycle, Jesus was understood to refer to the wine before he referred to the bread (see chapters 1, 2 and 3). From its origins in Jesus' movement as instruction of the twelve, the source known as "Q" developed in the environment of Syria in a markedly apocalyptic direction.

The Jacobean program would prove to be reasonably adaptable. After the destruction of the Temple, Jews generally celebrated a modified Seder, without a lamb, presumably accommodating to an earlier practice in the Diaspora. Still, the implications of James' position are evident: an extension of the Torah to the "last supper," as to a paschal meal, would carry with it the consequence that "no uncircumcised person shall eat of it" (Exodus 12:48). In other words, it would constitute a further, logical development of the exclusionary policy of James, as reflected in Galatians 2 and Acts 15: only the circumcised could truly celebrate eucharist, and even then, only at Passover. The relatively privileged position of Jews among Christian Jews and Jewish Christians alike was therefore maintained and regularized.

The Jacobean revision of the Petrine cycle was promulgated in Greek by Judas Barsabbas and Silas in Antioch after the council c. A.D. 49. After A.D. 70, "the little apocalypse," a Syrian addition to the Jacobean revision, was composed; it is a response to James' martyrdom and the Temple's destruction. The compiler may have

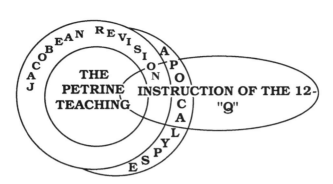

Figure 1.

been Silas, who under a more current form of his name (Silvanus) was involved in several sorts of apocalyptic speculation (cf. 1 Thessalonians 1:1; 2 Thessalonians 1:1; 1 Peter 5:12). In any case, the Jacobean revision of the Petrine cycle would have included (prior to any apocalyptic addendum) the insistence that the twelve alone could provide the sense of the parables, a collection of such parables, a note of Jesus' rejection by his own neighbors, a commissioning of the twelve, and the paschal interpretation of the eucharist within a more detailed story of the passion than the Petrine cycle had offered.

The primitive cycles or revisions of tradition (Petrine, Jacobean, instructional ["Q"], and apocalyptic) were amalgamated into the Hellenistic catechesis reflected in the Synoptic Gospels, probably first of all in Antioch. The relationship among the sources of the catechesis is represented schematically in figure 1. The most likely exponent of the unified catechesis is Barnabas. His standing is consistent with the wide acceptance of the Synoptic tradition, and the greater accommodation to Jacobean influence in the Synoptics as compared to Paul would be characteristic of Barnabas. But the Synoptic eucharist addresses the needs of its overwhelmingly Hellenistic constituency, in presenting the last supper as a well ordered symposium, a sacrifice for sin which offered its benefits to all who joined themselves to the heroic martyr's witness.

The Synoptic catechesis was a paradigm which was then developed and published in Rome (Mark, c. A.D. 71), Damascus (Matthew, c. A.D. 80), and Antioch itself (Luke, c. A.D. 90). The spine of each Gospel is the narrative catechesis of the Petrine cycle, supplemented by Jacobean revision of that catechesis, the apocalyp-

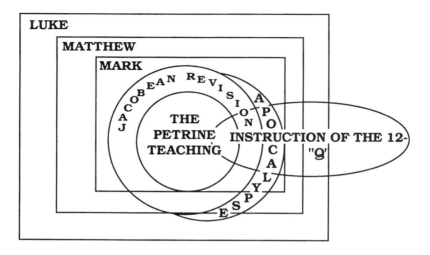

Figure 2.

tic addendum of Judas Barsabbas and Silas, and the instruction of
the twelve with its addenda (''Q''). Their similarities and differences are best understood as functions of the particular sort of
catechesis (preparation of catechumens) which was current in each
community. No Synoptic Gospel is simply a copy of another; rather,
each represents the choices among varying traditions, written
and/or oral, and the development of those tradition which had taken
place in a given locality, as represented in figure 2.[1]

Thomas (from Edessa, during the second century) represents a
different ordering principle, based upon the mishnaic genre of the
instruction of the twelve, rather than the Petrine catechesis. The absence of the last supper from *Thomas* shows by contrast the influence
of the Petrine cycle upon the Synoptic tradition and Paul. The same
can not quite be said of John. Although there is formally no counterpart of the last supper, the substance and theology of the Synoptic
tradition (if not of the Synoptic Gospels themselves) are reflected.
The Johannine Gospel associates the Synoptic *haggadah* of the feeding of the 5,000 with Passover (6:4) and then fully develops the
quasi-magical exposition of the eucharistic bread as *manna* which
Paul in 1 Corinthians 10 only tentatively indulged (John 6:26-59).

---

[1] For a further elaboration, see *Profiles of a Rabbi. Synoptic Opportunities in Reading
About Jesus*: Brown Judaic Studies 177 (Atlanta: Scholars Press, 1989).

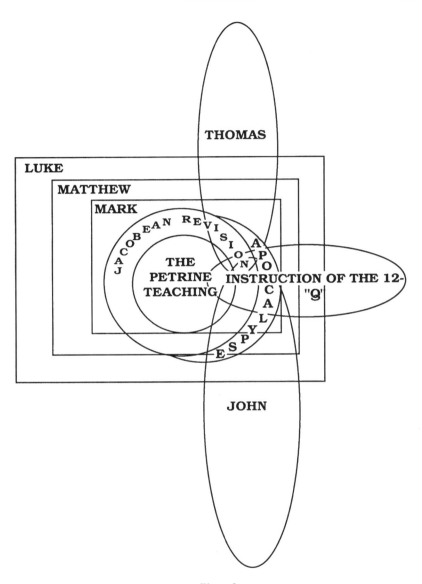

Figure 3.

The Johannine "last supper" is swallowed up in a heroic symposium in chapter 13, because for John it is truer to say that Jesus *is* the bread of eucharist than to say that he instituted eucharist. The discursive style of John to some extent imitates that of "Q," as does

Thomas, but in both cases the earlier developments of Christian catechesis are reflected (see figure 3). Neither John nor *Thomas* represents a single source of Jesus' teaching, but both documents show that the genre of instruction proved to be a useful vehicle of theological reflection. The Revelation accomplishes a similar aim by adopting the genre of prophecy: the Johannine paschal lamb becomes a primary category of meaning in a new, visual idiom.

The Practice of Eucharist

Our analysis suggests that considerations of practice—involving issues such as what was to be done with what, by whom, in which order, with what meaning and feeling—were formative of the eucharistic texts of the New Testament. Sequential interaction in types of eucharist is apparent even within the most primitive phases of the movement. During Jesus' own career, common meals altered in significance from occasions of purity in anticipation of the kingdom to surrogates of sacrifice.

Because the interaction is sequential, the sense of each type is plain only in the light of what went before. Even Jesus' practice in its first stage is sensible only within the cultural context of early Judaic practice. And the issue of cultic replacement which arose at the end of his career is understandable only within the context of what his meals had been and what his distinctive teaching regarding purity was. Generative exegesis enables us to see, not only how one practice became another (and therefore how traditions were transformed), but how the relationship between one practice and another established tendencies in the development of practices and their traditions.

Those tendencies were diverse, and do not constitute a simple, linear direction. The Petrine cycle presented its new Moses as an emblem of the purity God sought in his Temple, in accordance with a social setting more focused on Jerusalem than Jesus' had been. The Jacobean revision of the Petrine cycle introduced a limitation upon the understanding of purity which caused conflict among the practices and constituencies of the early Church. Non-Jews had no essential role in eucharist, in the literally paschal view of James' circle. Paul resisted the Jacobean revision, while the Synoptic tradition incorporated what had been a limitation as one element in a hero's preparation of a paschal symposium designed to benefit *all* who would follow him. John and the Revelation transmuted Passover into the symbol of Christ's personal body and blood, and therefore made eucharist into a Mystery.

The assumption within this developmental sequence is that eucharist is a communal meal in which the gathering attends to the kingdom according to the teaching of Jesus. But only the first type in the sequence makes that apparent. From that point onward, the fundamental issue concerns who should participate in the meal. At type 2, those in sympathy with the administration of the Temple are excluded. At type 3, acceptance of Jesus as offering a covenant of purity is demanded, while type 4 requires circumcision of male participants. Type 5 is inclusive relative to type 4, and is intentionally so, but its implicit requirement is that one accept the Synoptic account of Jesus' noble death as a sacrifice for sin. Type 6, finally, is knowingly and explicitly exclusive of Judaism in its portrayal of bread and wine as Jesus' personal body and blood.

A sequential reading of the pattern of development, then, reveals a common thread which is woven into the cloth of differing and sometimes conflicting social constituencies. But there is no question of one meaning simply producing the next, through the sequence. Rather, the meaning attributed to the meal within each constituency was, within the practice of that community, the *only* significance of the eucharist. The meal which was for Jesus a feast of the kingdom and then a provisional surrogate of sacrifice was for the Petrine cycle a covenantal sacrifice, for the Jacobean revision a Passover, for the Synoptic tradition a heroic *ḥaṭaʾat*, and for the Johannine synthesis the flesh and blood of the son of man.

For the appropriate group, each type was exactly what eucharist was, definitively and exclusively. There is no evidence that any community conceived of its practice as derivative, or as the explanation of a more primitive meaning; each practice was taken to be the standard, conveyed within the catechesis of the particular group. Eucharist was not, at base, a practice with a stable meaning which was variously expressed within the communities which contributed to the New Testament. Just as the development of practice was non-linear, subject to the particulars of the social constituencies in which the traditions were framed, so the meanings attributed to eucharist are only sensible as related to those constituencies.

A generative exegesis of eucharistic texts, therefore, may not conclude with a single meaning which is alleged to have occasioned the others. One of the principal findings of such an approach is rather that meaning itself is to some extent epiphenomenal, a consequence of a definable practice with its own initial sense being introduced into a fresh environment of people who in turn take up the practice as they understand it and produce their own meanings. The sense with which a practice is mediated to a community is therefore one measure of what that community will finally produce as its practice, but the initial meaning does not determine the final meaning.

The meanings conveyed by words must be the point of departure for a generative exegesis, because those meanings are our only access to what produced the texts to hand. But having gained that access, it becomes evident that eucharist is not a matter of the development of a single, basic meaning within several different environments. Those environments have themselves produced various meanings under the influence of a definable practice.

Eucharist was not simply handed on as a tradition. Eucharistic traditions were rather the catalyst which permitted communities to crystallize their own practice in oral or textual form. What they crystallized was a function of the practice which had been learned, palpable gestures with specified objects and previous meanings, along with the meaning and the emotional response which the community discovered in eucharist. There is no history of the tradition apart from a history of meaning, a history of emotional response, a history of practice: the practical result of a generative exegesis of eucharistic texts is that practice itself is an appropriate focus in understanding the New Testament.

APPENDICES

THE PHARISEES IN A RECENT DISPUTE

Consideration of a recent contribution from E.P. Sanders, *Jewish Law from Jesus to the Mishnah*, permits us to characterize Pharisaic concerns with the purity of food more precisely than has been possible before. Initially, however, we must clear up a rhetorical aporia in his third "Study," which is entitled "Did the Pharisees Eat Ordinary Food in Purity?" Recent investigations, most especially those of Jacob Neusner, would lead one to expect the answer "yes." Resoundingly and repeatedly, Sanders insists the answer is "no." The problem is that when Sanders says "no" in response to the question he poses, he means "yes."

What causes the confusion is that, while addressing his thematic question, Sanders is principally concerned to establish that Neusner's definition of the Pharisees "is entirely wrong" (p. 167, cf. 131, 173, 176, 232, 234, 235, 246, 248).[1] In fact, the disagreement with Neusner is a matter of assessing the kind and degree of purity the Pharisees observed, not in denying an interest in purity. That disagreement is informative, but a hasty reading of Sanders's presentation might lead some readers to conclude his difference with Neusner is more substantial than actually is the case.

What Sanders is concerned to deny is that "the Pharisees ate ordinary food at their own tables as if they were priests in the Temple" (p. 131, cf. 163-4). As he points out, if that were literally the case, the Pharisees could not have permitted any impure person to touch their food (p. 150; cf. Leviticus 7:19-21). Such a policy would have had consequences ranging from inconvenient to inhuman, for example as applied to women during their menstrual flow, men who experienced nocturnal emissions of semen, members of both sexes who suffered unusual discharges from their genitals, and "lepers." Perhaps the greatest difficulty posed by such a construction is that

---

[1] As in each citation of Sanders's work, unless otherwise specified, the references are to *Jewish Law from Jesus to the Mishnah. Five Studies* (London: SCM and New York: Trinity Press International, 1990).

of women after childbirth: a woman who bore a male child was not to touch a holy object (קֹדֶשׁ) or approach the sanctuary for forty days altogether (Leviticus 12:4), and eighty days in the case of a female child (v. 5). If, then, the Pharisees actually defined their meals as holy in the sense of Leviticus 12, they banned their women from their tables and their food when nutrition was vital to maternal health. As it happens, such a policy would not be without precedent, judged from the perspective of ethnographic studies, which document the withdrawal of certain normally key foods from women post-partem.[2] In such cases, of course, there are methods of coping with the apparently rigorous denial, such as substituting other foods or simple cheating. Sanders's court of appeal is common sense, rather than anthropology, but it would indeed seem odd to imagine that the systematic substitution of foods a month or two post partem, or the systematic evasion of a ban during the same period, would have been completely ignored in Mishnah.

As Sanders has it (p. 197), the potential problem posed by Leviticus 12 is resolved in the Mishnah (Niddah 10:6, 7): the קֹדֶשׁ of Leviticus 12:4 is taken to refer to most holy things eaten within the Temple, so that the stricture would not be applied to ordinary food. The passage is more subtle than Sanders indicates, although a more rigorous exegesis supports some of his general contentions. The issue initially is whether a woman during the period of blood-purifying (דַּם טוֹהַר, cf. דְּמֵי טָהֳרָה in Leviticus 12:4) is to pour water for the paschal offering. That interest is signal within the Mishnah, since there was an imperative that all the assembly of the congregation of Israel should slaughter the lamb (Pesaḥim 5:5, citing Exodus 12:6).[3] For that reason, a woman post-partem was initially (בָּרִאשׁוֹנָה) permitted to pour water for the Passover. But then the view was taken that, in regard to holy things (לְקֳדָשִׁים), she was comparable to someone who touched another who was corpse-unclean (so beth Hillel) or to someone who was himself corpse-unclean (so beth Shammai; Niddah 10:6).

The passage certainly does not refer to holy things as what priests

---

[2] Cf. Harris, pp. 236-242.

[3] There is some discussion of those with a genital flow, menstruants, and women post-partem eating lambs prepared in uncleanness (Pesaḥim 9:4), that is already susceptible of impurity. The proposition is rejected, but it is notable that Eliezer even countenances such people entering the Temple.

eat in the Temple: the reference is to what might be associated with an act of offering in the Temple. Actual consumption, as a matter of fact, would normally occur outside the Temple in the case of the lamb at Passover. The general argument, which Sanders supports, that the Pharisees were concerned with the conduct of the sacrificial cult, is confirmed here, but that concern is evidently broader than the specification of what priests eat and where they eat it. Moreover, Niddah 10:7 goes on to state that a woman post-partem may eat second tithe (a form of sacrifice; cf. Deuteronomy 14:22-29, from which the notion of a second tithe seems primarily to have emerged),[4] separate the priests' share of dough (חַלָּה), and prepare the heave-offering (תְּרוּמָה; Niddah 10:7). She is pure for some activities, including sacrificial eating, but not others. And eating the second tithe is by no stretch of the imagination portrayed as the activity of greatest sanctity. The underlying assumption of the passage is that there is a hierarchy of sanctity, of what belongs to God in his Temple, and an associated hierarchy of purity, of what rightly pertains to Israel in its land.[5] One must know what sort of holy object or gesture is at issue before one can know the appropriate point of intersection with Israel's purity: then one can say when, how, and by whom the pure becomes sacred.

Although Sanders has misconstrued Niddah 10:6, 7, his general observation, that the Pharisees were concerned with the regulation of the cult in the Temple, is unexceptionable and a matter of common consensus. Moreover, he is correct in asserting that the Pharisees "thought that priests' food had to be *handled* in purity" (p. 150, cf. pp. 193-195). The passage from Niddah shows, how-

---

[4] So Freyne, pp. 190-198; cf. Joachim Jeremias (tr. F.H. Cave and C.H. Cave), *Jerusalem in the Time of Jesus: An Investigation into Economic and Social Conditions during the New Testament Period* (London: SCM, 1969) 134-138, who cites Deuteronomy 26:12 in the LXX, Jubilees 32:8-14 and Tobit 1:6-8 in Sinaiticus as the earliest explicit evidence.

[5] Shabbath 14a provides an interesting illustration, in a dictum attributed to Joshua: "One who eats food of the first degree or eats food of the second degree is [himself in] the second degree; of the third degree, [in] the second degree in respect of *qodesh*, but not in the second degree in respect of *terumah*, this referring to *hullin* subjected to the purity of *terumah*" (cf. the predictably stricter construction of Eliezer). The dictum is an explicit instance in which, *pace* Sanders, ordinary food is related directly to strictures of priestly food. Cf. Tosephta Demai 2:2, cited in Gedalyahu Alon, "The Bounds of the Laws of Levitical Cleanness," *Jews, Judaism and the Classical World* (tr. I. Abrahams; Jerusalem: Magnes, 1977) 190-234, 207.

ever, that the issues of priests' food (the share of dough and heave-offering generally) and second tithe (a biblically mandated sacrifice) are treated as of lesser sanctity than Passover, since a woman during the period of the blood of purification might handle the first and eat the second, but could not touch the third.[6] The hierarchy of concerns rests less on eating *per se* (whether priestly or lay) than on the understanding of the degree of proximity to the conduct of the cult a given object or activity involves. The greater the sanctity implied, the greater the purity required (cf. Ḥagigah 2:7 for an explicit articulation of the principle).

Once the foundations of the Pharisaic concern with purity are laid bare, the dichotomy Sanders attempts to maintain between "priestly" purity and "ordinary" purity (pp. 163, 164, 176) is seen to be untenable. Sanders himself writes:

> . . . the suitability of food for an ordinary Israelite was a necessary but by no means a sufficient condition for its acceptibility (*sic!*) by the priests (p. 176).

Two sorts of propriety (one of purity, the other of sanctity) are indeed related; that has been one of the seminal insights of Neusner's contributions. But a woman post-partem could not prepare the Passover, which she was evidently impure for, although she could prepare (the implicitly less sacred) priests' food in the case of heave-offering. The systemic issue is proximity to sacrifice in the Temple. Normally, priests enjoy greater proximity to the cult in Mishnah's scheme; regular practice comports with genealogical claims of sanctity involved in the Torah. But the cases of Passover and heave-offering in Niddah 10:6, 7 show that priestly sanctity was taken to be relative to sacred function, and not inherent. Moreover, the sacred and the pure cannot be related by a single continuum: there are categories of clean, edible animals which would not be offered in the Temple (cf. Deuteronomy 14:5 with 12:15-19). Purity is not

---

[6] An unanswered question here is whether a woman during that period might eat Passover, since the ordinary remedy for those who were impure at the time of Passover in Nissan was to prepared a second, one month later (during Iyar). The extensive time required for purification after childbirth would not assure that the Passover of Iyar would meet the case; for the same reason women with unusual flows (Pesaḥim 8:5; 9:4) constitute only a partial analogy. In Babli, the problem is nonetheless resolved at the end of a discussion attributed to Rabina, the Babylonian Amora (Pesaḥim 90b), by assimilating the category of a woman after childbirth to that of a menstruant: both are excluded from eating Passover.

a condition which is sufficient or necessary to establish sanctity: it is simply beside the point, because the pure and holy are intersecting continua, not gradations along a single plane.

The conceptual problem of Sanders's analysis is that there are not two purities, the one of Israel and the other of priests; there are rather greater and lesser degrees of purity which, within Mishnah, must be coordinated with the sanctity of given moments. Sanders in fact recognizes that the Pharisees located their own meals within a continuum, one of whose extremes intersected the sanctity of the Temple. He admits, almost as a matter of course, that the Pharisees did insist that holy food be handled in a state of purity (pp. 136, 137, 193-199,[7] 229) and the consideration of Niddah 10:6, 7 above has already established the point: the sanctity of the Passover was such that a woman post-partem might not be involved in preparing it, although she might routinely set aside *t^erumah*. The concerns of sanctity clearly influenced constructions of purity, and unless one appreciates that the two continua are interacting in the literature, confusion must be the result. The same consideration applies to the Pharisaic extension of the definition of impurity from a corpse, and their attempt to avoid the extended area. Sanders himself calls the teaching "a kind of gesture towards living like priests" (p. 166, 190), but does not observe that his remark undercuts his own argument.

Sanders sometimes tries to explain away the Pharisaic concern with purity which he himself documents. He accepts, for example, a closer connection between the Pharisees and the Ḥaverim than he formerly maintained (p. 154). He cites Demai 2:2, where one who undertakes to be faithful (הַמְקַבֵּל עָלָיו לִהְיוֹת נֶאֱמָן) must tithe what he eats, what he sells, and what he buys, and not accept hospitality from an עַם הָאָרֶץ. Demai 2:3 is of particular interest to Sanders (cf. pp. 34, 155, 165, 202, 238, 350 n. 10, 358 n. 5); it specifies that a חָבֵר must not sell an עַם הָאָרֶץ wet or dry produce, and must not buy wet produce from him.[8] That stricture clearly reflects a construction of purity among the *ḥaverim* which sets them apart from other

---

[7] His citations of Isaiah 66:20 and *Damascus Document* 11:18-20 are quite useful by way of precedent.

[8] The passage goes on to make the rule against hospitality more reciprocal, insofar as he cannot have an עַם הָאָרֶץ as a guest when that person is wearing his own (probably impure) garments.

Jews by impinging upon the foods one might eat and trade, and the commerce and fellowship one might enjoy. The formulation of the strictures so far considered perhaps derives from the second century, but Sanders plausibly relates the concern in regard to wet produce to the discussion in Demai 6:6 of a limitation of the market of olives (pp. 33, 163, 165, 202, 231, 237, 238, 250, 304, 350 n. 10). The operative point is that olives become moist, and therefore susceptible of impurity (as the Mishnah understands Leviticus, cf. the tractate Makhshirin); on the same basis, one would not buy wet produce from an עַם הָאָרֶץ, or provide him with produce which was either wet or might become so.[9]

As Sanders points out, the biblical precedent for a concern with that sort of impurity is provided in Leviticus 11:32-38 (cf. pp. 148, 172 [in respect of the tractate Makhshirin], 200-202), *a passage which Sanders admits the Pharisees interpreted to construe intentionally moist food generally as susceptible of impurity from swarming insects and animals.* Leviticus speaks of only wetted seeds (v. 38) and of food wetted from an unclean vessel (v. 34): Pharisaic practice makes moist food as such the issue. Sanders considers Mishnaic discussions of how much of a swarming thing needed to touch food for it to be rendered unclean, and concludes that the Levitical ordinance was "not *extended* but *reduced*" by the Pharisees (pp. 200, 201). Although he repeatedly appeals to a social construction of history in his book, he apparently judges the extension or reduction of requirements of purity, not by common practice (such as among the עַמְמֵי הָאָרֶץ), but by his own idealized understanding of what a strict construction of Leviticus should have produced. Yet in social terms, if one group of people restricts their consumption of food, their trade, and their fellowship with groups of the same religious system on the grounds of purity,[10] what can their policy be called but an extension of notions of cleanness and uncleanness?

Sanders gives us Pharisees who are not concerned with priestly purity, except when they are, and who do not care for their own purity, except when they do. His distinction between "priestly" purity and "ordinary purity" is heuristically useful, but misleading at the

---

[9] Just that point is emphasized by Alon, "The Bounds," 207, 208. Cf. also Eduyoth 1:14, with its assumption that the earthenware vessel of an עַם הָאָרֶץ is of suspect purity, and Sanders pp. 189, 192, 231, 250.

[10] Cf. Sanders's final description of the Pharisees, pp. 240, 248.

level of a systematic understanding of the practices he describes. He
acknowledges that Pharisees kept their own "ordinary" food pure
(p. 148, 172), although he does not consider that doing so in areas
of significant non-Jewish trade, such as Galilee, might have made
the Pharisees stand out, even from their Jewish contemporaries.[11]
He accepts that their hand washing "may be a pharisaic innovation" (pp. 203, 204) derived from their concern for the handling of
priestly food (p. 229), that their fine-tuning of the definition of that
impurity which derived from those with genital discharges mediated
between priestly and ordinary practice (pp. 205, 206), and that they
promulgated a distinctive design of bath for the purpose of purification which diverged from priestly norms (pp. 214-227).[12] Moreover, he accepts that there was a line of development in the Pharisees' practice which ran "from washing hands before handling the
priests' food to washing hands before their own special meals and
sabbaths" (pp. 229, 230).

Sanders explicitly heads one of his sections, "Ordinary food in
purity" (p. 231): he shows that the answer to the question posed by
the title of his chapter ("Did the Pharisees Eat Ordinary Food in
Purity?") is "yes." He also shows that the Pharisees' "ordinary"
food was unlike the common run of the ordinary (p. 233), and that
they attempted to influence the conduct of worship in the Temple,
and particularly the preparation of foodstuffs for such worship. All
such traits strike him as amounting to a "'minor gesture'" towards
living as priests (p. 232), although he then qualifies the assertion,
acknowledging that the "word 'minor', however, probably misleads
with regard to their own intention" (p. 235). The only reason for
the confusion is that his purpose is more to deny Neusner's influence
upon him than to characterize the position of the Pharisees:

> The full analogy between the altar and the common table which
> Neusner proposes is neither implied in Leviticus nor specified in
> pharisaic material (p. 176).

He strains out "full," the adjectival gnat, and silently gulps down
the substantive camel.[13] His argument simply confirms the insight

---

[11] Cf. Freyne, pp. 168-175, 256, 257.

[12] A related issue is observed by Sanders to lie behind the destruction of a
trough in the Temple (p. 227, citing Mikwaoth 4:5).

[13] Sanders also asserts that the focus of the Pharisees was not "the purity of
their own food" (p. 242); rather "study probably consumed more time than any-

that the Pharisees were possessed of a characteristic concern with purity which made them appear distinctive, and which they attempted to influence others with (p. 247). Any appearance to the contrary is an artifact of Sanders's rhetorical stance.

The importance of Sanders's contribution, once it is appreciated how he says what he says, is that it marks a definitive shift in the secondary literature: there is now broad agreement that Neusner is correct, and that the issue of purity marked out Pharisaic practice from the practice of priests and of Jews generally. Moreover, Sanders has documented within Mishnah what has sometimes been disputed, that the Pharisaic construction of purity defined persons who might be approached as well as foods that might be handled.[14]

---

thing else" (p. 236, cf. pp. 244, 247, 252). That position, or rather that return to a position one might have thought discredited long ago, is not defended by argument.

[14] Cf. Gedalyahu Alon, "The Levitical Uncleanness of the Gentiles," *Jews, Judaism*, 146-189, and "The Bounds," with its brilliant discussion of the concept of "extension." Alon himself uses the term in quotation marks and does not confuse the refinement of principles with greater stringency or legalism, a confusion which appears to burden Sanders's analysis.

THE CONSTRUCTION OY MH...EΩΣ [AN] IN ASSEVERATIONS OF JESUS

In Matthew 5:26//Luke 12:59, the warning that you will not leave the prison until you have paid your last penny is no promise of departure after payment, but an injunction to avoid Roman litigation (cf. Matthew 5:25; Luke 12:57, 58), which might cost you both your wealth and your freedom. The statement in Matthew 23:39 and Luke 13:35, ''You will not see me until you say, Blessed is he who comes in the name of the Lord,'' is manifestly odd. Within the narrative context, it is evident that Jesus *will* be seen in Jerusalem; within the context of early Christian eschatology, it is equally plain that joining in Psalm 118 *will not* effect an appearance of the son of man. In other words, the apparently causal relationship between the phrases breaks down on closer inspection. Their linkage is rather in their assertion together: you will one day join in saying the (eschatological) Hallel, and I will not show my face in Jerusalem. So understood, Matthew 26:29//Mark 14:25//Luke 22:18 would mean both that Jesus envisaged drinking new wine in the feast of the kingdom, and that he bound himself not to drink wine which was not associated with the celebration of the kingdom.

The passages which have been cited are adduced by Beyer as among those in which the emphasis must surely be taken to fall on what comes after ''until,''[1] and that is an important insight. It is equally important to recognize that the usage is congruent with that of the Septuagint. Genesis 28:15, cited in chapter 1, instances the usage of οὐ μή...ἕως for לא-עד, as one might expect, and somewhat similar cases are presented in Genesis 19:22; 29:8; Numbers 23:24b; Ezra 4:21; Nehemiah 13:19. In fact, however, the last

---

[1] Klaus Beyer, *Semitische Syntax im Neuen Testament*: Studien zur Umwelt des Neuen Testaments 1 (Göttingen: Vandenhoeck und Ruprecht, 1962) 132, 133 (n. 1). There are other examples cited from the Synoptics, but they do not belong to the category of asseverations. They are simply assertions (cf. Matthew 24:39) or imperatives (cf. Matthew 17:9); Beyer's work may be consulted for other instances outside the Synoptics.

usages cited do not repeat the pattern of οὐ μή with ἕως [ἄν]; the redundant negation does not appear, and the temporal particle varies (between ἕως in Genesis 19:22; 29:8; Numbers 23:24b through ἕως ὀπίσω in 2 Esdras 23:19 and ὅπως in 2 Esdras 4:21). In most of those cases, moreover, an evidently temporal and causal relationship between the phrases does obtain. The single exception to that rule might be instructive. Ezra 4:21 in Aramaic reads:

וקריתא דך לא תתבנא עד-מני טעמא יתשׂם.

The Septuagint at 2 Esdras 4:21 gives us:

καὶ ἡ πόλις ἐκείνη οὐκ οἰκοδομηθήσεται ἔτι, ὅπως ἀπὸ τῆς γνώμης.

The translators clearly evidence an awareness that לא-עד need not be taken in a temporal sense.[2] Unfortunately, Beyer does not distinguish between temporal and non-temporal usages of the construction, and even conflates the usage of עד-אם/εἰ-ἕως (in Psalm 132:3-5) within his list. But the evidence of the Septuagint appears clear: לא-עד need not be taken in a temporal sense, and οὐ μή-ἕως might be the rendering when it is not to be so taken.

Beyer's conflation of usages, and of the same basic usage with distinctive meanings, obscures a crucial feature of the Septuagintal meaning of οὐ μή-ἕως. Not only, as we have seen, may the construction be used to convey a non-temporal usage of לא-עד; in Isaiah 55:11, the construction is *introduced* in order to render לא-כי אם, and the meaning is clearly atemporal, an insistence that God's word will not return to him empty, but accomplish what he desires. Just as in the cases of Jesus' sayings, the phrases coordinated by οὐ μή and ἕως amount to vigorous assertions in tandem: God's word will perform what he desires and will not return empty to him (ever). The usage of the construction in the Septuagint demonstrates that it may be used without a temporal reference, and even that a translator might introduce the usage οὐ μή-ἕως simply in order to render two coordinated assertions, one positive and one negative.

Beyer observes that the usage of ''until'' is not to be pressed temporally:

---

[2] It may be of interest that, in an appearance of the idiom in Leviticus Rabbah 24:3, the Aramaic adds specific reference to time (זמן) in order to assure the temporal sense of the construction.

Jedoch bezeichnet "bis" auch nach einer Negation im Sem. und im Griech. öfters nur die Grenze, innerhalb derer die Haupthandlung betrachtet wird, ohne dass damit gesagt sein soll, dass sich danach etwas ändert...

He then instances Genesis 28:15; Isaiah 22:14; 42:4, among other passages; the second of his examples is an instance of the type we have noted above, in that οὐκ-ἕως renders עַד-אִם. The cognate examples from the Synoptics he proposes include 16:28//Mark 9:1//Luke 9:27;[3] Matthew 24:34//Luke 21:32; Matthew 5:18; 10:23.[4] He is correct in insisting that the construction opens the possibility that the intended meaning simply involves assertion (by means of the clause following ἕως) and negation (by means of the clause following οὐ μή), without the postulation of a temporal relationship between the two.

Other considerations will also need to be brought to bear, to determine whether or to what extent a temporal aspect is operative within the usage. It is of note, for example, that the Markan parallel of Matthew 24:34//Luke 21:32 employs, not οὐ μή-ἕως, but οὐ μή-μέχρις οὗ (Mark 13:30), an emphatically temporal construction. Similar usages of the relative pronoun (but with ἕως) are associated with vigorously temporal assertions in Acts 23:12, 14, 21.[5] By that criterion, the usage in Luke 22:16, οὐ μή-ἕως ὅτου, and in v. 18, οὐ μή-ἕως οὗ, should be taken as in the nature of vows of abstinence, as is suggested in chapter 1.[6]

---

3 Beyer's observation occasioned my exegesis of the passage, on the understanding that those who would not taste death were figures such as Moses and Elijah, who stood as guarantors that God's kingdom will come in power. Cf. *God in Strength. Jesus' Announcement of the Kingdom*: Studien zum Neuen Testament und seiner Umwelt 1 (Freistadt: Plöchl, 1979, reprinted within "The Biblical Seminar;" Sheffield: Sheffield Academic Press, 1987); "The Transfiguration: Dominical Assurance and Apostolic Vision," *New Testament Studies* 27 (1980) 115-124.

4 Beyer also cites Matthew 1:25; 1 Corinthians 4:5, but the formal hallmarks of the dominical asseveration are not present, the sayings are not attributed to Jesus, and the meaning of the verses may in fact include a temporal dimension.

5 John 13:38 marches in the opposite direction, by employing οὐ μή-ἕως when the Synoptics do not (cf. Matthew 26:34; Mark 14:30; Luke 22:34; the last usage being the closest approximation to John's). John perhaps represents a diminished sensibility of the meaning of the locution.

6 The sense is similar to Luke 1:26, although the construction is different.

JESUS' PURPOSE IN JERUSALEM:
PETER RICHARDSON'S CONTRIBUTION REGARDING
THE HALF SHEKEL

In an article which appeared just after the publication of *The Temple of Jesus*, Peter Richardson has made a crucial contribution to the understanding of Jesus' perspective upon the collection of the half shekel.[1] He shows conclusively that the Tyrian shekel was not—as is frequently maintained—aniconic: "The coins uniformly have the god Melkart (or Herakles) on the obverse and a Tyrian (Ptolemaic) eagle on the reverse (see illustrations), with the inscription 'Tyre the holy and inviolable.'"[2] Richardson surmises that such coins would have been offensive to many Jews, Jesus included: "I can almost hear Jesus—and for that matter the revolutionaries in 66 CE—say, then give to Melkart what is his and don't sully the Temple with foreign gods."[3]

Richardson's analysis amounts to an independent argument for assessing Jesus on the basis of a categorical concern for purity, and he raises the possibility (which I was developing at nearly the same time) that Jesus objected to the selling of pigeons in the Temple "on the grounds of ritual cleanness" (p. 521, see also pp. 522, 523). That purity was a focal issue within Jesus' activity, and that it was a determinative concern in what transpired in Jerusalem, is common ground in Richardson's analysis and my own. We have both identified Jesus in historical terms as a teacher of purity.

The points at which we differ are nonetheless important. Where Richardson makes the image on the Tyrian shekel the object of Jesus' concern, I understand Matthew 17:24-27 (for reasons discussed in chapter 2) as an argument against any required tax levied by the Temple upon Israelites. There is also, in my opinion, a problem of

---

[1] Peter Richardson, "Why Turn the Tables? Jesus' Protest in the Temple Precincts," *Society of Biblical Literature 1992 Seminar Papers* (ed. E.H. Lovering; Atlanta: Scholars, 1992) 507-523.

[2] P. 514, see pp. 513-518.

[3] P. 519.

anachronism manifest in any direct comparison between Jesus and the revolutionaries of A.D. 66: after all, the revolt against Rome did in fact involve striking coins, an issue Jesus famously steered clear of (see Matthew 22:15-22//Mark 12:13-17//Luke 20:20-26).[4]

Richardson makes the image on the shekel Jesus' motivation, although there is no saying of Jesus which addresses the matter, and—as Richardson acknowledges—"no explicit evidence . . . suggests Tyrian shekels were found to be repugnant" by teachers of his period (p. 518). The coins may have been seen as far from ideal, as the minting of coins by the revolutionaries who came after Jesus might suggest, but they were silver, while "Jewish authorities, almost uniformly, were forbidden during the whole period of foreign domination from minting silver coins" (p. 515). If something corresponding to the "shekel of the sanctuary" (Exodus 30:13) was to be contributed in silver (see Exodus 38:25, 26), options were therefore limited, and the Tyrian shekel was of consistent quality, and did not bear Roman symbols. Moreover, the ancient connection between Tyre and the foundation of the Temple (see 1 Kings 5:15-32; 7:13-51) may have been held to have been a precedent for the custom. But whatever the discussion that stood behind the custom, as Richardson says, "The simple fact is that Roman coinage was not used for Temple dues and Tyrian coinage was" (p. 517). Precisely because that was a simple fact, it seems strained to me to attribute to Jesus an idiosyncratic scruple over the coin, when the relevant tradition (Matthew 17:24-27) concerns taxing Israelites as Israelites, not the instrument of payment.

Richardson acknowledges (p. 520), but does not solve, a serious defect in the reasoning we must attribute to Jesus on the theory he aimed to remove Tyrian shekels from the Temple. Every year, money changing—for the sake of collecting the tax—went on publicly throughout Israel. The process commenced a full month before Passover, with a proclamation (Shekalim 1:1), and exchanges were set up in the provinces ten days *before* they were set up in the Temple (Shekalim 1:3). According to Josephus the tax was also gathered among those resident outside the land of Israel (*War* VII, 218; *Antiquities* XVIII, 312), so that the procedure itself would not have been stopped by the sort of interruption the Gospels in aggregate

---

[4] For a discussion of the problem of such anachronism in the analysis of S.G.F. Brandon, cf. *The Temple of Jesus*, 92-100, 128, 138.

describe. If Jesus focused his attention on money changing in the Temple alone, then, he could not have interrupted the collection of the half shekel generally. Failing in that purpose, he also would not have stopped the iconic shekels being brought into the Temple, which is what Richardson supposes his motivation was.

But then, had Jesus succeeded in preventing the collection of the half shekel generally, he would have interfered with the many purposes which it was designed to support.[5] The upkeep of the Temple appears to have been countenanced by Jesus, on virtually any sensible reading of his position,[6] and maintenance for the building and its personnel was provided out of the tax. A programmatic attempt on Jesus' part to cleanse the Temple of Tyrian shekels would have been inconsistent with his overall loyalty to cultic institutions, as well as hopelessly unrealistic.

There is no evidence that Jesus objected to the image on the Tyrian shekel as such; turning over the tables in the Temple would have prevented neither the collection of the half shekel nor the introduction of the Tyrian shekel into the treasury; Jesus in any case was not motivated by a desire to interfere with the physical maintenance of the Temple. Jesus may well have objected to the tax of a half shekel, as Matthew 17:24-27 suggests. But it is by no means certain that he did, and even *if* he did, a single onslaught of the sort described in the Gospels would not have amounted to an effective protest against it. On the other hand, Jesus' action in the Temple is comprehensible within the concerns of Pharisaic Judaism. It was an occupation designed to prevent the sacrifice of animals acquired on the site, in trading which involved commerce within the Temple and obscured the understanding that those animals were fully the property of Israel (as distinct from the priesthood or the Temple). His action, of course, might well have upset financial arrangements for the sale of such animals,[7] but such incidental disturbance is to be distin-

---

[5] Cf. Exodus 30:11-16; Nehemiah 10:33, 34; 2 Chronicles 24:4-14; Josephus, *Jewish War* VII, 218; *Antiquities* XVIII, 312; Philo, *De specialibus legibus* I, 76-78; Shekalim 4:1-6.

[6] Cf. Matthew 5:23, 24; 23:16-23; Matthew 8:1-4//Mark 1:40-45//Luke 5:12-16 cf. 17:11-19. It is by no means necessary to hold such traditions accurately reflect Jesus' position in order to appreciate that their attribution to him makes it unlikely he opposed the institution of the Temple as such as well as necessary provisions for it.

[7] Cf. the arrangement envisaged in Shekalim 5:4, and the reference to κέρμα in John 2:15, where the term refers to money of lesser value than was probably in-

guished from a deliberate attempt to prevent the collection of the half shekel, which would have required coordinated activity throughout Israel (and beyond).

In his emphasis upon the issue of the image on the Tyrian shekel, Richardson is inclined to diminish the importance of the contention over where animals for sacrifice were to be sold. He does acknowledge that Jesus may have objected to selling pigeons in the outer court on the grounds of purity (p. 521). But the matter for him is strictly one of pigeons, in that he takes the Johannine reference to sheep and oxen (2:14, 15) to be incorrect.[8] It is, of course, conceivable that the contention was simply over the vending of birds, and that the inclusion of other animals in the description is an example of Christian exaggeration. But before that argument is accepted, it should be borne in mind that, while John alone mentions sheep and oxen in so many words, Matthew (21:12) and Mark (11:15) refer to those selling and buying in the Temple before they mention the "seats" of the dove vendors. The natural inference is that both Gospels are first citing commercial activity in general, and then physical arrangements which attended the keeping of doves in particular.[9]

Which animals were involved in the trade to which Jesus took exception cannot not be determined precisely; indeed, Luke merely refers to vending in the most general of terms (19:43). But Luke does not mention the tables of the moneychangers at all: that may be an indication that they represent embellishment in the passage, rather than the vendors of various animals. After all, the Synoptics (Matthew 21:13//Mark 11:17//Luke 19:46), John (2:16) and *Thomas* (1. 64.12[10]) all agree that Jesus spoke against commercial activity in

---

volved in the exchange for shekels, and more likely associated with trade in animals. The latter passage is treated of in Chilton, "[ὡς] φραγέλλιον ἐκ σχοινίων [John 2:15]," *Templum Amicitiae. Essays on the Second Temple presented to Ernst Bammel* (ed. W. Horbury; Sheffield: Sheffield Academic Press, 1991) 330-344.

[8] P. 521, citing Sanders by way of support, and Joseph Klausner to the effect that the sale of doves and pigeons, although ordinarily located on the Mount of Olives, took place in the Royal Basilica during Jesus' time in Jerusalem. That is just the sort of observation (mediated through the work of Victor Eppstein) which lies behind my analysis.

[9] So, for example, Alan Hugh McNeile, *The Gospel according to St. Matthew* (London: Macmillan, 1957 [from 1915]) 298, 299 and Henry Barclay Swete, *The Gospel according to St Mark* (London: Macmillan, 1915 [from 1909]) 255, 256.

[10] For the probable association of the saying with the Temple in the tradition prior to *Thomas*, see *The Temple of Jesus*, 118.

the Temple. Why should we not proceed on the supposition that such a consideration brought him into conflict with the authorities there during the period of Caiaphas' innovation?

Finally, to begin with the issue of vending animals, and to understand the reference to the moneychangers as an embellishment, makes better sense both of Jesus' activity and the development of the Gospels. If Jesus led a revolt against the collection of the Tyrian shekel, his effort was ill conceived and doomed to failure from the outset. But if Jesus was motivated by a particular theory of purity (as discussed in chapter 2), it was natural for him—as it was for any teacher concerned with purity—to teach in the vicinity of the Temple. The innovation of Caiaphas would particularly have offended him, given his definition of purity in terms of what was offered directly by forgiven Israel. Monetary surrogacy in sacrifice seemed to him an offence. His occupation of the Temple was aimed against the wares and the currency of cultic commercialism. Within the traditions of early Christianity, once the events of Jesus' last days were placed during the season of Passover (see chapter 4), it was natural to associate a dispute over money with the collection of the half shekel. In that the collection of the half shekel had been a feature of Judaism which was considered typical (as well as contentious) within the Graeco-Roman world,[11] and because the *fiscus iudaicus* kept the memory of the institution alive, the identification of the coins of the vendors with the Tyrian shekels of the moneychangers was a natural development.

---

[11] See E. Mary Smallwood, *The Jews under Roman Rule*: Studies in Judaism in Late Antiquity 20 (Leiden: Brill, 1976) 143 and Chilton, "A Coin of Three Realms (Matthew 17.24-27)," *The Bible in Three Dimensions. Essays in celebration of forty years of Biblical Studies in the University of Sheffield*: Journal for the Study of the Old Testament, Supplement Series 87 (eds D. J.A. Clines, S.E. Fowl, S.E. Porter; Sheffield: JSOT, 1990) 269-282, 272, 273.

ARAMAIC RETROVERSIONS OF JESUS' SAYINGS

Within chapter 1, it has been argued that a dominical saying best explains the formation of Matthew 26:29//Mark 14:25//Luke 22:18). The foundational saying plainly speaks the language of anticipation, and warrants that each meal is a pledge that the kingdom is to come: "I shall again not drink of the fruit of the vine until I drink it new in the kingdom of God."[1]

The promise is conveyed by means of a Semitic locution which stresses that the kingdom will come and that Jesus will drink wine in no way but in its celebration, as has been discussed, and is easily rendered in Aramaic:

לָא עוֹד אִשְׁתֵּי מִפְּרִי גָפְנָא עַד דִּי אִשְׁתֵּיה חֲדַתָּא בְּמַלְכָתָא אֱלָהָא.

An introductory formula such as בְּקָשְׁתָּא אָמַרְנָא לְכוֹן ("In truth, I say to you") may have been used at an Aramaic stage in the transmission of the saying, or ἀμὴν λέγω ὑμῖν may have been introduced at a latter stage.[2] In either case, the intention of the saying within its originating context was to assure Jesus' followers that each meal taken in fellowship was a warrant of the festal kingdom which was shortly to come, and Jesus himself undertook to consume wine in no other way.

Retroversion into Aramaic is only to be recommended when the literary history of a given passage commends an Aramaic tradition as the most plausible explanation for the present form of the text. In the present case, the locution οὐ μή-ἕως, the asseveration "amen," and the reference to the kingdom of God may all be taken to suggest that the originating language of the saying was not Greek, and the probability that Jesus was the original speaker may also be taken to encourage retroversion into Aramaic.

---

[1] Cf. Appendix 2, "The construction οὐ μή...ἕως [ἄν] in asseverations of Jesus."

[2] Cf. Chilton, "'Amen': an Approach through Syriac Gospels," *Zeitschrift für die neutestamentliche Wissenschaft* 69 (1978) 203-211 and *Targumic Approaches to the Gospels. Essays in the Mutual Definition of Judaism and Christianity*: Studies in Judaism (Lanham and London: University Press of America, 1986) 15-23.

Where possible, the forms and vocabulary chosen here have been attested in written sources in Palestinian Aramaic from the period of Jesus, among his immediate predecessors and successors.[3] That is clearly the appropriate procedure, when the interest is in any sense philological. It is also appropriate to invoke later sources in Aramaic, where it is a question of attempting to elucidate the early Judaism of which Jesus and his movement were one product, because there is a dearth of contemporary sources.[4] In the present treatment, our initial approach has been along the lines of the meanings inferred within the probable circles of transmission which produced the Gospels. But now that it is a question of retroversion into Aramaic, the grammatical and lexical forms should obvious derive from the first century.[5]

The Genesis Apocryphon attests several of the words proposed here (often in the same forms) as Jesus' usages: בְּקָשְׁתָא (2.5, 22 [cf. 7, 10, 18]); אמר (2.2); אִשְׁתֵּי (21.20);[6] מִפְּרִי (2.15);[7] בְּמַלְכְּתָא (21.2). Other elements are attested elsewhere (or as well, in the case of בְּמַלְכְּתָא) in the scrolls from Qumran: לכון (4Q Enoch Giants[a] 2.6; 1Q Unidentified 8.2); לָא עוֹד (4Q Testuz 2); בְּמַלְכְּתָא (1Q Testament Levi 1.1, 2; 3.1; 4Q Pseudo-Daniel 4; 4Q Nabonidus 1.2;[8] 11Q Targum Job 11.1; 30.5; 4Q "Messianic" Text 1.10; 4Q Visions Amran 2.6). The terms אֱלָהָא, לָא, and עַד are ubiquitous.

The absence of certain words from the Palestinian corpus ought simply to serve as a reminder that the corpus is both slight and defective. The construction לֹא-עַד is endemic within Hebrew, Biblical Aramaic, Mishnaic Hebrew, and Targumic Aramaic; it requires no attestation at Qumran in order to be presupposed. The fact that גֶּפְנָא does not appear, while כרמא does (*Genesis Apocryphon* 12.13),

---

[3] Cf. Joseph A. Fitzmyer and Daniel J. Harrington, *A Manual of Palestinian Aramaic Texts*: Biblica et Orientalia (Rome: Biblical Institute Press, 1978).

[4] Cf. Chilton, *A Galilean Rabbi and His Bible. Jesus' own interpretation of Isaiah* (London: SPCK, 1984).

[5] Given the state of the published evidence, the pointing of the consonantal retroversions here proposed is inferential.

[6] If, after all, one wanted to accept μεθ' ὑμῶν from Matthew 26:29 as dominical, עמכון in 5/6 Ḥever Letter of Bar Kokba 11.2 would provide a precedent (although not an antecedent!).

[7] The form has inclined me away from the usage of separated prepositions, as from a later period.

[8] In view of this passage and similar usages, I prefer not to use דִי between אֱלָהָא and בְּמַלְכְּתָא.

should not prevent us from seeing that a first century speaker of Aramaic did not need to use the word for an entire vineyard in order to refer to grape juice. The absence of the term "new" (חֲדַתָּא) is likewise simply bad luck. One always needs to bear in mind that the Palestinian texts, occasional, fragmentary, and countervailing as they frequently are, may only be held to be a standard of the sort of Aramaic Jesus may plausibly be held to have spoken. They do not constitute a Rosetta Stone for the decoding of his teaching.

In his commentary on Luke, Joseph Fitzmyer retroverts both Luke 22:19b, 20 and Mark 14:22, 23 into Aramaic.[9] The difficulty with such exercises is that they give the appearance that traditions are primitive without engaging in any argument to that effect. In Fitzmyer's case, the retroversion conflates the dominical meaning with the Petrine emphasis on the theme of the covenant of which the meal is a memorial (cf. chapter 3). For that matter, Fitzmyer accepts the Jacobean chronology too readily, as well as the order of bread before wine (cf. chapter 4). Finally, Fitzmyer even retroverts "which is given for you" (Luke 22:19, clearly a phrase from a late development in eucharistic theology, and christology),[10] "new covenant" (Luke 22:20), "for you" (in the Lukan expansion regarding the "cup," 22:20), and "for many" (in the Markan expasion regarding the "blood," 14:24), all of which represent explanatory developments within the Hellenistic environment of the Synoptic tradition (cf. chapter 5).

The sole justification Fitzmyer provides for his global retroversion is the general statement that the Lukan wording "is often judged today as an echo of an Antiochene liturgy" while Mark "may reflect a Jerusalem liturgy."[11] Inasmuch as the Gospels as a whole may be held to be an "echo" of Christian practice, or to "reflect" it, there is no reason not to translate whatever Synoptic text one pleases into Aramaic, but the exercise obviously does not amount to an analysis of what is translated. Fitzmyer is linguistically and philologically correct in insisting upon the usage of texts of Middle Aramaic (rather than Byzantine or Targumic Aramaic) in

---

[9] Cf. Joseph A. Fitzmyer, *The Gospel According to Luke (X-XXIV)*: The Anchor Bible 28 A (Garden City: Doubleday, 1985) 1394.

[10] Cf. Perrin, "The Use of παραδιδόναι in Connection with the Passion of Jesus in the New Testament," *Der Ruf Jesu und die Antwort der Gemeinde* (eds E. Lohse, C. Burchard, B. Schaller; Göttingen: Vandenhoeck und Ruprecht, 1970) 204-212.

[11] Fitzmyer, p. 1393.

retroversions of Jesus' sayings, but his work is of lesser usefulness in deciding what should be retroverted and why. He translates into good, early Aramaic what fashion dictates should be so rendered, with the result that Christian theology from Petrine, Jacobean and Hellenistic phases in the development of the movement is attributed to Jesus.

Fitzmyer's Aramaic may be trusted, then, but his literary history is simplistic. He provides wording which he collates against the texts of Palestinian Aramaic which he edited, although at times he must retrovert unattested forms, as I have done above. For the present purpose, his collation is simply accepted.[12] After we have removed the later material which he unwisely retroverted, we are left with the following saying of Jesus, as analyzed in chapter 2:

דֵין דַּמִי דִי שְׁפִיךְ
דֵין בְּסְרִי הוּא.

For reasons discussed in chapter 3, at the Cephan stage of transmission, the saying became:

דֵין בְּסְרִי הוּא עֲבִידוּ דָא לְדָכְרָנִי
דֵין דַּמִי דִי קַיָמָא הוּא דִי שְׁפִיךְ.

The retroversion would account for a notably clumsy Greek text on the basis of an Aramaic couplet characterized by assonance in the first line, alliteration in the second, and—most importantly—a symmetrical structure of four beats per line. Certain features of the formulation, which are awkward in Greek, are easily understood as Aramaic expansions of the dominical saying. Τὸ αἷμά μου τῆς διαθήκης, which has spawned a literature all its own, has been produced by appending דִי קַיָמָא to דֵין דַּמִי; formally, the device is all the more natural because דִי already appeared in the dominical saying. Similarly, הוּא in the statement about blood (which produces an extraneous ἐστιν in Greek) has been picked up from the statement about flesh and repeated, in accordance with the ritual tendency of the Cephan/Petrine eucharist. In terms of phonology, the Aramaic retroversion makes sense as poetry, while the Greek texts do not. הוּא in the first line offers the vowel which will provide the dominant

---

[12] Cf. Fitzmyer, p. 1394, for a specification of the corresponding language in the texts from Qumran and Ḥever, such as I have provided for the retroversion above.

assonance, and its introduction in the second line underlines the device. The repetition of רִי results in the emergence of alliteration as the structuring principle of the second line. More important, from the point of view of Aramaic aesthetics, is the meter of the retroversion: at four beats each, the lines constitute a proverbial couplet, while the dominical saying is simply a declarative statement.

THE PAULINE ΙΛΑΣΤΗΡΙΟΝ AND THE OFFERING OF THE NATIONS

A recent monograph on Romans 3:25 provides a suitable point of departure for grasping the sense of ἱλαστήριον within the sacrificial context of Paul's thought.

Douglas A. Campbell[1] initially joins the side of the debate which construes the meaning of the term in respect of general propitiation,[2] rather than in respect of the כפרת on the ark of the covenant. That argument is unexceptional: Manson's suggestion that Paul wrote Romans under the influence of the festival of Yom Kippur, and that ἱλαστήριον is to be read accordingly, is a tissue of speculation.[3] But having rejected Manson's reading of ἱλαστήριον, Campbell proceeds to argue that "Paul evokes the singular and supremely atoning resonance of *Yom Kippur*, rather than the much more general, pagan idea of propitiatory sacrifice which was repetitive."[4] The line of argumentation is only possible because a notion from the secondary literature, Manson's suggestion, is taken up, although

---

[1] *The Rhetoric of Righteousness in Romans 3:21-26*: Journal for the Study of the New Testament Supplement Series 65 (Sheffield: Sheffield Academic Press, 1992) 107-113. The present treatment of Campbell's position is developed more fully in Chilton, "Aramaic and Targumic Antecedents of Pauline 'Justification'" (forthcoming).

[2] So Adolf Deissmann (tr. A. Grieve), *Bible Studies* (Edinburgh: Clark, 1901) 124-135.

[3] Cf. "ΙΛΑΣΤΗΡΙΟΝ," *Journal of Theological Studies* 46 (1945) 1-10. The attempt of David Hill to read the letter in respect of Hanukkah represents a further abstraction of such speculation; he argues that since Tabernacles, which was linked with Yom Kippur, was the occasion of 2 Corinthians, another feast most have been the occasion of Romans! (Cf. *Greek Words and Hebrew Meanings* [Cambridge: Cambridge University Press, 1967] 43-47). As Campbell points out (pp. 219-228, and cf. p. 109 n. 3), Hill's acceptance of an early dating of 4 Maccabees is credulous. Ulrich Wilkens is perhaps the ablest representative of Manson's position, cf. *Der Brief an die Römer*: Evangelisch-Katholischen Kommentar (Zürich: Benziger, 1978) 193. Campbell supports C.E.B. Cranfield's more sober assessment; cf. *The Epistle to the Romans* 2: The International Critical Commentary (Edinburgh: Clark, 1986) 214, 215. Campbell also takes up Cranfield's view that the 3:21-26 represents Paul's own prose (cf. pp. 199, 200).

[4] Cf. Campbell, p. 131, within pp. 130-133.

the thesis within which the suggestion is a corollary is rejected. The parts are rejected individually, but the whole remains as a phantom.

The only direct support Campbell cites for such a reading within Romans is that "Christ is often depicted in priestly and cultic terms."[5] Earlier, he had referred to such depictions within a characterization of "a scarlet thread of Levitical imagery running through Romans."[6] But the scarlet thread of Christian thought, which conceives of Jesus' death as a replacement of the imagery of Yom Kippur, runs from Hebrews 9, not from Paul.[7] Hebrews is the document which—more than any other in the New Testament—avails itself of cultic language, and it uses that language to argue that an irrevocable change of the sacrificial economy has taken place.

Chapter 9 of Hebrews imagines the "first" scheme of sacrifice, with the menorah, the table and presented bread in the holy place, and the holy of holies empty, but for the gold censer and the ark.[8] The mention of the censer as being in the holy of holies fixes the point in time of which the author speaks: it can only be the day of atonement (or, as we would say, appeasement[9]), when the high

---

[5] Cf. Campbell, p. 132, citing 5:2; 8:3, 34; 15:8.

[6] Cf. Campbell, p. 17. The reference to scarlet here would be a play on words, if the reference were self-conscious (cf. the discussion of Yoma in both the Mishnah and Talmud in chapter 3).

[7] Similarly, Campbell's emphasis throughout upon "expiation," as distinct from "propitiation," is characteristic of debates within Protestantism which are predicated upon Hebrews, cf. especially pp. 188, 189.

[8] For a consideration of the terminological problems, cf. Harold W. Attridge, *The Epistle to the Hebrews*: Hermeneia (Philadelphia, 1989) 230 and Brooke Foss Westcott, *The Epistle to the Hebrews* (London: Macmillan, 1909) 244-252.

[9] The translation of כפר has long has been a matter of dispute. The traditional translation, "to make atonement," is misleading, since it invokes a notion of being at one with the deity, which is at home amongst the Reformers in England during the sixteenth century, but not amongst the ancient Hebrews, for whom such a notion (even if conceivable) would be dangerous. G.B. Gray, *Sacrifice in the Old Testament* (Oxford: Clarendon, 1925) 67-77 establishes that the quest for a rendering along the lines of etymology is fruitless, and suggests that in the Priestly source and Ezekiel the meaning of the term is technical, that is, contextually defined. (By way of contrast, cf. Baruch A. Levine, *In the Presence of the Lord. A Study of Cult and Some Cultic Terms in Ancient Israel*: Studies in Judaism in Late Antiquity 5 [Leiden: Brill, 1974] 56). He proposes "to make expiation" as a better translation, and his proposal is followed in the New English Bible. The division of sacrificial effects upon the divine into propitiation and expiation, however, frequently appears artificial, particularly as perpetuated by scholars of the Hebrew scriptures. It seems wiser to think in terms of appeasement, and to allow that the mechanism of appeasement is left open. In any case, כפר clearly bears such a meaning at Genesis

priest made his single visit to that sanctum, censer in hand.[10]

That precise moment is only specified in order to be fixed, frozen forever. The movement of ordinary priests, in and out of the holy place, the "first tabernacle" (v. 6) while the high priest could only enter "the second tabernacle," the holy of holies (v. 7), once a year, was designed by the spirit of God as a parable: the way into the holy of holies could not be revealed while the first Temple, the first tabernacle and its service, continued (vv. 8-10). That way could only be opened, after the Temple was destroyed, by Christ, who became high priest and passed through "the greater and more perfect tabernacle" of his body (v. 11) by the power of his own blood (v. 12) so that he could find eternal redemption in the sanctuary.

Signal motifs within the Gospels are developed in the passage. The identification of Jesus' death and the destruction of the Temple, which the Gospels achieve in narrative terms, is assumed to be complete; it is not even clear what exactly the author made of the interim between the two events. Moreover, the passage takes it for granted that Jesus' body was a kind of "tabernacle," an instrument of sacrifice (v. 11), apparently because the Gospels speak of his offering his body and his blood in the words of institution. (And John, of course, actually has Jesus refer to "the temple of his body," 2:21.)[11] "Body" and "blood" no longer relate to the normative pragmata of Israel's worship: they are uniquely the high priest's self-immolating means to an end. The Temple of Jesus, the place where all Israel was truly to offer of its own, has in Hebrews become a purely ideological construct. There is nothing to be done pragmatically, and no change of affect to be experienced moment by moment, because sacrifice is finished. The high priest has entered once for all (v. 12) within the innermost recess of sanctity.

32:21 (v. 20 in the English Bible), where the reference is to Jacob's maneuver in order to appease Esau, and the gifts involved are collectively called מנחה. Levine, pp. 56-63, supports such a reading, on the basis that כפר refers etymologically (cf. the analogy in Akkadian usage), not to covering (as is frequently argued), but to the wiping away of wrath. He also cites Proverbs 16:14 and Isaiah 28:18. In any case, Greek ἵλεως, whatever might be said in respect of כפר, is straightforwardly affective in its meaning, as will feature in the discussion below.

[10] Attridge, pp. 232-235, follows other commentators in taking the θυμιατήριον as an altar, and so charges Hebrews with a "minor (sic!) anomaly," but he points out himself that "censer" would be the more straightforward rendering, with the diction of the Septuagint.

[11] Cf. Westcott, pp. 258-260.

But Paul did not conceive of that death as a replacement of the cult, for the simple reason that Paul believed he had a role to play within the service of the Temple. His preaching of the Gospel is depicted in Romans 15:16 as a kind of priestly service (ἱερουργοῦντα τὸ εὐαγγέλιον τοῦ θεοῦ), in that it is to result in "the offering of the nations, pleasing, sanctified in holy spirit" (ἡ προσφορὰ τῶν ἐθνῶν, εὐπρόσδεκτος, ἡγιασμένη ἐν πνεύματι ἁγίῳ, 15:16). Contextually, Paul's characterization of his own ministry as sacrificial is associated with his "serving the saints in Jerusalem" (15:25), by means of a collection in Macedonia and Asia for the poorer community in return for its spiritual treasure (vv. 26, 27). That done, Paul expects to come to Rome "in the fullness of Christ's blessing," and to proceed to Spain (vv. 28, 29), there (presumably) to engage in the same priestly service (cf. v. 19). Paul's program is known conventionally as the collection,[12] after Romans 15:26, 1 Corinthians 16:1, 2, 2 Corinthians 8, 9 and Galatians 2:10, and the assumption has been that the purpose of the program was purely practical: Paul agreed to provide material support in exchange for recognition by Peter, James, and John (cf. Galatians 2:9), and used priestly language as a rhetorical device.

Paul was unquestionably capable of using cultic language as metaphor. Romans 12:1 provides the example of the addressees being called to present their bodies as "a living sacrifice, holy and acceptable to God." Indeed, Romans 15:16 itself can only refer to Paul's priestly service metaphorically, as the means by which the offering of the nations might be completed. But is "the offering of the nations" itself to be taken only as a metaphor? Two standard commentaries suggest that should be the understanding as matter of course. C.E.B. Cranfield reads the metaphor explicitly within the context of a cultic theology of the significance of Jesus' death:

> The sacrifice offered to God by Christ, which Paul has here in mind, consists of the Gentile Christians who have been sanctified by the gift of the Holy Spirit...(cf. Cranfield, p. 757)

Otto Michel links the passage more strictly with 12:1, and takes it that, in both cases, the cult is transcended eschatologically:

---

[12] Cf. Victor Paul Furnish, *II Corinthians*: Anchor Bible (Garden City: Doubleday, 1984) 408-413.

Das Besondere an dieser Bildsprache des Paulus besteht darin, dass der Begriff auf den eschatologischen Vollzug der Heilsgeschichte hinweist. *Was der Kultus besagen will, erfüllt sich in der Endgeschichte.*[13]

Both of these exegeses rely upon the invocation of contexts which may indeed be recovered from Paul's theology, but which are not explicit here. It is, of course, impossible to exclude the meanings which Cranfield and Michel suggest, but it is striking that neither commentator considers the possibility that Paul might speak of an actual offering, provided by Gentile Christians for sacrifice in Jerusalem. That meaning should not be excluded, unless the straightforward sense of the words is found to be implausible.

The hope of a climactic disclosure of divine power, signalled in the willingness of nations to worship on Mount Zion, is certainly attested within sources extant by the first century. Chief among them, from the point of view of its influence upon the New Testament, is the book of Zechariah. It has been argued that Zechariah provided the point of departure for Jesus' inclusive program of purity and forgiveness as the occasions of the kingdom.[14] Jesus is said to have mentioned the prophet by name (cf. Matthew 23:34-36; Luke 11:49-51).[15] The book programmatically concerns the establishment of restored worship in the Temple, especially at the feast of Sukkoth (14:16-19). "All the nations" are to go up to Jerusalem annually for worship (v. 16), and the transformation of which that worship is part involves the provision of "living waters" from the city (v. 8, cf. John 4:10, 14). That image is related to an earlier "foun-

---

[13] Otto Michel, *Der Brief an die Römer*: Kritisch-exegetischer Kommentar über das Neue Testament (Göttingen: Vandenhoeck & Ruprecht, 1966) 458. He cites Isaiah 66:20 (pp. 457, 458), although—as he rightly points out—the issue there in play is the return of those of Israel from the Diaspora.

[14] *The Temple of Jesus*, chapter 7, "The Sacrificial Program of Jesus."

[15] Indeed, the saying (from "Q") is at least as securely attested as his references to Isaiah (cf. Matthew 13:14; 15:7; Mark 7:6). The importance of Zechariah in assessing Jesus' purpose has been stressed in Joachim Jeremias (tr. S.H. Hooke), *Jesus' Promise to the Nations*: Studies in Biblical Theology (London: SCM, 1958) 65-70; Cecil Roth, "The cleansing of the temple and Zechariah XIV 21," *Novum Testamentum* 4 (1960) 174-181. It is a commonplace of criticism to suggest that Matthew and Luke may originally have referred to Zechariah the priest in 2 Chronicles 24:20-22 (and cf. Zechariah, son of Baris, in *Jewish War* IV, 334-344), but the identification with the prophet, the son of Barachiah, is unambiguous in Matthew (and some witnesses to Luke). That the figure in mind is a product of haggadic embellishment, however, appears evident, and may draw upon the recollection of several people named "Zechariah."

tain opened for the house of David and the inhabitants of Jerusalem in view of sin and uncleanness'' (13:1). Here we see the association of forgiveness and purity which is a feature of Jesus' program, as well as the notion of an immediate release, without any mention of sacrifice, from what keeps Israel from God. (There is, incidentally, also an indication of how the issue of Davidic ancestry might have featured in Jesus' ministry, quite aside from any messianic claim.)[16] God himself is held to arrange the purity he requires, so that the sacrifice he desires might take place.

Zechariah features the commissioning of a priest (3, cf. Matthew 16:18, 19),[17] an oracle against swearing (5:3, 4[18], cf. Matthew 5:33-37), a vision of a king humbly riding an ass (9:9, cf. Matthew 21:1-9; Mark 11:1-10; Luke 19:28-40; John 12:12-19), the prophetic receipt of thirty shekels of silver in witness against the owners of sheep (11:4-17, cf. Matthew 26:14-16; 27:3-10; Mark 14:10, 11; Luke 22:3-6). It is obvious that the connections between Jesus' ministry and Zechariah do not amount to a common agenda, and Matthew clearly reflects a tendency to increase the fit between the two. But the similarities may be suggestive of Jesus' appropriation of Zechariah's prophecy of eschatological purity, as a final, more fundamental connection would indicate. The climactic vision of Zechariah insists that every vessel in Jerusalem will belong to the LORD, and become a fit vessel for sacrifice. As part of that insistence, the text asserts that no trader will be allowed in the Temple (14:20, 21). In the light of Zechariah, Jesus' occupation of the Temple appears an enactment of prophetic purity in the face of a commercial innovation,[19] a vigorous insistence that God would prepare his own people and vessels for eschatological worship.

Notably, the Targum of Zechariah specifically includes reference to God's kingdom at 14:9,[20] and that might represent another, pro-

---

[16] Cf. Chilton, ''Jesus *ben David*: reflections on the *Davidssohnfrage*,'' *Journal for the Study of the New Testament* 14 (1982) 88-112.

[17] Cf. ''Shebna, Eliakim, and the Promise to Peter,'' *Targumic Approaches*, 63-80 and *The Social World of Formative Christianity and Judaism* (eds J. Neusner, P. Borgen, E.S. Frerichs, R. Horsley; Philadelphia: Fortress, 1989) 311-326.

[18] V. 3 refers simply to swearing, not to swearing deceitfully, as in v. 4, despite the impression given in the RSV.

[19] Cf. *The Temple of Jesus*, chapter 7, ''Jesus' Occupation of the Temple.''

[20] Cf. Kevin J. Cathcart and Robert P. Gordon, *The Targum of the Minor Prophets*: The Aramaic Bible 14 (Wilmington: Glazier, 1989). As the editors indicate, the significance of the reference was earlier established in my article, ''Regnum Dei

grammatic link with Jesus. In any case, it is clear that Jesus understood the essential affect of sacrifice to derive from a purity and a forgiveness which God extended to Israel in anticipation of the climax of worship. In those understandings, Jesus was no doubt unusual in his immediate application of a prophetic program to the actual Temple, but far from unique. His precise demands concerning the provision of animals as offerings, however, show how the issue of purity was for him pragmatic, as well as affective. And it was in that Pharisaic vein—as we have seen—that he confronted the authorities in the Temple with the claim that their management was a scandal, and that the direct provision of animals by a forgiven, purified Israel was what was required for the experience of holiness and the reality of the covenant to be achieved.

Whether or not Jesus' program was a precedent for Paul's, the mere existence of Zechariah, which Paul does at least allude to,[21] opens the possibility that Paul might have included an actual offering from the Gentiles in Jerusalem as a part of his program, and therefore as part of his meaning in Romans 15:16. The relationship discussed in chapter 5 between Zechariah 9:11 and 1 Corinthians 11:25//Luke 22:20 points in the same direction. The reading of the Targum of Zechariah is particularly pertinent at this point, quite aside from the question of its relationship to Jesus' preaching. Over the past ten years, a consensus has emerged regarding the dating of Targum Jonathan, a consensus which the series, "the Aramaic Bible," has both confirmed and helped to establish. In a work published in 1982, I suggested that the Targum of Isaiah should be understood to have developed in two principal stages, with the gathering and development of translations during the period between A.D. 70 and A.D. 135, and then again during the fourth century.[22] A

Deus Est," *Scottish Journal of Theology* 31 (1978) 261-270, cf. *Targumic Approaches to the Gospels*, 99-107.

[21] Cf. Romans 8:36; 1 Corinthians 2:11; 11:25; 13:5; 14:25.

[22] Cf. *The Glory of Israel. The Theology and Provenience of the Isaiah Targum*: Journal for the Study of the Old Testament Supplements 23 (Sheffield: JSOT, 1982). It might be mentioned, in the interests of accuracy, that the date printed on the title page is an error. (Churgin's work suffered a similar fate, although the error involved misplacing his book by a decade! Cf. P. Churgin, *Targum Jonathan to the Prophets*: Yale Oriental Series [New Haven: Yale University Press, 1927]). In a condensed form, my conclusion are available in *The Isaiah Targum. Introduction, Translation, Apparatus, and Notes*: The Aramaic Bible 11 (Wilmington: Glazier and Edinburgh: Clark, 1987) xiii-xxx.

version—perhaps incomplete—of Isaiah in Aramaic was composed by a meturgeman who flourished between A.D. 70 and 135.[23] That work was completed by another meturgeman, associated with Rabbi Joseph bar Ḥiyya of Pumbeditha, who died in 333.[24] Throughout the process, however, the communal nature of the interpretative work of the meturgeman was acknowledged; insofar as individuals were involved, they spoke as the voice of synagogues and of schools. My analysis of those phases as exegetical frameworks within the document, manifested in characteristic theologoumena, has been a matter for some discussion, but it is gratifying to see that the pattern of phases which I identified in the Targum of Isaiah has been confirmed in the cases of the Targums of the Former Prophets, of Jeremiah, Ezekiel, and the Minor Prophets.[25] The emphasis within the fourteenth chapter of the Targum of Zechariah upon the inclusion of the nations in eschatological worship, and that within the Tannaitic framework (or phase) of the document, demonstrates that the motif which the Hebrew text and the Septuagint represent translated quite well within the concerns of the meturgemanin.

The Targum of Zechariah need not be dated as its editors suggest in order to establish the possibility that Paul might have invoked its theme. That theme is present in the biblical text independently of Zechariah, within the book of Tobit (13:8-11 in Vaticanus, Alexandrinus, and Venetus):

λεγέτωσαν πάντες καὶ ἐξομολογείσθωσαν αὐτῷ ἐν Ιερσολύμοις,
Ιεροσόλυμα πόλις ἁγία

---

[23] Within that early framework, materials were incorporated which appear to reflect the interpretations of earlier periods, including the period of Jesus, cf. Chilton, *A Galilean Rabbi and his Bible. Jesus' Use of the Interpreted Scripture of His Time*: Good News Studies 8 (Wilmington: Glazier, 1986; also published with the subtitle, *Jesus' own interpretation of Isaiah*; London: SPCK, 1984).

[24] *The Glory of Israel*, pp. 2, 3; *The Isaiah Targum*, p. xxi. For the sections of the Targum most representative of each meturgeman; cf. *The Isaiah Targum*, p. xxiv.

[25] The model I developed for the Targum of Isaiah is applied in D.J. Harrington and A.J. Saldarini, *Targum Jonathan of the Former Prophets*: The Aramaic Bible 10 (Wilmington: Glazier and Edinburgh: Clark, 1987) 3; Robert Hayward, *The Targum of Jeremiah*: The Aramaic Bible 12 (Wilmington: Glazier and Edinburgh: Clark, 1987) 38; S.H. Levey, *The Targum of Ezekiel*: The Aramaic Bible 13 (Wilmington: Glazier and Edinburgh: Clark, 1987) 3, 4; Cathcart and Gordon, *op. cit.*, pp. 12-14. Levey's acceptance of the paradigm is especially noteworthy, in that he had earlier argued that Targum Jonathan (especially Isaiah) should be placed within the period of the ascendancy of Islam, cf. "The Date of Targum Jonathan to the Prophets," *Vetus Testamentum* 21 (1971) 186-196.

μαστιγώσει ἐπὶ τὰ ἔργα τῶν υἱῶν σου,
καὶ πάλιν ἐλεήσει τοὺς υἱῶν τῶν δικαίων.
ἐξομολογοῦ τῷ κυρίῳ ἀγαθῶς
καὶ εὐλόγει τὸν βασιλέα τῶν αἰώνων,
ἵνα πάλιν ἡ σκηκὴ αὐτοῦ οἰκοδομηθῇ ἐν σοὶ μετὰ χαρᾶς.
καὶ εὐφράναι ἐν σοὶ τοὺς αἰχμαλώτους
καὶ ἀγαπήσαι ἐν σοὶ τοὺς ταλαιπώρους
εἰς πάσας τὰς γενεὰς τοῦ αἰῶνος.
ἔθνη πολλὰ μακρόθεν ἥξει πρὸς τὸ ὄνομα κυρίου του θεοῦ
δῶρα ἐν χερσὶν ἔχοντες καὶ δῶρα τῷ βασιλεῖ τοῦ οὐρανοῦ,
γενεαὶ γενεῶν δώσουσίν σοι ἀγαλλίασιν.[26]

It is evident that, within Hellenistic Judaism, the consolation of Jerusalem and the sacrificial recognition of God as king by the nations were motifs which could be and were associated. The significance of the prominence of a similar theme in the Targum of Zechariah shows that the association was not merely Hellenistic, and that it survived through the first century.

In Sinaiticus, an alteration is introduced into the reading of v. 11. Instead of ἔθνη πολλὰ μακρόθεν ἥξει πρὸς τὸ ὄνομα κυρίου του θεοῦ, we find ἔθνη πολλὰ μακρόθεν ἥξει σοι καὶ κάτοικοι πάντων τῶν ἐσχάτων τῆς γῆς πρὸς τὸ ὄνομα τὸ ἅγιόν σου. The appearance of the parallelism in Sinaiticus is characteristic of the paraphrastic form of the text which Hanhart calls $\mathfrak{G}^{II}$, but it serves the purpose here of making it clear beyond any doubt that worship by Gentiles, not simply Jews living abroad, is at issue.

Both the idea and its phrasing are striking for another reason. The phrase, ''all the inhabitants of the earth,'' appears innovatively within the Targum of Isaiah 24:16:

> From the *sanctuary, whence joy is about to go forth to all the inhabitants* of the earth, we hear *a* song for the righteous.

The same wording appears in 38:11 (cf. 2:3), within the song of Hezekiah; typically, the meturgemanin managed to duplicate the diction exactly, by innovating at different points in order to produce the same slogan: ''*all* the inhabitants of the *earth*.''[27] The emphatic inclusion of the Gentiles (''all the inhabitants of the earth'') within

---

[26] Cf. the edition of Robert Hanhart, *Tobit*: Septuaginta VIII,5 (Göttingen: Vandenhoeck & Ruprecht, 1985).

[27] As in the Glazier edition, italics indicate Targumic innovations, as compared to a Hebrew *Vorlage* which was virtually identical to the Masoretic Text.

the eschatological worship of the Temple is therefore not only attested in the Targum, as in Sinaiticus' version of Tobit, it is attested as
a characteristic motif. And the same phrase precisely is associated
with the kingdom of God in Targum Jonathan, notably—and in an
innovative fashion—at Zechariah 14:9.[28] The sanctuary, the kingdom, and all the inhabitants of the earth are therefore associated
within the Targum as the climax of God's revelation; Sinaiticus'
Tobit demonstrates that the first and third elements were linked by
the first century, while Matthew 8:11, 12 shows that the second and
the third were also paired by that time. More generally, Jubilees
4:26 establishes that the global range of the sanctuary was an expectation within early Judaism.[29]

Targum Jonathan, together with Tobit and Jubilees, establishes
quite clearly that an expectation of global worship in the Temple was
a feature of early Judaism, so that it is within the range of plausibility that Paul aimed to promote a literal offering of the nations by
means of his collection for the needs of the church in Jerusalem. The
book of Acts is at pains to exculpate Paul from the charge that he
introduced Gentiles into the precincts of the Temple (21:27-30), but
precisely that accusation, mounted by Jews from Asia who were in
a position to know what Paul intended (v. 27), is what in Acts
produces the attempt to kill Paul, and his subsequent (as it turned
out, definitive) arrest (vv. 31f.). Acts may certainly not be consulted
as a straightforwardly historical source, but the confused picture it
conveys at this point may be said to be consistent with the finding
from Paul's own letters that he intended that Gentiles should be
joined within the sacrificial worship of Israel.[30]

Paul's assertion in Romans 3:25, that God appointed Jesus a
ἱλαστήριον διὰ πίστεως ἐν τῷ αὐτοῦ αἵματι,[31] is therefore not to be
understood as positing a formal replacement of the cult by Jesus'

---

[28] Cf. "Regnum Dei Deus Est."

[29] Cf. *The Glory of Israel*, "'Sanctuary' (מקדשא)," 18-24, and 130 n. 9.

[30] Particularly, the hypothesis explains why Paul, in Romans 9-11, is at pains
to include all believers within the ambit of Israel at a moment of historic weakness
in the Jewish community in Rome, cf. Chilton, "Romans 9-11 as Scriptural Interpretation and Dialogue with Judaism," *Ex Auditu* 4 (1988) 27-37.

[31] Cranfield (p. 210) rightly asserts that it is only natural to read the phrase
concerning blood with the noun ἱλαστήριον. Campbell's attempt to separate the
two, on the grounds that the proposition διά is the structural key of the sentence,
relies on a mechanical understanding of Paul's rhetoric which is not shown to be
Paul's own.

death.[32] The standard references to similar usages in 2 Maccabees (3:33) and 4 Maccabees (6:28, 29; 17:20-22) ought long ago to have warned commentators against any reading which involves such notions, whether in the key of Hebrews (as in Cranfield's reading) or in the key of a transcendent eschatology (as in Michel's reading). 2 Maccabees 3:33, after all, simply speaks of a high priest "making appeasement" (ποιουμένου δὲ τοῦ ἀρχιερέως τὸν ἱλασμόν) by cultic means. That usage is an extension of the Septuagintal equation between ἵλεως and such verbs as סָלַח, נָחַם, נָשָׂא, רִחַם, and כִּפֶּר, where the emphasis falls on the divine affect involved in forgiveness.[33]

Even 4 Maccabees, which is probably too late a composition to be used as representing the milieu which was the matrix of Paul's thought, maintains a distinction between God's pleasure in sacrifice, and the means of that sacrifice. In 6:28, 29, God is asked to be pleased with his people (ἵλεως γενοῦ τῷ ἔθνει) by Eleazar, and to make his blood their purification (καθάρσιον) and his life their ransom (ἀντίψυχον). The plea is that heroic martyrdom be accepted in an unusual way in the light of a radical challenge to the usual means of sacrifice. Then, in chapter seventeen, it is said of the seven brothers that, in the manner of Eleazar, they purified the homeland in that they became a ransom of the sin of the nation (17:21, τὴν πατρίδα καθαρισθῆναι ὥσπερ ἀντίψυχον γεγονότας τῆς τοῦ ἔθνους ἁμαρτίας). The language of purification and ransom is consistently used, in chapters six and seventeen, to refer to the deaths of martyrs in cultic terms, but on the understanding that such terms need carefully to be spelled out. In chapter six, ἵλεως is used to speak of God's willingness to consider their deaths within those terms; 17:22 presents a resumé of the theme, in stating that through the blood of those pious men and the appeasement of their death (καὶ διὰ τοῦ αἵματος τῶν εὐσεβῶν ἐκείνων καὶ τοῦ ἱλαστηρίου τοῦ θανάτου αὐτῶν), God determined to save Israel. That salvation, of course,

---

[32] Cranfield's rendering (cf. pp. 214-217), as "a propitiatory sacrifice," although inspired by an appropriate skepticism of Manson's position, is too redolent of Hebrews to suit the Pauline context.

[33] Cf. F. Büchsel, "ἵλεως...," *Theologisches Worterbuch zum Neuen Testament* III (ed. G. Kittel; Stuttgart: Kohlhammer, 1938) 300, 301; cf. the article by J. Herrmann on ἱλάσκομαι, pp. 301-324, where particular attention is devoted to connections with various forms of כפר (cf. Psalms 64[65]:3; 77[78]:38; 78[79]:9). Within the present context, the rendering of חטאה by ἱλασμός at Ezekiel 44:27, and of כפרים by the same term at Leviticus 25:9; Numbers 5:8, might especially be noted.

did not require or involve the permanent replacement of cultic sacrifice, but its reestablishment in the Temple. 4 Maccabees envisages the restoration of cultic sacrifice in the Temple as a result of the sort of heroic sacrifice that is praised.

The usage of the Septuagint, and particularly of 2 Maccabees and 4 Maccabees, militates against the complete identification of the ἱλαστήριον of Romans 3:25 with the כפרת of Leviticus 16, as—of course—does the absence of the definite article in Paul's usage. There is naturally a relationship between the two, because the ἱλαστήριον of Leviticus 16 (vv. 2, 13, 14, 15) is where the high priest makes appeasement (ἐξιλάσεται, v. 16, cf. vv. 17, 18, 20); that connection is achieved in both the Masoretic Text and Neophyti by means of the root כפר. Taken together, Neophyti and the Septuagint demonstrate that the כפרת/ἱλαστήριον was understood to be the place where God was appeased,[34] the occasion of efficacious sacrifice. That also explains why the Greek term appears for עֲזָרָה at Ezekiel 43:14, 17, 20.

Jesus for Paul is a ἱλαστήριον because he provides the occasion on which God may be appeased, an opportunity for the correct offering of sacrifice in Jerusalem. The notion of Jesus' "blood" as atoning, of course, reenforces the emphasis upon the significance of his death as a *hata*ʾ*at* which has already been observed. Jesus can be a ἱλαστήριον "in his blood" in a straightforward sense. When the term "blood" is taken prosaically, of Jesus' lifeblood, the image is skewed: one is left wondering how Jesus can be placed in belief in his own blood. But when his "blood" is understood eucharistically, in accordance with the Petrine tradition which is Paul's matrix, the sense is clearer: the "blood" shared in eucharist is a place where consecration through faith occurs. Jesus is designated ἱλαστήριον in the sense of the site of sacrificial appeasement.[35]

---

[34] Cf. also בֵּית כַּפּוֹרֵי at Leviticus 16:2 in Onqelos, and the use of מכפרין in respect of the altar in 2QJN 8.5.

[35] Cf. Campbell, pp. 107-113, 112.

BIBLIOGRAPHY

Paul J. Achtemeier, *Mark*: Proclamation Commentaries (Philadelphia: Fortress, 1986)

Gedalyahu Alon, "The Bounds of the Laws of Levitical Cleanness," *Jews, Judaism and the Classical World* (tr. I. Abrahams; Jerusalem: Magnes, 1977) 190-234

——, "The Levitical Uncleanness of the Gentiles," *Jews, Judaism*, 146-189

Gary A. Anderson, *Sacrifices and Offerings in Ancient Israel. Studies in their Social and Political Importance*: Harvard Semitic Monographs 41 (Atlanta: Scholars, 1987)

Hugh Anderson, "4 Maccabees," *The Old Testament Pseudepigrapha* 2 (ed. J.H. Charlesworth; Garden City: Doubeday, 1985) 531-564

Samuel Angus, *The Mystery-Religions and Christianity. A Study in the Religious Background of Early Christianity* (London: Murray, 1925)

Harold W. Attridge, *The Epistle to the Hebrews*: Hermeneia (Philadelphia, 1989)

Caroline Bammel, "Die Einheit des Glaubens und die Mannigfaltigkeit der Bräuche in der christlichen Ueberlieferung nach Irenäus," *La Tradizione: Forme e Modi*: Studi Ephemeridis "Augustiniaun" 31 (Rome: Institutum Patristicum "Augustinianum," 1990) 283-292

Ernst Bammel, "Gottes ΔΙΑΘΗΚΗ (Gal. III.15-17) und das jüdische Rechtsdenken," *New Testament Studies* 6 (1959/1960) 313-319

——, "Hirsch und Wellhausen," *Christentumsgeschichte und Wahrheitsbewusstsein: Studien zur Theologie Emanuel Hirschs* (ed. J. Ringleben; Berlin: de Gruyter, 1991) 37-62

C.K. Barrett, *The Gospel according to St John* (London: SPCK, 1960)

Walter Bauer, *A Greek-English Lexicon of the New Testament and Other Early Christian Literature* (translation and edition by F. Arndt, F.W. Gingrich, F.W. Danker; Chicago: University of Chicago Press, 1979)

Christopher Begg, "'Josephus' Portrayal of the Disappearances of Enoch, Elijah and Moses': Some Observations," *Journal of Biblical Literature* 109 (1990) 691-693

Catherine Bell, *Ritual Theory, Ritual Practice* (New York: Oxford University Press, 1992)

Hans Dieter Betz, *Galatians*: Hermeneia (Philadelphia: Fortress, 1979)

Herman Wolfgang Beyer, "βλασφημέω..." *Theological Dictionary of the New Testament* I (ed. G. Kittel, tr. G.W. Bromiley; Grand Rapids: Eerdmans, 1978) 621-625

Klaus Beyer, *Semitische Syntax im Neuen Testament*: Studien zur Umwelt des Neuen Testaments 1 (Göttingen: Vandenhoeck und Ruprecht, 1962)

L. Blau, "Bath Ḳol," *The Jewish Encyclopedia* (ed. I. Singer; New York: Funk and Wagnalls, 1903) 588-592

Baruch M. Bokser, *The Origins of the Seder. The Passover Rite and Early Rabbinic Judaism* (Berkeley: University of California Press, 1984)

——, "Unleavened Bread and Passover, Feasts of," *Anchor Bible Dictionary* 6 (ed. D.N. Freedman; New York: Doubleday, 1992) 755-765

Roger P. Booth, *Jesus and the Laws of Purity. Tradition and Legal History in Mark 7*:

Journal for the Study of the New Testament Supplement 13 (Sheffield: JSOT, 1989)

Günther Bornkamm, Gerhard Barth, Heinz Joachim Held (tr. P. Scott), *Tradition and Interpretation in Matthew* (London: SCM, 1963)

John W. Bowman, *The Gospel of Mark. The New Christian Passover Haggadah*: Studia Post-Biblica (Leiden: Brill, 1965)

Raymond E. Brown, *The Gospel according to John (i-xii)*: The Anchor Bible (Garden City: Doubleday, 1966)

Raymond E. Brown and John P. Meier, *Antioch and Rome. New Testament Cradles of Catholic Christianity* (New York: Paulist, 1983)

F.F. Bruce, "The Book of Zechariah and the Passion Narrative," *Bulletin of the John Rylands Library* 43 (1960-61) 336-353

Adolf Büchler, *Studies in Sin and Atonement* (New York: Ktav, 1967)

Douglas A. Campbell, *The Rhetoric of Righteousness in Romans 3.21-26*: Journal for the Study of the New Testament Supplements 65 (Sheffield: Sheffield Academic Press, 1992)

Kevin J. Cathcart and Robert P. Gordon, *The Targum of the Minor Prophets*: The Aramaic Bible 14 (Wilmington: Glazier, 1989)

R.H. Charles, *A Critical and Exegetical Commentary on the Revelation of St. John* 1, 2: The International Critical Commentary (New York: Scribner's, 1920)

Bruce Chilton, "'Amen': an Approach through Syriac Gospels," *Zeitschrift für die neutestamentliche Wissenschaft* 69 (1978) 203-211 and *Targumic Approaches to the Gospels. Essays in the Mutual Definition of Judaism and Christianity*: Studies in Judaism (Lanham and London: University Press of America, 1986) 15-23

——, "Aramaic and Targumic Antecedents of Pauline 'Justification'" (forthcoming)

——, "A Coin of Three Realms (Matthew 17.24-27)," *The Bible in Three Dimensions. Essays in celebration of forty years of Biblical Studies in the University of Sheffield*: Journal for the Study of the Old Testament, Supplement Series 87 (eds D.J.A. Clines, S.E. Fowl, S.E. Porter; Sheffield: JSOT, 1990) 269-282

——, "Forgiving at and Swearing by the Temple," *Forum* 7.1/2 (1991) 45-50

——, *A Galilean Rabbi and His Bible. Jesus' own interpretation of Isaiah* (London: SPCK, 1984) and, with the subtitle *Jesus' Use of the Interpreted Scripture of His Time*, (Wilmington: Glazier, 1984)

——, *The Glory of Israel. The Theology and Provenience of the Isaiah Targum*: Journal for the Study of the Old Testament Supplements 23 (Sheffield: JSOT, 1982)

——, *God in Strength. Jesus' Announcement of the Kingdom*: Studien zum Neuen Testament und seiner Umwelt 1 (Freistadt: Plöchl, 1979, reprinted within "The Biblical Seminar;" Sheffield: Sheffield Academic Press, 1987)

——, *The Isaiah Targum*: The Aramaic Bible 11 (Wilmington: Glazier and Edinburgh: Clark, 1987)

——, "Jesus and the Repentance of E.P. Sanders," *Tyndale Bulletin* 39 (1988) 1-18

——, "Jesus *ben David*: reflections on the *Davidssohnfrage*," *Journal for the Study of the New Testament* 14 (1982) 88-112

——, *Profiles of a Rabbi. Synoptic Opportunities in Reading About Jesus*: Brown Judaic Studies 177 (Atlanta: Scholars Press, 1989)

——, "Regnum Dei Deus Est," *Scottish Journal of Theology* 31 (1978) 261-270, and *Targumic Approaches to the Gospels*, 99-107

——, "Romans 9-11 as Scriptural Interpretation and Dialogue with Judaism," *Ex Auditu* 4 (1988) 27-37

——, "Shebna, Eliakim, and the Promise to Peter," *Targumic Approaches*, 63-80 and *The Social World of Formative Christianity and Judaism* (eds J. Neusner, P. Borgen, E.S. Frerichs, R. Horsley; Philadelphia: Fortress, 1989) 311-326

——, *The Temple of Jesus. His Sacrificial Program within a Cultural History of Sacrifice* (University Park: The Pennsylvania State University Press, 1992)

——, "The Transfiguration: Dominical Assurance and Apostolic Vision," *New Testament Studies* 27 (1980) 115-124

——, "Typologies of *memra* and the fourth Gospel," *Targum Studies* 1 (1992) 89-100

Francis L. Cohen, "Hallel," *The Jewish Encyclopedia* 6 (New York: Funk and Wagnalls, 1906) 176-178

Hans Conzelmann (tr. J.W. Leitch), *1 Corinthians*: Hermeneia (Philadelphia: Fortress, 1975)

C.E.B. Cranfield, *The Epistle to the Romans* 2: The International Critical Commentary (Edinburgh: Clark, 1986)

——, *The Gospel according to St Mark*: The Cambridge Greek Testament Commentary (Cambridge: Cambridge University Press, 1963)

Oscar Cullmann, "πέτρα," *Theological Dictionary of the New Testament* VI (ed. G. Friedrich, tr. G. W Bromiley; Grand Rapids, 1979) 95-99

Oscar Cullmann and F.J. Leenhardt, *Essays on the Lord's Supper*: Ecumenical Studies in Worship 1 (tr. J.G. Davies; Richmond: John Knox, 1958)

Elian Cuvillier, "Tradition et rédaction en Marc 7:1-23," *Novum Testamentum* 34 (1992) 169-192

W.D. Davies and Dale C. Allison, *A Critical and Exegetical Commentary on the Gospel according to Saint Matthew* II: The International Critical Commentary (Edinburgh: Clark, 1991)

Adolf Deissmann (tr. A. Grieve), *Bible Studies* (Edinburgh: Clark, 1901)

Gregory Dix, *The Shape of the Liturgy* (Westminster: Dacre, 1954)

C.H. Dodd, *Historical Tradition in the Fourth Gospel* (Cambridge: Cambridge University Press, 1965)

Karl P. Donfried, "Peter," *The Anchor Bible Dictionary* 5 (eds D.N. Freedman and others; New York: Doubleday, 1992) 251-263

Mary Douglas, *Purity and Danger. An Analysis of Concepts of Pollution and Taboo* (New York: Praeger, 1966)

Victor Eppstein, "The historicity of the Gospel account of the Cleansing of the Temple," *Zeitschrift für die neutestamentliche Wissenschaft* 55 (1964) 42-58

Zeev W. Falk, "Notes and Observations on Talmudic Vows," *Harvard Theological Review* 59 (1966) 309-312

Gordon D. Fee, *The First Epistle to the Corinthians*: The New International Commentary (Grand Rapids: Eerdmans, 1987)

Elisabeth Schüssler Fiorenza, "The Quest for the Johannine School: The Book of Revelation and the Fourth Gospel," *The Book of Revelation, Justice and Judgment* (Philadelphia: Fortress, 1989) 85-113

Joseph A. Fitzmyer, *The Gospel According to Luke (I-IX)*: The Anchor Bible 28 (Garden City: Doubleday, 1981)

——, *The Gospel According to Luke (X-XXIV)*: The Anchor Bible 28 A (Garden City: Doubleday, 1985)

Joseph A. Fitzmyer and Daniel J. Harrington, *A Manual of Palestinian Aramaic Texts*: Biblica et Orientalia (Rome: Biblical Institute Press, 1978)

Georg Fohrer, "Σιών, Ἰερουσαλήμ...,: *Theological Dictionary of the New Testament* VII (eds G. Kittel, G. Friedrich, tr. G.W. Bromiley; Grand Rapids: Eerdmans, 1971) 292-319

Robert Tomson Fortna, *The Fourth Gospel and Its Predecessor. From Narrative Source to Present Gospel* (Philadelphia: Fortress, 1988)

Sean Freyne, *Galilee, Jesus and the Gospels: Literary Approaches and Historical Investigations* (Philadelphia: Fortress, 1988)

Jöram Friberg, "Numbers and Counting," *Anchor Bible Dictionary* 4 (ed. D.N.

Freedman; New York: Doubleday, 1992) 1139-1146

Victor Paul Furnish, *II Corinthians*: Anchor Bible (Garden City: Doubleday, 1984)

Theodor H. Gaster, *The Dead Sea Scriptures In English With Introduction and Notes* (Garden City: Anchor/Doubleday, 1976)

Joachim Gnilka, *Das Evangelium nach Markus* 2: Evangelisch-Katholischer Kommentar zum Neuen Testament (Köln and Neukirchen-Vluyn: Benziger and Neukirchener, 1979)

G.B. Gray, *Sacrifice in the Old Testament* (Oxford: Clarendon, 1925)

Ernst Haenchen (tr. Robert W. Funk), *John* 1, 2: Hermeneia (Philadelphia: Fortress, 1984)

Robert Hanhart, *Tobit*: Septuaginta VIII,5 (Göttingen: Vandenhoeck & Ruprecht, 1985)

Anthony Tyrrell Hanson, *The Prophetic Gospel. A Study of John and the Old Testament* (Edinburgh: Clark, 1991)

Douglas R.A. Hare, *The Son of Man Tradition* (Minneapolis: Fortress, 1990)

D.J. Harrington and A.J. Saldarini, *Targum Jonathan of the Former Prophets*: The Aramaic Bible 10 (Wilmington: Glazier and Edinburgh: Clark, 1987)

Marvin Harris, *Good to Eat: Riddles of Food and Culture* (New York: Simon and Schuster, 1985)

Robert Hayward, *The Targum of Jeremiah*: The Aramaic Bible 12 (Wilmington: Glazier and Edinburgh: Clark, 1987)

Fritz Herrenbrück, *Jesus und die Zöllner. Historische und neutestamentlich-exegetische Untersuchungen*: WUNT 41 (Tübingen: Mohr, 1990)

A.J.B. Higgins, *The Lord's Supper in the New Testament*: Studies in Biblical Theology 6 (London: SCM, 1960)

Emanuel Hirsch, *Frühgeschichte des Evangeliums* (Tübingen: Mohr, 1941)

Otfried Hofius, *Jesu Tischgemeinschaft mit den Sündern* (Calwer: Stuttgart, 1967)

William Horbury, "The Temple Tax," *Jesus and the Politics of His Day* (ed. E. Bammel and C.F.D. Moule; Cambridge: Cambridge University Press, 1984) 265-286

Richard A. Horsley, *Jesus and the Spiral of Violence. Popular Jewish Resistance in Roman Palestine* (San Francisco: Harper & Row, 1987)

Wolfgang Huber, *Passa und Osten: Untersuchungen zur Osterfeier der alten Kirche*: Beiheft zur Zeitschrift für die neutestamentliche Wissenschaft 35 (Berlin: Töpelmann, 1969)

Philip Edgcumbe Hughes, *The Book of the Revelation. A Commentary* (Grand Rapids: Eerdmans, 1990)

F.J. Foakes Jackson and Kirsopp Lake, "The Disciples in Jerusalem and the Rise of Gentile Christianity," *The Beginnings of Christianity* I (Grand Rapids: Baker, 1979) 300-320

Joachim Jeremias, "ἀμνός, ἀρήν, ἀρνίον," *Theological Dictionary of the New Testament* I (ed. G. Kittel, tr. G.W. Bromiley; Eerdmans: Grand Rapids, 1978) 338-241

——, (tr. A. Ehrhardt), *The Eucharistic Words of Jesus* (New York: Macmillan, 1955)

——, (tr. N. Perrin), *The Eucharistic Words of Jesus* (London: SCM, 1964)

——, (tr. F.H. Cave and C.H. Cave), *Jerusalem in the Time of Jesus: An Investigation into Economic and Social Conditions during the New Testament Period* (London: SCM, 1969)

——, (tr. S.H. Hooke), *Jesus' Promise to the Nations*: Studies in Biblical Theology (London: SCM, 1958)

E. Kautzsch, *Gesenius' Hebrew Grammar* (tr. A.E. Cowley; Oxford: Clarendon, 1974)

A.C. Kenny, "The Transfiguration and the Agony in the Garden," *Catholic Biblical Quarterly* 19 (1957) 444-452

Hans-Josef Klauck (tr. E. Ewert), "Lord's Super," *The Anchor Bible Dictionary* 4 (ed. D.N. Freedman and others; New York: Doubleday, 1992) 362-372

Michael A. Knibb, *The Qumran Community*: Cambridge Commentaries on Writings of the Jewish and Christian World 200 BC to AD 200 (Cambridge: Cambridge University Press, 1987)

Kirsopp Lake, "The Apostolic Council of Jerusalem," *The Acts of the Apostles* V (eds F.J. Foakes Jackson and K. Lake; Grand Rapids: Baker, 1979) 195-212

Kirsopp Lake and Henry J. Cadbury, *The Beginnings of Christianity. Part I, The Acts of the Apostles: Vol. IV English Translation and Commentary* (eds F.J. Foakes Jackson and K. Lake; Grand Rapids: Baker, 1979)

William L. Lane, *The Gospel according to Mark*: The New London Commentary (London: Marshall, Morgan & Scott, 1974)

Bernhard Lang, "Der Becher als Bundeszeichen: 'Bund' und 'neuer Bund' in den neutestamentlichen Abendmahlstexten," *Der neue Bund im Alten. Studien zur Bundestheologie der beiden Testamente* (ed. E. Zenger; Freiburg: Herder, 1993) 199-212

——, "The Roots of the Eucharist in Jesus' Praxis," *Society of Biblical Literature 1992 Seminar Papers* (ed. E.H. Lovering; Atlanta: Scholars, 1992) 467-472

Roger Le Déaut, *La nuit pascale. Essai sur la signification de la Pâque juive à partir du Targum d'Exode XII 42*: Analecta Biblica 22 (Rome: Pontifical Biblical Institute, 1963)

Xavier Léon-Dufour, *Le partage du pain eucharistique selon le Nouveau Testament* (Paris: Editions du Seuil, 1982)

S.H. Levey, *The Targum of Ezekiel*: The Aramaic Bible 13 (Wilmington: Glazier and Edinburgh: Clark, 1987)

Baruch A. Levine, *In the Presence of the Lord. A Study of Cult and Some Cultic Terms in Ancient Israel*: Studies in Judaism in Late Antiquity 5 (Leiden: Brill, 1974)

Lee I. Levine, *The Rabbinic Class of Roman Palestine in Late Antiquity* (New York: The Jewish Theological Seminary, 1989)

Henry George Liddell and Robert Scott, *A Greek-English Lexicon* (Oxford: Clarendon, 1901)

Saul L. Lieberman, *Hellenism in Jewish Palestine. Studies in the Literary Transmission, Beliefs and Manners in Palestine in the I Century B.C.E.—IV Century C.E.*: Texts and Studies 18 (New York: Jewish Theological Seminary of America, 1962)

Hans Lietzmann (tr. D.H.G. Reeve), *Mass and Lord's Supper. A Study in the History of Liturgy* (Leiden: Brill, 1979)

——, *Messe und Herrenmahl. Eine Studie zur Geschichte und Liturgie*: Arbeiten zur Kirchengeschichte 8 (Bonn: Marcus und Weber, 1926)

Barnabas Lindars, *Jesus Son of Man. A Fresh Examination of the Son of Man Sayings in the Gospels in the Light of Recent Research* (Grand Rapids: Eerdmans, 1983)

Burton Mack, *A Myth of Innocence. Mark and Christian Origins* (Philadelphia: Fortress, 1988)

Alan Hugh McNeile, *The Gospel According to St. Matthew* (London: Macmillan, 1957 [from 1915])

Frederic W. Madden, *Coins of the Jews* (London: Trübner, 1881)

T.W. Manson, "ΙΛΑΣΤΗΡΙΟΝ," *Journal of Theological Studies* 46 (1945) 1-10

Benjamin Mazar (tr. G. Cornfeld), *The Mountain of the Lord* (Garden City: Doubleday, 1975)

Wayne A. Meeks and Robert L. Wilken, *Jews and Christians in Antioch in the First Four Centuries of the Common Era*: Society of Biblical Literature Sources for Biblical Study 13 (Missoula: Scholars, 1978)

Ben F. Meyer, "A Caricature of Joachim Jeremias and his Scholarly Work," *Journal of Biblical Literature* 110 (1991) 451-462

Otto Michel, *Der Brief an die Römer*: Kritisch-exegetischer Kommentar über das Neue Testament (Göttingen: Vandenhoeck & Ruprecht, 1966)

Matti Myllykoski, *Die letzten Tage Jesu. Markus und Johannes, ihre Traditionen und die historische Frage*, I: Suomalaisen Tiedeakatemian Toimituksia Annales Academiae Scientiarum Fennicae B.256 (Helsinki: Suomalainen Tiedeakatemia, 1991)

David A. Neale, *None but the Sinners. Religious Categories in the Gospel of Luke*: Journal for the Study of the New Testament Supplement 58 (Sheffield: Sheffield Academic Press, 1991)

Jacob Neusner, "Josephus' Pharisees: A Complete Repertoire," *Josephus, Judaism, and Christianity* (ed. L.H. Feldman and G. Hata; Detroit: Wayne State University Press, 1987) 274-292

——, *The Peripatetic Saying. The Problem of the Thrice-Told Tale in Talmudic Literature*: Brown Judaic Studies 89 (Chico: Scholars, 1985)

Martin Noth (tr. J.D. Martin), *Numbers: A Commentary* (Philadelphia: Westminster, 1968

Robert F. O'Toole, "Last Supper," *The Anchor Bible Dictionary* 4 (ed. D.N. Freedman and others; New York: Doubleday, 1992) 234-241

Norman Perrin, "The Use of παραδιδόναι in Connection with the Passion of Jesus in the New Testament," *Der Ruf Jesu und die Antwort der Gemeinde* (eds E. Lohse, C. Burchard, B. Schaller; Göttingen: Vandenhoeck und Ruprecht, 1970) 204-212

Rudolf Pesch, *Das Markusevangelium II. Teil*: Herders Theologischer Kommentar zum Neuen Testament (Freiburg: Herder, 1980)

A. Plummer, *An Exegetical Commentary on the Gospel according to S. Matthew* (New York: Scribner, 1910)

M.H. Pope, "Number, Numbering, Numbers," *The Interpreter's Dictionary of the Bible* 3 (New York: Abingdon, 1962) 561-567

K.H. Rengstorf, "κορβᾶν, κορβανᾶς," *Theological Dictionary of the New Testament* III (ed. G. Kittel, tr. G.W. Bromiley; Grand Rapids: Eerdmans, 1978) 860-866

Peter Richardson, "Why Turn the Tables? Jesus' Protest in the Temple Precincts," *Society of Biblical Literature 1992 Seminar Papers* (ed. E.H. Lovering; Atlanta: Scholars, 1992) 507-523

Cecil Roth, "The cleansing of the temple and Zechariah XIV 21," *Novum Testamentum* 4 (1960) 174-181

Eugen Ruckstuhl, "Jakobus (Herrenbruder)," *Theologische Realenzyklopädie* (Berlin: de Gruyter, 1987) 485-488

Kurt Rudolf (tr. M.J. O'Connell), "Mystery Religions," *The Encyclopedia of Religion* 10 (ed. M. Eliade; New York: Macmillan, 1987) 230-239

E.P. Sanders, *Jesus and Judaism* (Philadelphia: Fortress, 1985)

——, *Jewish Law from Jesus to the Mishnah. Five Studies* (London: SCM and New York: Trinity Press International, 1990)

Rudolf Schnackenburg (tr. D. Smith and G.A. Kon), *The Gospel according to St John*, volume three: Herder's Theological Commentary on the New Testament (London: Burns & Oates, 1982)

Albert Schweitzer (tr. A.J. Mattill), *The Problem of the Lord's Supper according to the Scholarly Research of the Nineteenth Century and the Historical Accounts. I. The Lord's Supper in Relationship to the Life of Jesus and the History of the Early Church* (Macon: Mercer University Press, 1982)

Eduard Schweizer, "σῶμα κτλ. D. The New Testament," *Theological Dictionary of the New Testament* VII (ed. G. Freidrich, tr. G.W. Bromiley; Grand Rapids: Eerdmans, 1979) 1057-1081

David Seeley, *The Noble Death: Graeco-Roman Martyrology and Paul's Concept of Salva-*

tion: Journal for the Study of the New Testament Supplement 28 (Sheffield: Sheffield Academic Press, 1990)

J.B. Segal, *The Hebrew Passover from the earliest times to A.D. 70*: London Oriental Series 12 (London: Oxford University Press, 1963)

E. Mary Smallwood, *The Jews under Roman Rule*: Studies in Judaism in Late Antiquity 20 (Leiden: Brill, 1976)

Dennis E. Smith, "Table Fellowship as a Literary Motif in the Gospel of Luke," *Journal of Biblical Literature* 106 (1987) 613-638

Morton Smith, "The Dead Sea Sect in Relation to Ancient Judaism," *New Testament Studies* 7 (1960-1961) 347-360

Preserved Smith, *A Short History of Christian Theophagy* (Chicago: Open Court, 1922)

Burnett Hillman Streeter, *The Four Gospels. A Study of Origins* (London: Macmillan, 1924)

Henry Barclay Swete, *The Gospel according to St Mark* (London: Macmillan, 1915 [from 1909])

James Tabor, "Martyr, Martyrdom," *The Anchor Bible Dictionary* 4 (ed. D.N. Freeman *et al.*; New York: Doubleday, 1992) 574-579

Charles Taylor, *The Teaching of the Twelve Apostles* (Cambridge: Deighton Bell, 1886)

Nicholas Taylor, *Paul, Antioch and Jerusalem. A Study in Relationship and Authority in Earliest Christianity*: Journal for the Study of the New Testament Supplements 66 (Sheffield: Sheffield Academic Press, 1992)

Vincent Taylor, *The Gospel according to St. Mark* (London: Macmillan, 1966)

William Temple, *Readings in St. John's Gospel* (New York: Macmillan, 1939)

Gerd Theissen (tr. L.M. Maloney), *The Gospels in Context. Social and Political History in the Synoptic Tradition* (Minneapolis: Fortress, 1991)

Marianna Torgovnick, *Gone Primitive: Savage Intellelects, Modern Lives* (Chicago: University of Chicago, 1990)

John T. Townsend, "The New Testament, the Early Church, and Anti-Semitism," *From Ancient Israel to Modern Judaism: Intellect in Quest of Understanding* I: Brown Judaic Studies 159 (eds J. Neusner, E.S. Frerichs, N.M. Sarna; Atlanta: Scholars, 1989) 171-186

Brooke Foss Westcott, *The Epistle to the Hebrews* (London: Macmillan, 1909)

Ulrich Wilkens, *Der Brief an die Römer*: Evangelisch-Katholischen Kommentar (Zürich: Benziger, 1978)

A.G. Wright, "The Widow's Mites: Praise or Lament?—A Matter of Context," *Catholic Biblical Quarterly* 44 (1982) 256-265

David P. Wright, "Unclean and Clean (OT)," *Anchor Bible Dictionary* 6 (ed. D.N. Freedman; New York: Doubleday, 1992) 729-741

——, *The Disposal of Impurity. Elimination Rites in the Bible and in Hittite and Mesopotamian Literatures*: Society of Biblical Literature Dissertation Series 101 (Atlanta: Scholars, 1987)

INDEX

SUPPLEMENTS TO NOVUM TESTAMENTUM

ISSN 0167-9732

22. GABOURY, A. *La Stucture des Évangiles synoptiques*. La structure-type à l'origine des synoptiques. 1970. ISBN 90 04 01602 3
23. GASTON, L. *No Stone on Another*. Studies in the Significance of the Fall of Jerusalem in the Synoptic Gospels. 1970. ISBN 90 04 01603 1
24. *Studies in John*. Presented to Professor Dr. J.N. Sevenster on the Occasion of His Seventieth Birthday. 1970. ISBN 90 04 03091 3
25. STORY, C.I.K. *The Nature of Truth in the 'Gospel of Truth', and in the Writings of Justin Martyr*. A Study of the Pattern of Orthodoxy in the Middle of the Second Christian Century. 1970. ISBN 90 04 01605 8
26. GIBBS, J.G. *Creation and Redemption*. A Study in Pauline Theology. 1971. ISBN 90 04 01606 6
27. MUSSIES, G. *The Morphology of Koine Greek As Used in the Apocalypse of St. John*. A Study in Bilingualism. 1971. ISBN 90 04 02656 8
28. AUNE, D.E. *The Cultic Setting of Realized Eschatology in Early Christianity*. 1972. ISBN 90 04 03341 6
29. UNNIK, W.C. VAN. *Sparsa Collecta*. The Collected Essays of W.C. van Unnik Part 1. Evangelia, Paulina, Acta. 1973. ISBN 90 04 03660 1
30. UNNIK, W.C. VAN. *Sparsa Collecta*. The Collected Essays of W.C. van Unnik Part 2. I Peter, Canon, Corpus Hellenisticum, Generalia. 1980. ISBN 90 04 06261 0
31. UNNIK, W.C. VAN. *Sparsa Collecta*. The Collected Essays of W.C. van Unnik Part 3. Patristica, Gnostica, Liturgica. 1983. ISBN 90 04 06262 9
33. AUNE D.E. (ed.) *Studies in New Testament and Early Christian Literature*. Essays in Honor of Allen P. Wikgren. 1972. ISBN 90 04 03504 4
34. HAGNER, D.A. *The Use of the Old and New Testaments in Clement of Rome*. 1973. ISBN 90 04 03636 9
35. GUNTHER, J.J. *St. Paul's Opponents and Their Background*. A Study of Apocalyptic and Jewish Sectarian Teachings. 1973. ISBN 90 04 03738 1
36. KLIJN, A.F.J. & G.J. REININK (eds.) *Patristic Evidence for Jewish-Christian Sects*. 1973. ISBN 90 04 03763 2
37. REILING, J. *Hermas and Christian Prophecy*. A Study of The Eleventh Mandate. 1973. ISBN 90 04 03771 3
38. DONFRIED, K.P. *The Setting of Second Clement in Early Christianity*. 1974. ISBN 90 04 03895 7
39. ROON, A. VAN. *The Authenticity of Ephesians*. 1974. ISBN 90 04 03971 6
40. KEMMLER, D.W. *Faith and Human Reason*. A Study of Paul's Method of Preaching as Illustrated by 1-2 Thessalonians and Acts 17, 2-4. 1975. ISBN 90 04 04209 1
42. PANCARO, S. *The Law in the Fourth Gospel*. The Torah and the Gospel, Moses and Jesus, Judaism and Christianity According to John. 1975. ISBN 90 04 04309 8
43. CLAVIER, H. *Les variétés de la pensée biblique et le problème de son unité*. Esquisse d'une théologie de la Bible sur les textes originaux et dans leur contexte historique. 1976. ISBN 90 04 04465 5
44. ELLIOTT, J.K.E. (ed.) *Studies in New Testament Language and Text*. Essays in Honour of George D. Kilpatrick on the Occasion of His Sixty-fifth Birthday. 1976.

ISBN 90 04 04386 1

45. PANAGOPOULOS, J. (ed.) *Prophetic Vocation in the New Testament and Today*. 1977. ISBN 90 04 04923 1

46. KLIJN, A.F.J. *Seth in Jewish, Christian and Gnostic Literature*. 1977. ISBN 90 04 05245 3

47. BAARDA, T., A.F.J. KLIJN & W.C. VAN UNNIK (eds.) *Miscellanea Neotestamentica*. I. Studia ad Novum Testamentum Praesertim Pertinentia a Sociis Sodalicii Batavi c.n. Studiosorum Novi Testamenti Conventus Anno MCMLXXVI Quintum Lustrum Feliciter Complentis Suscepta. 1978. ISBN 90 04 05685 8

48. BAARDA, T., A.F.J. KLIJN & W.C. VAN UNNIK (eds.) *Miscellanea Neotestamentica*. II. 1978. ISBN 90 04 05686 6

49. O'BRIEN, P.T. *Introductory Thanksgivings in the Letters of Paul*. 1977. ISBN 90 04 05265 8

50. BOUSSET, D.W. *Religionsgeschichtliche Studien*. Aufsätze zur Religionsgeschichte des hellenistischen Zeitalters. Hrsg. von A.F. Verheule. 1979. ISBN 90 04 05845 1

51. COOK, M.J. *Mark's Treatment of the Jewish Leaders*. 1978. ISBN 90 04 05785 4

52. GARLAND, D.E. *The Intention of Matthew 23*. 1979. ISBN 90 04 05912 1

53. MOXNES, H. *Theology in Conflict*. Studies in Paul's Understanding of God in Romans. 1980. ISBN 90 04 06140 1

55. MENKEN, M.J.J. *Numerical Literary Techniques in John*. The Fourth Evangelist's Use of Numbers of Words and Syllables. 1985. ISBN 90 04 07427 9

56. SKARSAUNE, O. *The Proof From Prophecy*. A Study in Justin Martyr's Proof-Text Tradition: Text-type, Provenance, Theological Profile. 1987. ISBN 90 04 07468 6

59. WILKINS, M.J. *The Concept of Disciple in Matthew's Gospel, as Reflected in the Use of the Term 'Mathetes'*. 1988. ISBN 90 04 08689 7

60. MILLER, E.L. *Salvation-History in the Prologue of John*. The Significance of John 1: 3-4. 1989. ISBN 90 04 08692 7

61. THIELMAN, F. *From Plight to Solution*. A Jewish Framework for Understanding Paul's View of the Law in Galatians and Romans. 1989. ISBN 90 04 09176 9

64. STERLING, G.E. *Historiography and Self-Definition*. Josephos, Luke-Acts and Apologetic Historiography. 1992. ISBN 90 04 09501 2

65. BOTHA, J.E. *Jesus and the Samaritan Woman*. A Speech Act Reading of John 4:1-42. 1991. ISBN 90 04 09505 5

66. KUCK, D.W. *Judgment and Community Conflict*. Paul's Use of Apologetic Judgment Language in 1 Corinthians 3:5-4:5. 1992. ISBN 90 04 09510 1

67. SCHNEIDER, G. *Jesusüberlieferung und Christologie*. Neutestamentliche Aufsätze 1970-1990. 1992. ISBN 90 04 09555 1

68. SEIFRID, M.A. *Justification by Faith*. The Origin and Development of a Central Pauline Theme. 1992. ISBN 90 04 09521 7

69. NEWMAN, C.C. *Paul's Glory-Christology*. Tradition and Rhetoric. 1992. ISBN 90 04 09463 6

70. IRELAND, D.J. *Stewardship and the Kingdom of God*. An Historical, Exegetical, and Contextual Study of the Parable of the Unjust Steward in Luke 16: 1-13. 1992. ISBN 90 04 09600 0

71. ELLIOTT, J.K. *The Language and Style of the Gospel of Mark*. An Edition of C.H. Turner's "Notes on Marcan Usage" together with other comparable studies. 1993. ISBN 90 0409767 8

72. CHILTON, B. *A Feast of Meanings*. Eucharistic Theologies from Jesus through Johannine Circles. 1994. ISBN 90 04 09949 2

73. GUTHRIE, G.H. *The Structure of Hebrews*. A Text-Linguistic Analysis. 1994. ISBN 90 04 09866 6